the overselling of
Population Aging

the overselling of
Population Aging

Apocalyptic Demography, Intergenerational Challenges, and Social Policy

edited by Ellen M. Gee
and Gloria M. Gutman

OXFORD

UNIVERSITY PRESS

OXFORD
UNIVERSITY PRESS

70 Wynford Drive, Don Mills, Ontario M3C 1J9
www.oupcan.com

Oxford University Press is a department of the University of Oxford.
It furthers the University's objective of excellence in research, scholarship,
and education by publishing worldwide in
Oxford New York

Athens Auckland Bangkok Bogotá Buenos Aires Calcutta
Cape Town Chennai Dar es Salaam Delhi Florence Hong Kong Istanbul
Karachi Kuala Lumpur Madrid Melbourne Mexico City Mumbai
Nairobi Paris São Paulo Singapore Taipei Tokyo Toronto Warsaw
with associated companies in Berlin Ibadan

Oxford is a trade mark of Oxford University Press
in the UK and in certain other countries
Published in Canada
by Oxford University Press

Copyright © Oxford University Press Canada 2000
The moral rights of the author have been asserted
Database right Oxford University Press (maker)
First published 2000

Canadian Cataloguing in Publication Data

Main entry under title:

The overselling of population aging : apocalyptic demography,
intergenerational challenges, and social policy
(Studies in Canadian population)
Includes bibliographical references and index.
ISBN 0-19-541465-9

1. Aged – Canada – Social conditions.   2. Aging – Social aspects – Canada.
3. Aged – Government Policy – Canada.   4. Canada – Social policy.
5. Canada – Population.   I. Gee, Ellen Margaret Thomas, 1950– .
II. Gutman, Gloria M. (Gloria Margaret), 1939– .   III. Series.

HQ1064.C2093 2000   305.26'0971   C99-932953-7

Cover & Text Design: Tearney McMurtry
1 2 3 4 - 03 02 01 00

This book is printed on permanent (acid-free) paper ∞
Printed in Canada

Contents

Contributors

YVES CARRIÈRE, trained in the Department of Demography at the University of Montreal, is an Assistant Professor of Gerontology at Simon Fraser University. His research interests include healthy life expectancy, formal and informal support networks, and policy issues.

ELLEN M. GEE is Professor and Chair of the Department of Sociology and Anthropology at Simon Fraser University. She has published extensively in the areas of Canadian demography, sociology of aging, and sociology of families. She serves on the editorial boards of the *Journal of Women and Aging* and *Canadian Studies in Population*; formerly she was associate editor of *Canadian Public Policy* and Social Science Divisional Chair of the Canadian Association on Gerontology.

GLORIA M. GUTMAN is Professor and Director of the Gerontology Research Centre and Gerontology Program at Simon Fraser University. A past President of the Canadian Association on Gerontology, she is currently Chair-Elect of the International Association of Gerontology. Her research interests include seniors' housing, long-term care, health promotion, and environmental design.

SUSAN A. McDANIEL is Professor of Sociology at the University of Alberta. An elected Fellow of the Royal Society of Canada, she is the author of over 150 research articles, book chapters, and research reports on social policy, gender inequalities, demography, and sociology of families. Among her many distinctions, this former President of the Canadian Population Society was recently awarded the Gordin Kaplan Award for outstanding research at the University of Alberta. She is currently editor of *Current Sociology*.

LYNN McDONALD is Professor in the Faculty of Social Work at the University of Toronto, as well as Director of the Centre for Applied Social Research. She has published extensively in the areas of older workers, retirement, and elder abuse. She was recently appointed to the Social Sciences and Humanities Council of Canada, and is a former Chair of the Canadian Association on Gerontology, Social Welfare Division.

ANNE MARTIN-MATTHEWS is a Professor of Family Science in the School of Social Work and Family Studies, and Associate Dean (Research and Graduate Studies) in the Faculty of Arts at the University of British Columbia. Her areas of research expertise include widowhood, aging in rural environments, marital status transitions in later life, and work-family responsibilities among employed caregivers. Founder of the Gerontology Research Centre at the University of Guelph, she is currently Editor-in-Chief of the *Canadian Journal on Aging,* and is a former Social Science Divisional Chair of the Canadian Association on Gerontology.

BARBARA A. MITCHELL is an Assistant Professor in the Department of Sociology and Anthropology and in the Gerontology Program at Simon Fraser University. Her primary research areas are life-course transitions, intergenerational relationships, health promotion, and social policy.

MICHAEL J. PRINCE is Lansdowne Professor of Social Policy and Assistant Dean of Human and Social Development at the University of Victoria. His research interests include Canadian social policy, public-sector budgeting, retirement income and pension reform issues, and organization and practice of policy analysis.

CAROLYN J. ROSENTHAL is Professor of Gerontology and Sociology and Director of the Office of Gerontological Studies at McMaster University. She specializes in aging families, and has published extensively on intergenerational relationships, social support, and paid work-family responsibilities. She served as Editor, Social Sciences, for the *Canadian Journal on Aging*, and is a past Chair of the Social Science Division of the Canadian Association on Gerontology.

LILLIAN ZIMMERMAN is currently a Research Associate at the Gerontology Research Centre at Simon Fraser University, with research interests focusing on women and retirement, public pensions, and intergenerational issues. She is a retired faculty member at Douglas College in New Westminster, BC, who specialized in adult education.

Foreword

LILLIAN ZIMMERMAN

This is a good time to be growing old for most people in Western industrialized countries. Great benefits accrue from advances in medicine and health care, from increased longevity, from remarkable technological achievements including communications and the dissemination of information worldwide. As an older Canadian woman, I have experienced and benefited from these developments.

It is disquieting to now observe the dismantling of our systems of social support in Canada and the speed with which it is taking place. It is especially ironic to be told that the unravelling of our support programs is attributable to the threat of population aging. We are familiar with projections that the number of Canadians over 65 years will increase from the current 12 per cent to 18 per cent of the population by the year 2021. Instead of hailing this as the accomplishment it will be, we are told instead that our public system of pensions and health care will be unable to sustain the drain that increased numbers of older persons will impose.

This negative view of population aging has been accompanied by an equally disturbing development of myths and stereotypes about older Canadians—depicting them as wealthy, selfish, and uncaring. These portrayals have taken hold in public perceptions. We appear to have borrowed the notion of a conflict between generations from the United States. Such US headlines as 'Robbing Poor Peter to Pay Aging Paul' are echoed in Canada. This stereotyping of older persons contains two contradictory scenarios (Katz, 1996). On the one hand, the old are seen as healthy, financially secure, and comfortably living lives of luxury; on the other hand, they are viewed as a massive, dependent burden on the welfare system. In both cases, the elderly are seen as taking a disproportionate share of society's resources and disrupting intergenerational relations in the process.

While Canadian social researchers have critiqued stereotypes of the aged and simplistic notions about the negative implications of population aging, and have pointed out the contributions that older Canadians make in private (as contrasted to public) intergenerational transfers, this research has not received the attention it deserves. At the same time, alarmist and politically motivated views of population abound. In an attempt to correct this situation, a conference organized by Gloria Gutman and me, entitled 'The Overselling of Population Aging: Apocalyptic Demography and Intergenerational Challenges', was held in May 1998 at Simon Fraser University. The papers presented at this conference are contained in this book.

Reference

Katz, Stephen. 1996. *Disciplining Old Age: The Formation of Gerontological Knowledge.* Charlottesville: University Press of Virginia.

Introduction

ELLEN M. GEE AND GLORIA M. GUTMAN

A number of terms have surfaced—apocalyptic demography, voodoo demography, and alarmist demography—to refer to an increasingly held view that demographic factors determine human affairs. While demography does influence the social environment, it does not determine it—this is what the 'holy writ' of apocalyptic demography fails to understand. We use the term 'holy writ' advisedly because apocalyptic demography has an ideological hue. For many, it is accepted fact that population aging has negative consequences for society and for intergenerational relations, i.e., that increasing numbers and proportions of elderly translate into the need for major cuts in social policies and programs, and that generational tensions are bound to escalate.

The idea that population aging is negative originated in the United States,[1] where it took form in two ways—in academic discourse and in political action. With regard to the latter, AGE (Americans for Generational Equity) formed an important lobby group, arguing for reforms to present social policy that it viewed as privileging the aged at the expense of the young (Longman, 1987). With regard to academic work, apocalyptic demography has taken many forms. One of the earliest and most influential expressions appeared in Samuel Preston's (1984) presidential address to the Population Association of America, in which he pitted youth against elderly as beneficiaries of public policy measures. Also, Kotlikoff's (1993) work has been influential; his generational accounting framework focuses on ways to reform social and economic policy so that supposed intergenerational inequities—again viewed as favouring elders— are addressed. An extreme example is evident in the writings of medical ethicist Daniel Callahan (1987), who argues that population aging will incur such an escalation in health-care costs that health care should be rationed to, and/or withheld from, elders.

The fear that population aging has dire social and economic consequences has spread from the United States to become a worldwide phenomenon, and Canada has not been immune from the globalization of apocalyptic demography. In the early 1990s, Marshall et al. could justifiably boast that Canada had not fallen prey to its ideology (although Susan McDaniel, as early as 1987, had the insight to observe its nascent beginnings in the Canadian social policy arena). However, this claim can no longer be made. While apocalyptic demography has not dominated academic research, it has made inroads. Examples may be found in a sociology/demography doctoral dissertation based on Preston's framework (Ng, 1992), in a Statistics Canada volume that examines generational accounting in the Canadian context (Corak, 1998), and in research by senior Canadian demographers Jacques Henripin (1994) and Anatole Romaniuc (1998), who argue for increased fertility to counteract what they view as extreme negative economic implications of population aging. And apocalyptic demography got a big boost with the publication of University of Toronto economist/demographer David Foot's 1996 best-seller *Boom, Bust, and Echo.*[2]

But academicians have not been the real culprits in the ascendency of apocalyptic demography in Canada. Indeed, a good deal of research by Canadian social scientists is aimed directly at slaying the myths associated with apocalyptic demographic thinking. Some work has focused on assessing the impact of population aging on government expenditures, finding that its effects are relatively minor (Fellegi, 1988; Murphy and Wolfson, 1991). Robert Evans and his colleagues at the University of British Columbia have been at the forefront of research showing that population aging does not necessarily lead to major increases in health-care costs (Barer et al., 1987, 1995; Evans, 1987); McDonald shows that population aging will not strain the labour force (McDonald and Chen, 1994) and pension systems (McDonald, 1997) as much as we are led to believe; McDaniel (1987) points to alarmist demographic thinking in social policy while Marshall (1993) critiques the apocalyptic demography underlying Canadian health policy; and Katz (1992), Northcott (1994), and Robertson (1997) variously examine the causes and effects of socially constructed rhetoric about the negativity of population aging. Taken as a whole, this research should not be construed as suggesting that population aging contains no social policy challenges. Rather, the point is that population aging is not itself a 'crisis', nor does it cause one; it is one aspect of a whole set of changes in our society (Gee and McDaniel, 1994).

Thus, Canadian social scientists have created a considerable body of research that shows apocalyptic demography for what it is—a set of beliefs that does not stand up to empirical examination. Still, these beliefs have taken hold in the minds of the public and policy-makers. This represents an example of what Stacy (1999: 18) refers to as 'virtual social science', that is, 'the application of . . . public relations and mass media to culturally construct social scientific "truth"'. Our social researchers have failed to 'get the message out'.

This book seeks to correct the mythology of apocalyptic demography. It does so by carefully considering this ideology in relation to the facts of population aging, in relation to social policy developments, and with special attention paid to intergenerational issues.

Taken together, the eight chapters provide a solid base for confronting apocalyptic demography for what it is—a mechanism used to meet largely political goals. The message of this book is that population aging is a very complex phenomenon, particularly with regard to intergenerational relationships. The contributors to this volume—all well-respected social researchers whose work centres on some aspect of population aging—each reveal a part of the complexity of population aging and together clearly show the dangers and follies of apocalyptic demography.

Notes

1. In Western thought, the view that demographic change can and will have catastrophic social consequences gained credence through the writings of the nineteenth-century English minister, Reverend Thomas Malthus. However, his focus was on population growth, not population aging.
2. Foot's book represents a bit of a twist to apocalyptic demography. With Foot, the characteristic pessimism of apocalyptic demography is absent—after all, his focus is on the profits that individuals can make in an aging population. However, demographic determinism is present, as evidenced in his unsubstantiated claim that two-thirds of what happens to a person in his/her life results from the timing of his/her birth.

References

Barer, Morris L., Robert G. Evans, Clyde Hertzman, and Jonathan Lomas. 1987. 'Aging and Health Care Utilization: New Evidence on Old Fallacies', *Social Science and Medicine* 24: 851–62.

————, ————, and ————. 1995. 'Avalanche or Glacier? Health Care and the Demographic Rhetoric', *Canadian Journal on Aging* 14: 193–224.

Callahan, Daniel. 1987. *Setting Limits: Medical Goals in an Aging Society.* New York: Simon and Schuster.

Corak, Miles, ed. 1998. *Government Finances and Generational Equity.* Ottawa: Statistics Canada, Catalogue No. 68–513–XPB.

Fellegi, Ivan. 1988. 'Can We Afford an Aging Population?', *Canadian Economic Observer* (Oct.): 4.1–4.34.

Foot, David K., with Daniel Stoffman. 1996. *Boom, Bust, and Echo: How to Profit from the Coming Demographic Shift.* Toronto: MacFarlane Walter & Ross.

Gee, Ellen M., and Susan A. McDaniel. 1994. 'Social Policy for an Aging Society', in V. Marshall and B. McPherson, eds, *Aging: Canadian Perspectives.* Peterborough, Ont.: Broadview Press, 219–31.

Evans, Robert G. 1987. 'Hang Together or Hang Separately? The Viability of a Universal Health Care System in an Aging Society', *Canadian Public Policy* 13: 165–80.

Henripin, Jacques. 1994. 'The Financial Consequences of Population Aging', *Canadian Public Policy* 20: 78–94.

Katz, Stephen. 1992. 'Alarmist Demography: Power, Knowledge, and the Elderly Population', *Journal of Aging Studies* 6: 203–25.

Kotlikoff, Lawrence J. 1993. *Generational Accounting: Knowing Who Pays, and When, For What We Spend.* New York: Free Press.

Longman, Philip. 1987. *Born to Pay: The New Politics of Aging in America.* Boston: Houghton Mifflin.

McDaniel, Susan A. 1987. 'Demographic Aging as a Guiding Paradigm in Canada's Welfare State', *Canadian Public Policy* 13: 330–6.

McDonald, Lynn. 1997. 'Pension Questions that are Politically Out-of-the-Question', *Canadian Journal on Aging* 16: 393–9.

——— and Mervin Y.T. Chen. 1994. 'The Youth Freeze and the Retirement Bulge: Older Workers and the Impending Labour Shortage', in V. Marshall and B. McPherson, eds, *Aging: Canadian Perspectives.* Peterborough, Ont.: Broadview Press, 113–39.

Marshall, Victor W. 1993. 'A Critique of Canadian Aging and Health Policy', *Journal of Canadian Studies* 28: 153–65.

———, Faye L. Cook, and Joanne G. Marshall. 1993. 'Conflict Over Intergenerational Equity: Rhetoric and Reality in a Comparative Context', in V.L. Bengtson and W.A. Achenbaum, eds, *The Changing Contract Across Generations.* New York: Aldine DeGruyter, 101–40.

Murphy, Brian B. and Michael C. Wolfson. 1991. 'When the Baby Boom Grows Old: Impacts on Canada's Public Sector', *Statistical Journal* 8: 25–43.

Ng, Edward D.M. 1992. 'Dependents and Resource Allocation in an Aging Society: An Examination of the Preston Argument in Canada', Ph.D. dissertation, University of Western Ontario.

Northcott, Herbert C. 1994. 'Public Perceptions of the Population Aging "Crisis"', *Canadian Public Policy* 20: 66–77.

Preston, Samuel H. 1984. 'Children and the Elderly: Divergent Paths for America's Dependents', *Demography* 21: 435–57.

Robertson, Ann. 1997. 'Beyond Apocalyptic Demography: Towards a Moral Economy of Interdependence', *Ageing and Society* 17: 425–46.

Romaniuc, Anatole. 1998. 'Age of Demographic Maturity and Population Policy Implications', paper presented at the annual meeting of the Canadian Population Society, Ottawa.

Stacey, Judith. 1999. 'Virtual Truth with a Vengeance', *Contemporary Sociology* 28: 18–23.

1 | Population and Politics
Voodoo Demography, Population Aging, and Canadian Social Policy

Ellen M. Gee

A Look at Voodoo or Apocalyptic Demography

We are constantly bombarded with words and images informing us that our changing demographics—in particular, our aging population—are the cause, and will continue to be the cause, of a leaner and meaner Canada. These words and images reflect the ideology of voodoo—or apocalyptic—demography[1] that has come to frame Canadians' views of their society, now and in the future. What is voodoo/apocalyptic demography? It is the oversimplified idea that population aging has catastrophic consequences for a society. More specifically, it embraces the view that increasing numbers (or 'hordes') of older people will bankrupt a society, due to their incessant demands on the health-care system and on public pensions. A closely aligned idea is that an aging society exacts an unfair price on younger segments of the population who have to pay to meet the needs of the burgeoning numbers of elders. This idea has come to be labelled 'intergenerational equity' (or 'inequity') (Longman, 1987). Intertwined in the intergenerational equity concept is an image of the elderly as well-off leisurers who golf and cruise, partly at public expense, and who have no regard for the situation of younger people. This image, too, comes with a label—the elderly are 'greedy geezers' (Binstock, 1994). Also, this generational unfairness is viewed as leading to intergenerational conflict, straining the Canadian social fabric.

I refer to apocalyptic demography as an ideology, using 'ideology' in the sense of a set of beliefs that justifies (or rationalizes) action. The *beliefs* converge on the idea that an aging population has negative implications for societal resources—which get funnelled to the sick, the old, and the retired at the expense of the healthy, the young, and the working. These beliefs are used to justify a certain course of *action*—a retrenchment of the old age welfare state (or the whole welfare state for that matter) in an effort to counteract the burden of population aging. It is important to think of apocalyptic demography *as an ideology*; that is, it contains two elements—beliefs and courses of action that stem from those beliefs. To fail to do so is to overlook the political implications of what at first glance might appear to be an objective representation of population data and trends.

My analysis of apocalyptic demography will encompass both its numerical or data side and its political consequences and agenda. However, as a preface, I present actual examples of it, as culled from Canadian newspapers.

PAINFUL DECISIONS MUST BE MADE TO ENSURE FUTURE OF SOCIAL PROGRAMS
If you think we are having a hard time affording our social programs today, just wait a few years. What is little understood is how the demographic clock is working against us and how fast it is ticking.
Peter Hadekel, *Montreal Gazette,* 10 Dec. 1994

GRANDMA! GRANDPA! GET BACK TO WORK!
Retirement isn't a birthright. Those who enjoy it haven't earned it.
Canadians enjoy retirement, and why not? Most retirees are having the time of their lives: long, lazy summers at the cottage, gambling jaunts to Vegas in the winter, golf all year round.
Peter Shawn Taylor, *Saturday Night*, June 1995

RAISE SENIORS' TAXES
Ottawa should hit older people and their estates with new taxes to pay down the national debt, says a top tax lawyer. Seniors have benefitted from a lifetime of economic growth boosted by government spending and it is now time for them to pay the country back. . . . The $500 billion federal debt 'belongs' to older Canadians, but younger generations are being asked to pay for it.
Toronto Star, 11 Nov. 1994

GREYER HORIZONS
. . . the deal between the generations is under severe threat, as the costs of state pensions rise. Many countries are running out of people to pay those contributions. . . . But the argument between the generations is not just about pensions. Medical expenses, too, will burgeon as people get older.
Barbara Beck, *Globe and Mail*, 29 Dec. 1995

VALUE FOR MONEY
Canadians have rarely received so few benefits for their tax dollars, and the difficult times are just beginning. The consequences of this will be profound: tense interregional conflict, *clashes between young and old people*, and, if things get really bad, class warfare. [italics added]
Edward Greenspoon, *Globe and Mail,* 3 Oct. 1996

PENSION PLAN PINS PROSPECTS ON MARKET
Faced with the daunting demographic challenges of an aging baby-boom . . . Canadians—younger ones in particular—are skeptical . . . the CPP will be around for their retirement. And they have every reason to worry.
Shawn Mccarthy and Rob Carrick, *Globe and Mail*, 11 Apr. 1998

PAYING FOR THE BOOMERS
Blame it on the baby boomers. Last week, Finance Minister Paul Martin announced that Canada Pension Plan contributions will increase to 9.9 percent of pensionable earnings.

Maclean's, 24 Feb. 1997

LETTER TO THE EDITOR
The old women lugging their pension-laden purses from store to store aren't suffering. It's the people who are too young for the pension who are hard up.

Toronto Star, 5 Dec. 1994

At least five themes can be detected in this material. One theme is the *homogenization* of persons on the basis of age, e.g., old people are basically the same— they are comfortably well off. A second theme is *age-blaming*. Interestingly, in one case the elderly are held responsible—the federal debt is their fault— whereas in another case the middle-aged (the baby boomers) are to blame—for increases in CPP contributions. A third theme is that the shifting age structure is considered to be a significant *social problem* (e.g., 'a daunting demographic challenge'; 'the demographic clock is working against us'). A fourth, and very prominent, theme is *intergenerational injustice*—an aging population exacts an unfair toll on its younger members (e.g., 'clashes between the young and the old'; 'the deal between the generations is under severe threat'; old women are richer than working folk). The last theme is the *intertwining of population aging and social policy* concerns: for example, demographic aging will make it harder for us to afford our social programs; the federal debt is the fault of seniors; public pension sustainability is threatened by the baby boomers. While all of these themes are telling, the fifth theme—the mixing of demographic change and social welfare policy issues, or of population and politics—lies at the heart of voodoo demography. Population aging has become an important tool for social policy reform that lines up with a neo-conservative political agenda.

A 'Deconstruction' of Apocalyptic Demography

A number of different approaches can be taken to deconstruct apocalyptic demography. The one used here employs the arithmetic tools that apocalyptic demography itself uses—in other words, I want to fight it on its own turf and with its own concepts.

Basically, apocalyptic demography depends on two quite simple measures. One is the measurement of the proportion of a population that is aged 65 and over. The other is what is termed 'dependency ratios'. Let us first turn, then, to the age structural changes that have occurred, and are expected to occur, in Canada. Figure 1.1 shows the familiar trend of population aging in this country. We can see a substantial growth in the percentage of people aged 65 and over

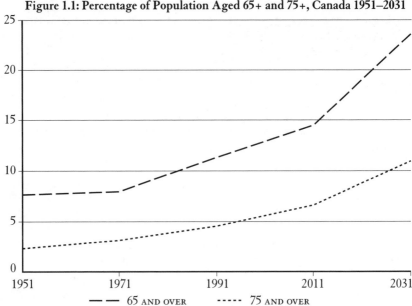

Figure 1.1: Percentage of Population Aged 65+ and 75+, Canada 1951–2031

— — 65 AND OVER   ····· 75 AND OVER

Projections based on medium assumptions regarding fertility, mortality, and migration.
Source: Adapted from Denton et al., 1998.

that has already occurred and will occur. We can also see an increase, although less marked, in the percentage of the population aged 75 and over. Murphy (1996) makes the point that older persons are steadily becoming more 'youthful'—look at a picture of your grandmother when she was your age and you will get the point. It may well be, then, that as we move into the next century, '75 and over' may come to mean the same thing as '65 and over' does now; if that is the case, the percentage of the elderly will be about the same as it is today—around 12 per cent. This is a bit of a demographic sleight of hand, though, because our social security system does not define the aged in that way. But it is an interesting point to consider, especially with regard to the arbitrary nature of 'aged' and 'elderly'.

Undoubtedly the favourite tool of voodoo demography is the dependency ratio (DR). This is simply the ratio of dependent persons to independent persons in a population. With regard to aging, the dependent population is defined as those aged 65 and over. The independent population is considered to be either all persons aged 20–64 or all persons aged 20–64 in the labour force.[2] Let's look at trends in the elderly DR, measured both ways.

Both DRs show the same general trend—an overall increase that escalates considerably after 2011. This post-2011 escalation shows the effects of the large baby-boom cohort, as its members enter the 65 and over age group. It is this

Table 1.1: Elderly Dependency Ratios, Based on Population and on
Labour Force, Canada, 1951–2041

Year	Elderly DR, based on Population*	Elderly DR, based on Labour Force**
1951	0.14	0.20
1961	0.15	0.20
1971	0.15	0.20
1981	0.16	0.19
1991	0.19	0.22
2001	0.21	0.25
2011	0.23	0.29
2021	0.32	0.40
2031	0.43	0.52
2041	0.46	0.57

* Proportion of population aged 65+ to population 20–64.
** Proportion of population aged 65+ to labour force aged 20–64.
Source: Adapted from Denton et al., 1998.

trend that fuels apocalyptic demography, but note two things. First, the increase in the elderly DR up to now has been really quite small; this is especially the case for the labour force-based elderly DR (for which increases in the elderly population have been partially counterbalanced by increases in the labour force participation of women). In other words, the concerns raised about the increasing burden of the older population that has supposedly led to government overspending in the last 10 or 20 years have to be seriously questioned—the increase in the elderly DR simply does not warrant these charges, which begin to look a lot like scapegoating. Second, while it is true that the elderly DR will increase in future years, the end result is nothing like we are led to believe. For example, in 2041 there will be approximately one-half an elderly person for every person in the working ages. While this is about double what it is today, it is nothing like the 'out of thin air' projections that there will be two or even three elderly persons for every person of working age.

But there is another dependent age group—children—and to get a fuller picture of dependency in the past, now, and in the future, we have to look at youth DRs as well as total DRs, which indicate the overall (youth plus elderly) dependency ratio (see Table 1.2).

We can see that the general trend in the youth DR is decline, except for the baby-boom years, which would be expected given the sustained fertility decline that commenced in Canada in the early 1970s. It can also be noted that the youth DR exceeds the elderly DR until 2031 or 2041 (depending on whether the DR is calculated on the total population aged 20–64 or on the labour force population

Table 1.2: Dependency Ratios, Based on Population and on Labour Force, Canada, 1951–2041

Year	Elderly DR	Youth DR	Total DR
	POPULATION		
1951	0.14	0.69	0.83
1961	0.15	0.82	0.96
1971	0.15	0.74	0.89
1981	0.16	0.54	0.71
1991	0.19	0.45	0.64
2001	0.21	0.41	0.62
2011	0.23	0.37	0.60
2021	0.32	0.36	0.68
2031	0.43	0.37	0.80
2041	0.46	0.36	0.82
	LABOUR FORCE		
1951	0.20	0.97	1.17
1961	0.20	1.12	1.32
1971	0.20	0.96	1.15
1981	0.19	0.64	0.83
1991	0.22	0.53	0.75
2001	0.25	0.50	0.75
2011	0.29	0.45	0.74
2021	0.40	0.45	0.85
2031	0.52	0.46	0.98
2041	0.57	0.45	1.02

Source: Adapted from Denton et al., 1998.

aged 20–64). Also, the trend in the youth DR reveals a sometimes overlooked fact. The large baby boom in Canada served to delay population aging here for some decades, in comparison with European countries, which have been dealing with populations with much higher elderly proportions than in Canada for many years now. For example, the population aged 65 and over is approaching 18 per cent in Sweden and is 16 per cent in the United Kingdom, Italy, and Germany (US Department of Commerce, 1993); we will not have a comparable percentage until around 2016.

If we look at the total DR, two important facts emerge. One, we are now at a historic low point in overall dependency. In other words, we have never had an age structure more favourable in terms of the ratio of the population in the non-working age groups to the population in the working age groups. Thus, any problems that Canada has with economic productivity, and with government debt and deficit, cannot be blamed on our demographics. Two, the projections regarding future total DRs indicate that, even in the 'terrible years' when the baby boom is old, our DR will not be as high as it was during the baby-boom years.

It is possible to argue that this is an overly optimistic interpretation, because the aged are much more of a burden on the public purse than are children, especially *vis-à-vis* pensions and health-care expenditures. Therefore, the elderly and children should not be treated as equal in their dependency effects. Things get a bit tricky here, because expenditures are both public and private, but the tendency has been to take account of public costs only, probably partly because the data are much more easy to obtain.

It has been estimated that per capita *public* expenditures are two to three times greater for the old than for the young (Clark and Spengler, 1980; Foot, 1989). If private expenditures were added in—in other words, if the total *social* costs of the dependent populations were calculated—the ratio would be somewhat smaller than this because of disproportionate private transfers to the young. Denton et al. (1998) have made a first attempt at estimating the relative social (private plus public) costs of the young and the old, and conclude that *total social costs for the elderly would have to be three times higher than for the young in Canada in order for our future overall dependency to exceed what we have already experienced* (during the baby-boom years). No one is suggesting that the total social costs of the elderly would be this much higher than for the young; therefore, our future age structure —although different in composition—will not be more 'costly' than what Canada has already had to deal with. This is, I think, very powerful ammunition against the predictions of apocalyptic demography with its vision of a future catastrophic age structure. It also exposes apocalyptic demography for what it is—a political tool for altering the Canadian social fabric and social contract. However, before embarking on a discussion of the blending of population and politics, a few words about dependency ratios are needed.

A Note on Dependency Ratios

Dependency ratios are far from perfect indicators of the costs of an age structure, and I would not be giving them so much attention if it were not for the fact that voodoo/apocalyptic demography relies on them so much. One of their shortcomings is the arbitrariness of defining everyone aged 65 and over (and under age 20) as dependent. Many teenagers work, as do some of the elderly population—recently released 1996 census data show that 372,415 persons aged 65 and over had employment income, with an average income of $20,446 (1995 dollars) (Statistics Canada, 1998). A related shortcoming is the assumption, in population-based DRs, that everyone aged 20–64 is productive. An even bigger problem exists with labour force-based DRs because they do not factor in the unwaged domestic labour of women (and men) and volunteer activities. So, for example, an elderly woman who is the primary caregiver for an ill husband, a homemaker, and a volunteer worker at a local arts organization is considered to be a dependant/non-provider/economic drain. Similarly, an elderly woman who looks after her grandchildren two or three days a week, so that her daughter can profitably work outside the home, is considered a dependant.

Volunteer activities and private assistance (or transfers) cannot be ignored. Prince and Chappell (1994) estimate that 20–50 per cent of Canadian seniors provide some form of formal voluntary activity, and it is especially likely to be direct service provision. McMullin and Marshall (1995) show that one-third of Canadians aged 65–74 and one-quarter of Canadians aged 75 and over provide assistance to friends. And most important of all, about 80 per cent of private cross-generational transfers occur within families, and it has been estimated that elders give over the course of their lives about 50 per cent more than they receive (Kronebusch and Schlesinger, 1994). When we move into these private domains of life, then, the definition of the aged as a dependent subpopulation becomes increasingly questionable.

Complicating the measurement of dependency is the growing underground economy, which has grown by leaps and bounds in the post-GST years. We do not know how much unregulated economic activity goes on, how it might differ by age, and its overall impact on the GDP (Pozo, 1996). But, clearly, some proportion of labour is not being taxed—among both dependent and independent age groups—and this has implications for the provision of government services.

Dependency ratios can be criticized along another, more theoretical dimension. They set up a false dichotomy between dependence and independence that needs to be examined (Robertson, 1997). This dichotomy can be traced to Western Enlightenment thought embracing individualism and its subvalues of self-reliance and self-sufficiency. Of course, no person is, or can be, totally self-reliant and self-sufficient, but the symbolism of individualism has been a powerful force in Western societies. We have been blinded from recognizing that:

> our very individuality exists only as a result of our embeddedness in a network of relationships both private and public. None of us is totally independent of our context—social, political, and economic; rather, we are located and live within complex webs of mutual dependence or interdependence. (Robertson, 1997: 436)

Through setting up dependence and independence as opposing concepts—as is the case with the DR—we make it more difficult to recognize and appreciate interdependence in social relationships, an interdependence that spans persons in the so-called dependent and independent age categories. Reciprocity is embedded in the concept of interdependence; it is the glue that binds people together in social relationships and to society as a whole. But recognizing reciprocity is not enough; it is also important for us to decommodify it (ibid.). Despite the fact we live in a capitalist, market-based economy, much of what transpires between individuals and across generations cannot be quantified in dollars and cents or be subjected to cost-benefit analyses. As Robertson (1997:

436) asks, 'how do we count or measure love, time, energy, kindness, commitment, shared memories, care—all the things which constellate human relationships and create community?'

Generational Accounting

Despite the conceptual importance of interdependence and the empirical point that not everything in social exchange can be measured in dollars, there is, at the same time, a counterforce seeking to quantify the generational contract. 'Generational accounting', first popularized by US economist Lawrence Kotlikoff (1993), concerns itself with measuring the lifetime tax burden on different age groups. The general idea is that if we can ensure that each generation carries the same tax burden—no more or no less than others—then all will be fair and right in the world. This is clearly linked to apocalyptic demography in that it is a mechanism to attempt to deal with the perceived crushing tax burden of the elderly and to ensure 'generational equity'.

A recent Statistics Canada publication edited by Miles Corak (1998), *Government Finances and Generational Equity*, applies the principles of generational accounting to the Canadian case. This is a disturbing turn of events for a number of reasons. One, it attempts to deal with generational relations in a strictly monetary way, whereas a wealth of social research shows that much of the social exchange that occurs between generations occurs along non-monetary dimensions. Another problem is that generational accounting is driven by a cost-containment mentality, which is not a good starting place for social policy—or at least it is one that should be questioned rather than taken for granted. Thus, generational accounting can be, and has been, used to justify reductions in government transfers (Good, 1995, in a Fraser Institute publication). Relatedly, as Osberg (1998: 137) points out, generational accounting takes into account only the costs of social programs, not their benefits:

> If only the costs of programs are counted, while benefits are not, it is clear that all programs will fail a cost-benefit evaluation. An agency like Statistics Canada can do a great deal to improve the debate on Intergenerational Equity in Canada, but one thing that I would argue that it should **not** do is to participate in . . . Generational Accounting exercises.

Another concern with the generational accounting framework lies in its assumption that redirecting transfers from one generation (e.g., the old) to another (e.g., children) will inevitably result in a fairer, more equitable society. Indeed, the international evidence suggests quite the contrary; it shows that nations that spend a lot on older people also spend a lot on children and youth (Myles, 1995). The poverty of children and youth is not caused by the pensions that older Canadians receive, and reducing the living standards of older Canadians will not lead to richer children. Hunsley (1997) has shown that the countries most successful in reducing poverty are those that do not target welfare expenditures to the poor (as is done in Canada, the US, the UK, and Australia). Rather, a more successful approach is to create equality of opportunity and to support family life *for all*.

Also, generational accounting fails to consider family-based transfers across generations. This is an important omission; as noted by McDaniel (1996a, 1997), in the past intergenerational transfers were almost always considered to be private family business—from parents to children (often sons), often through bequests. While these transfers were and are less private than often assumed—being influenced by laws and by social and economic policies that influence the ways that, and the degree to which, family members can assist one another—they are nevertheless an important element in the relations between generations and an element that we know very little about. Needless to say, generational accounting will not help us in understanding such transfers. Bengtson and Harootyan (1994: 233) argue that the future of intergenerational relationships is not nearly as pessimistic as some suggest because the 'prevalence, scope, and value of private intergenerational transfers are much greater than generally assumed.' They also note that these private transfers have been unrecognized by the media and by policy-makers.

A final problem with generational accounting that will be dealt with here[3] emanates from research findings by Wolfson et al. (1998: 119). Basically, they find more intragenerational variability than cross-generational variability:

> the very idea of framing the issue of the sustainability of government tax/transfer arrangements, including public pensions, in terms of generational equity may be seriously misleading. The reason, simply, is the vast heterogeneity within each generation. *This heterogeneity swamps generation.* . . . For example, if we examine 'winners' and 'losers' in terms of the net present value of their lifetime benefits in relation to taxes, each generation has substantial numbers of both. . . . It is certainly a major over-simplification to conclude that one generation or another is being unfairly treated by Canada's tax/transfer system. Individuals' life paths show such tremendous variety that birth cohort is unlikely to be a category or grouping with central political impact. [italics added]

Wolfson et al. make a powerful case, but their last sentence betrays a certain political naïvety—birth cohort or generation can be important politically, if the discourse of voodoo demography continues to hold sway.

Population and Politics

Apocalyptic demography demonstrates that population can become intertwined with politics to serve a political agenda. This is not the first time that this unhappy mixture has occurred; in this century, two other examples come to mind. One is the case of the eugenics movement in Canada, in which the control of reproduction was viewed as a way to preserve and improve the white race. Non-whites and less 'socially desirable' whites became the target of a campaign to lower their fertility. This movement gained its impetus from scientists and physicians; for example, E.W. McBride, McGill University's Strathcona Professor of Zoology in the early 1900s, wrote that 'All attempts to favour the slum population by encouraging their habits of reckless reproduction is throwing the support of their children on the State [which] places a heavier burden on the shoulders of the Nordic race, who form the bulk of the taxpayers' (McLaren, 1990: 24).

Even champions of the left, such as Tommy Douglas and J.S. Woodsworth, fell victim, early in their careers, to the ideas of the eugenicists. Tommy Douglas's MA thesis, 'The Problems of the Subnormal Family', submitted in 1933 to McMaster University, was a eugenics-based piece of research that viewed the mentally and physically subnormal as the cause of a good deal of the problems of the Depression, and saw remedies in such measures as health certification for marriage licences, the segregation of the unfit on sex-segregated state farms, and sterilization of the defective (ibid.). Woodsworth, later the founder of the CCF, in a characterization of pre-World War I immigrants in Winnipeg, described Scandinavians as 'clean-bodied' and 'serious-minded as a race' in contrast to Slavs, who were 'addicted to drunken sprees' and 'animalized' (ibid., 47). This is not to denigrate the memories of such notable Canadians as Douglas and Woodsworth, but rather to point out that even the intelligent and well-intentioned can be fooled by the 'ideas of the day' that appear to have scientific validity and purport to solve current problems. Those current problems were constructed as one of racial degeneration caused by two threats—the higher reproduction of the lower classes (who were labelled 'unfit') and the immigration to Canada of persons who were considered to be unsuitable due to their non-Nordic ethnic origins. Fertility and migration—two of the three basic demographic processes—were used as tools to preserve a type of Canada being jeopardized by the social and economic changes of the Industrial Revolution.

These ideas may seem foolish to us now, but their transformation into legislation is much more difficult to brush off. On the immigration front, the Oriental Exclusion Act placed severe hardships on Chinese and other Asians in Canada, who were unable to reunite with their families. Even worse, the eugenics movement led to sterilization legislation in British Columbia and Alberta that remained on the books until 1972 in both provinces. The Alberta legislation was more stringent, and we only have hard data for that province (because of lost and destroyed files in BC). We know that between 1928 and 1971, nearly 3,000 sterilizations occurred in Alberta; that teenage girls were the most likely to be sterilized; that Anglo-Saxons were underrepresented among those sterilized; and that in the last 25 years of the legislation, Indians and Métis, who comprised 2.5 per cent of Alberta's population, accounted for more than 25 per cent of the persons who were sterilized (ibid.).

At first glance, all of this may seem very remote from the issues involved in apocalyptic demography. But there are important points of parallelism: the problems of the day were conceptualized in strictly demographic terms (i.e., differential fertility, changing ethnic composition) whereas a much wider set of

factors was at play (i.e., the Depression, the social changes wrought by urbaniza-
tion and economic modernization); these demographic problems were deemed
to be costly to the public purse; and, accordingly, 'remedies' were sought to
lower public costs.

A second example of the intertwining of population and politics can be found
in the formulation of the 'population bomb' problem in the three decades or so
after World War II. It is true that populations in many Third World countries
were growing rapidly after the war—largely due to the introduction of technologies that lowered the death rate. However, it was the industrialized North
that defined the problem as a 'bomb' that had to be detonated, with massive
birth control aid as the detonating device. Millions of Western dollars (both
public and private monies, with the private sources large US-based foundations
like the Rockefeller Foundation) were spent on the delivery of birth control to
(largely) women in Third World countries, based on the assumption that lower
rates of population growth would positively influence economic development.
The birth control movement was generally a failure, as measured by declines in
fertility. But, on another level, it was hugely successful. Its success can only be
understood if one recognizes that the political motivation behind birth control
expenditures to the Third World was the exertion of Western influences in
'uncommitted' countries that could have easily fallen sway to Soviet development models. And it is not a coincidence that this funding dried up in the sunset
years of the USSR and when the support for birth control in other countries
became an obstacle to Ronald Reagan's domestic anti-abortion policies
(Hodgson, 1988).

This example is less directly relevant to the apocalyptic demography of the
present day, perhaps because of its foreign policy dimensions and international
context. Nevertheless, we again see a complex issue—in this case, Third World
development—oversimplified as a demographic problem, and we see demography being used to serve political ends.

Apocalyptic Demography and Social Policy

Let us now turn to some of the direct ways in which apocalyptic demography
has informed Canadian public policy—and how these claims stack up against
empirical evidence.

Government Debt/Deficit, Social Spending, and the Older Population

The fact that Canada now faces a huge debt and has experienced large deficits
until very recently is, of course, not news. However, the causes of the debt and
deficit are less well understood. It is 'accepted fact' that government spends too
much on social programs—such as pensions and health care—and that we now
have to cut down on this social spending (and this cutting down has been occurring for a number of years now). However, Lars Osberg and Pierre Fortin
(1996b), a leading team of Canadian economists, argue and provide evidence

that this accepted view is incorrect. They identify two time periods as important to the increase of Canada's debt-to-income ratio—the late 1970s and the period after 1988—each with different contributing factors. Gillepsie (1996) shows that the debt-to-income ratio problem of the late 1970s was caused by tax policy changes that led to reductions in personal income tax, corporate income tax, and the manufacturers' sales tax (thus decreasing national income). A number of economists point to the Bank of Canada as the major culprit in increasing post-1988 debt-to-income ratios (e.g., Fortin, 1996; Osberg and Fortin, 1996b; Rosenbluth, 1996; Van Audenrode, 1996). In 1988, the Bank of Canada altered monetary policy in favour of a zero-inflation regime. The resulting increases in interest rates (which added to our debt load) and decreases in economic growth (which meant a smaller income to service our debt as well as a greater need for employment insurance and social assistance payouts) contributed greatly to the Canadian debt and deficit. Rosenbluth (1996: 110) argues that a change in monetary policy to reduce interest rates (and thereby increase employment) would allow us to reduce our debt and maintain our social programs: 'the Canadian economy is far from bankrupt. It is government policy that is bankrupt.' Lastly, Fortin (1996) shows that anti-inflationary measures are the most important factor accounting for increased debt, with high world interest rates and slow economic productivity as secondary causes. Social spending on the aged (or any other group) is, in his words, 'definitely not a source of debt' (ibid., 26).

Economists of the classical school would disagree with this take on the factors responsible for the national debt. Nevertheless, enough substantive evidence, provided by leading Canadian economists, points to the negative effects of the Bank of Canada's monetary policies for us to question why the Bank of Canada as 'culprit' is never considered in the social policy discourse. It provides a credible alternative to voodoo/apocalyptic demography. It is perhaps important to point out, in this regard, that the Bank of Canada operates outside the influence of the democratic political process.

One might say that it really does not matter what caused our debt/deficit problems. They exist and reduced social spending is in the cards for all age groups. Yet, the identification of causes is critical in attacking the scapegoating that is part and parcel of apocalyptic demography.

Pensions and Population Aging

Most of the public debate around population aging has focused on pensions. The pension area brings out two of the strongest images of apocalyptic demography—the elderly as well-heeled 'greedy geezers' and the intergenerational injustice that will be brought on by the baby boomers.

Income and income security in later life are a huge topic, and chapters by Michael Prince and Lynn McDonald focus on it in some detail. Here, I just want to highlight important points with regard to apocalyptic demography.

First, the 'greedy geezer' stereotype is unwarranted. While we do have a small portion of highly visible well-off seniors, the Canadian aged as a whole are not rich. In a recent analysis of 1996 Survey of Consumer Finance data, Lochhead (1998) shows that 20 per cent of Canadian senior-headed households have less than $65 in annual pre-transfer income, i.e., income before the Old Age Security (OAS), Guaranteed Income Supplement (GIS), and Canada/Quebec Pension Plan (C/QPP), and that 40 per cent have less than $5,179 in pre-transfer income. It should also be remembered that the GIS was put in as a temporary measure in the late 1960s and was expected not to be needed when the C/QPP matured. However, the incomes of many seniors have remained so low that the GIS has never been rescinded and it is important in keeping many older Canadians out of poverty. Nearly 40 per cent of the elderly have such meagre incomes that they qualify for the GIS, and the combined OAS/GIS benefit does not lift the elderly living in larger cities out of poverty, and it barely does for others. As well, poverty continues to plague older unattached women, of whom nearly one-half live below the poverty line (Gee and Gutman, 1995).

Contribution rates to the Canada Pension Plan (shared equally by employers and employees) were increased in January 1998, with the goal of creating a five-year fund of money. This change has been presented as necessitated by our changing demographics. Let's see if the reason really is demographic.

The CPP operates on a 'pay-go' principle, with the contributions of today's workers paying the benefits of today's seniors, so there has never been a CPP fund in the same sense as there is with private pension plans. But there has been a potential fund, that is, the difference between what workers are contributing and what seniors are receiving. But that fund has been depleted over the years, not because of excessive benefits paid to seniors, but rather due to the borrowing of these funds by the provinces—at very low interest rates and generally not repaid—for all manner of things, such as building bridges and schools and preserving parks (Finlayson, 1988).

Thus, one problem is the transfer of potential pension benefits to other areas. This is not illegal; in fact, it was built into the original CPP legislation at the insistence of Ontario, which would not agree to sign this new pension scheme unless provincial borrowing was allowed. Such is the nature of Canadian federalism. Another problem is that the original contribution rates were set very low; in Myles's (1996: 55) words, our contribution rates are 'pitiably low' and 'by international and even American standards Canada is not even in the ballpark.'

These comments are not meant to imply that some increases in CPP contribution rates will not be required as the population ages. This is surely to be the case, and has been known for many years. The problem is that other causes are not mentioned. Another concern, highlighted by Prince (1996), is the political shift in pension reform, from a focus on expanding coverage to one of 'heading for cover'. The federal government now concentrates on affordability, neglecting issues of expansion in benefits (desperately needed by many, as data on seniors' incomes show), as well as problems with private pensions, such as increasingly inadequate coverage, especially in the private sector, and lack of indexation. The Senior's Benefit, examined by Lynn McDonald in Chapter 7, would have done little, except save the federal government money. It would have added 17 cents a day to the incomes of poorer seniors and was projected to save the government $2.1 billion in 2011 and $8.2 billion in 2030 (Brown, 1997).

Clearly, the message is that we are not to depend on public pensions and must save for our own retirement. The preferred vehicle is RRSPs—a partially privatized system that benefits the highly paid—although all evidence suggests that RRSPs will not play a key role for many Canadians in replacing pre-retirement income (Baldwin, 1996). McDonald (1995: 451) warns that our pension reforms are placing us on 'the brink of entrenching a two-tiered retirement system: one for the rich and one for the poor'. Our model of later-life income as social insurance is being replaced with a social welfare model. The pension reforms that will affect tomorrow's elderly are being driven by a neo-conservative ideology that will create hardship. The issue is not demography; rather, it is the failure of our policy-makers to recognize that the market-driven solutions that may have worked in the past will not work now. One could say that apocalyptic policy accompanies apocalyptic demography.

Today's workforce faces unemployment, downsizing and restructuring, and increased contract and part-time labour. As Marshall (1995: 48) states, 'rational individual-level planning for retirement is virtually impossible, [therefore] we must try to reverse the current trend of placing more and more responsibility for providing income security in retirement onto individuals.' This sentiment is echoed by demographers Rosenberg and Moore (1996), the authors of the 1991 Canadian census monograph on population aging. In my words, pension policy and economic realities for workers are on a collision course for reasons quite independent of demography. In more creative language, McDaniel (1996b) refers to the problem as one of 'serial employment and skinny government'.

Apocalyptic Demography and Health Care

There is no simple relationship between population age structure and health-care costs. While it seems obvious/intuitive that the older a population is, the more expensive are its health costs, the research evidence does not support this. For example, if we compare Canadian health costs and age structure with those of other developed countries, we see that while the Canadian population is quite 'young', we spend a higher proportion of our GDP on health than do many other 'much older' countries (Binstock, 1993).

Nevertheless, health-care costs have been escalating in the last few decades in Canada. The reason is not population aging. Barer et al. (1995) estimate that less than 5 per cent of the increase in BC health-care costs over a 12-year period is due to our changing age structure and that, overall, annual growth rates in the GDP of 1–2 per cent per year could accommodate the increases in costs. A major factor is increasing use of the health-care system. These increases have been substantial for all age groups, but have risen the most for persons aged 75 and over. Some ask if older people are receiving 'unnecessary' health care. Some evidence suggests that this might be the case, for example, Black et al. (1995), using Manitoba data for the period 1971–83, found that around one-half of the increase in consultations to specialist physicians was due to increased visits by elders in (self-reported) good health. But all gerontologists know that a very high proportion of the aged self-report they are in good health, meaning they are in good health 'for their age' (Gutman et al., 1999). Certainly, any 'overuse' of the medical/health system by elders (and others) should be curtailed, but we must be clear about what constitutes overuse and how much savings would be entailed. For example, one US-based study (Emanuel and Emanuel, 1994) finds that only 1 per cent of total national health-care expenditures would be saved if all aggressive treatment, hospice care, and advance directives were eliminated for persons aged 65 and over in their last year of life. Marshall (1997) argues that health-care reform aimed at reducing unnecessary use should be targeted at servicing patterns and not at the elderly *per se*.

But let us not forget two things. First, the Canadian health-care system is—despite, not because of, our demographics—very expensive. (This is in direct contrast to our income security system, which has minimal administrative costs; see Brown, 1997). The reasons for this are complex, having to do with the multiple linkages among needs, delivery, financing, organization, and management (Angus, 1996). This topic is outside the realm of what is being addressed here, but one point is important to emphasize. Available evidence shows that the successful control of health-care expenditures is more likely to occur in centralized health-care fiscal systems (ibid.). However, Canada and its provinces are committed to decentralization in health care, so we will have to be very careful that we are not making a costly policy error.

Second, despite our expensive formal health-care system, the large bulk of health care to the elderly is provided informally, largely by women. Attempts to reduce the formal costs of caring will thus place an even greater burden on women, who may themselves be frail and lack the financial resources to cope. Rosenthal (1994) argues that the health-care reform that is shifting elder care from institutions to the community carries along with it the yet unaddressed need for support for caregivers—support in the workplace, support in the form of formal services, and support with regard to available and high-quality institutions. And Aronson (1992) reminds us that many women caregivers really do not have a choice in the matter, given the prevailing gendered division of care labour. Health-care reform that traps and overworks women in an effort to save government dollars is not much of a bargain.

Conclusion

It is important to recognize voodoo/apocalyptic demography (and its components) for what it is—an ideology based on beliefs that do not hold up to the test of empirical research and that is leading us in regressive policy directions. It is attractive because (1) it provides a simple and intuitively plausible explanation for present-day problems and (2) it places blame on inexorable demographic change that we cannot do anything about. Together, these two qualities allow us to take what seems to be a simple path, even though it may be a path that creates a much degraded Canadian society. In many ways, voodoo demography can be considered as a kind of 'moral panic' (Thompson, 1998)—the consequences of population aging are being exaggerated to serve a political agenda.

I do not want to suggest that population aging does not carry challenges, even problems, for it certainly does. We will have to deal with important issues, a sampling of which include:

- What does/should retirement mean in a society in which one-quarter of the population is over the conventional retirement age of 65?
- How do we balance the age discrimination inherent in mandatory retirement with the health declines that make some seniors unable to work?
- What do we do about individual preferences for early retirement?
- How can we make work options more flexible for older people?
- What is the best way to deal with the long-term care needs of the frail elderly?
- How do we meet these needs without severely stressing their mostly female caregivers?
- How can we ensure equity for both caregivers and care-receivers?

Solutions to these challenges do not lie in the apocalyptic policy that accompanies apocalyptic demography. Rather, social policy in an aging society should recognize the past and present contributions of older persons at both the societal and familial (i.e., intergenenerational) levels and encourage them to continue to contribute; be based on the primacy of human (and not market) values; recognize the value of care work; and understand that failing to provide adequate incomes for the aged can be more costly in the long run.

Also, we face broader questions and problems; population aging is just one of many facets of a changing Canada. How can we ensure the economic productivity (an approximate 2–3 per cent annual growth in GDP) that will be necessary for a prosperous Canada in the face of globalization and the downward economic pressures and dislocations it imparts on developed countries? How can we ensure that societal resources are more equitably distributed, in the face of regional differences, changes in family structure, and a changing ethnic composition? How do we plan for a more knowledge- and information-intensive economy and the human capital educational requirements it will demand? If we place our attention on these matters and not let apocalyptic demography concerns overtake us, we will be far better equipped to deal with the twenty-first century and its changing age structure.

Notes

1. The terms 'voodoo demography' and 'apocalyptic demography' are used synonymously.

2. Dependency ratios based on the population are always lower than those based on the labour force because the population denominator is larger than the labour force denominator.
3. Other criticisms can be found in Marshall (1997).

References

Angus, Douglas E. 1966. 'Future Horizons for Health and Health Care: A Policy Perspective', in Canadian Federation of Demographers, *Towards the XXIst Century: Emerging Socio-Demographic Trends and Policy Issues in Canada*. Ottawa: Canadian Federation of Demographers, 11–22.

Aronson, Jane. 1992. 'Women's Sense of Responsibility for the Care of Old People: "But Who Else Is Going to Do It?"', *Gender and Society* 6: 8–29.

Baldwin, Bob. 1996. 'Income Security Prospects for Older Canadians', in A. Joshi and E. Berger, eds, *Aging Workforce, Income Security, and Retirement: Policy and Practical Implications*. Hamilton, Ont.: Office of Gerontological Studies, McMaster University, 69–74.

Barer, Morris L., Robert G. Evans, and Clyde Hertzman. 1995. 'Avalanche or Glacier?: Health Care and Demographic Rhetoric', *Canadian Journal of Aging* 14: 193–224.

Bengtson, Vern L., and R.A. Harootyan. 1994. *Intergenerational Linkages: Hidden Connections in American Society*. New York: Springer.

Black, Charlene, P. Noralou Roos, Betty Havens, and Linda McWilliam. 1995. 'Rising Use of Physician Services by the Elderly: The Contribution of Morbidity', *Canadian Journal on Aging* 14: 225–44.

Binstock, Robert H. 1993. 'Healthcare Costs Around the World: Is Aging a Fiscal "Black Hole"?', *Generations* 17, 4: 37–42.

————. 1994. 'Changing Criteria in Old-Age Programs: The Introduction of Economic Status and Need for Services', *Gerontologist* 34: 726–30.

Brown, Robert L. 1997. 'Economic Security for an Aging Canadian Population', Ph.D. thesis, Simon Fraser University.

Clark, R.L., and J.J. Spengler. 1980. 'Dependency Ratios: Their Use in Economic Analyses', in J.L. Simon and J. DaVanzo, eds, *Research in Population Economics*, vol. 2. Greenwich, Conn.: JAI Press, 63–76.

Corak, Miles, ed. 1998. *Government Finances and Generational Equity*. Ottawa: Statistics Canada Catalogue No. 68–513–XPB.

Denton, Frank T., Christine H. Feaver, and Byron G. Spencer. 1998. 'The Future Population of Canada, Its Age Distribution and Dependency Relations', *Canadian Journal on Aging* 17: 83–109.

Emanuel, E.J., and L.L. Emanuel. 1994. 'The Economics of Dying: The Illusion of Cost Savings at the End of Life', *New England Journal of Medicine* 330: 540–4.

Finlayson, Anne. 1988. *Whose Money Is It Anyway? The Showdown on Pensions*. Markham, Ont.: Viking/Penguin.

Foot, David K. 1989. 'Public Expenditure, Population Aging and Economic Dependency in Canada, 1921–2021', *Population Research and Policy Review* 8: 97–117.

Fortin, Pierre. 1996. 'The Canadian Fiscal Problem: The Macroeconomic Connection', in Osberg and Fortin (1996a: 26–38).

Gee, Ellen M., and Gloria M. Gutman. 1995. 'Introduction', Gee and Gutman, eds, *Rethinking Retirement*. Vancouver: Gerontology Research Centre, Simon Fraser University, 1–12.

Gillespie, W. Irwin. 1996. 'A Brief History of Government Borrowing in Canada', in Osberg and Fortin (1996a: 1–25).

Good, Christopher. 1995. 'The Generational Accounts of Canada', *Fraser Forum* (Aug.: special issue). Vancouver: Fraser Institute.

Gutman, G.M., A. Stark, A. Donald, and B.L. Beattie. 1999. 'The Contribution of Self-reported Health Ratings to Predicting Frailty, Institutionalization and Death Over a 5 Year Period', unpublished paper.

Hodgson, Dennis. 1988. 'Orthodoxy and Revisionism in American Demography', *Population and Development Review* 14: 541–69.

Hunsley, Terrance. 1997. *Lone Parent Incomes and Social Policy Outcomes: Canada in International Perspective*. Kingston, Ont.: Queen's University School of Policy Studies.

Kotlikoff, Lawrence J. 1993. *Generational Accounting: Knowing Who Pays, and When, For What We Spend*. New York: Free Press.

Kronebusch, Karl, and Mark Schlesinger. 1994. 'Intergenerational Transfers', in Bengtson and Harootyan (1994: 112–51).

Longman, Philip. 1987. *Born to Pay: The New Politics of Aging in America*. Boston: Houghton Mifflin.

Lochhead, Clarence. 1998. 'Who Benefits from Canada's Income Security Programs', *Insight* 21, 4: 9–12.

McDaniel, Susan A. 1996a. 'At the Heart of Social Solidarity', *Transition* 9 (Sept.): 9–11.

———. 1996b. 'Serial Employment and Skinny Government: Reforming Caring and Sharing in Canada at the Millennium', in Federation of Canadian Demographers, *Towards the XXIst Century: Emerging Socio-Demographic Trends and Policy Issues in Canada*. Ottawa: Canadian Federation of Demographers.

———. 1997. 'Intergenerational Transfers, Social Solidarity, and Social Policy: Unanswered Questions and Policy Challenges', *Canadian Journal on Aging/Canadian Public Policy* (Supplement): 1–21.

McDonald, Lynn. 1995. 'Retirement for the Rich and Retirement for the Poor: From Social Security to Social Welfare', *Canadian Journal on Aging* 14: 447–51.

McLaren, Angus. 1990. *Our Own Master Race: Eugenics in Canada, 1845–1945*. Toronto: McClellend & Stewart.

McMullin, Julie A., and Victor W. Marshall. 1995. 'Social Integration: Family,

Friends, and Social Support', in Marshall, McMullin, P.J. Ballantyne, J.F. Daciuk, and B.T. Wigdor, eds, *Contributions to Independence Over the Life Course*. Toronto: Centre for Studies in Aging, University of Toronto.

Marshall,Victor W. 1995. 'Rethinking Retirement: Issues for the Twenty-First Century', in E.M. Gee and G.M. Gutman, eds, *Rethinking Retirement*. Vancouver: Gerontology Research Centre, Simon Fraser University, 31–50.

————. 1997. 'The Generations: Contributions, Conflict, Equity', prepared for the Division of Aging and Seniors, Health Canada.

Murphy, Michael. 1996. 'Implications of an Aging Society and Changing Labour Market: Demographics', *Roundtable on Canada's Aging Society and Retirement Income System*. Ottawa: Caledon Institute of Social Policy.

Myles, John. 1995. 'Pensions and the Elderly', *Review of Income and Wealth* 41: 101–6.

————. 1996. 'Challenges Facing the Welfare State: Putting Pension Reform in Context', in A. Joshi and E. Berger, eds, *Aging Workforce, Income Security, and Retirement: Policy and Practical Implications*. Hamilton, Ont.: Office of Gerontological Studies, McMaster University, 51–6.

Osberg, Lars. 1998. 'Meaning and Measurement in Intergenerational Equity', in M. Corak, ed., *Government Finances and Generational Equity*. Ottawa: Statistics Canada Catalogue No. 68–513–XPB, 131–9.

———— and Pierre Fortin, eds. 1996a. *Unnecessary Debts*. Toronto: James Lorimer.

———— and ————. 1996b. 'Credibility Mountain', in Osberg and Fortin (1996a: 157–72).

Pozo, Susan, ed. 1996. *Exploring the Underground Economy: Studies of Illegal and Unreported Activity*. Kalamazoo, Mich.: W.E. Upjohn Institute for Employment Research.

Prince, Michael J. 1996. 'From Expanding Coverage to Heading for Cover: Shifts in the Politics and Policies of Canadian Pension Reform', in A. Joshi and E. Berger, eds, *Aging Workforce, Income Security, and Retirement: Policy and Practical Implications*. Hamilton, Ont.: Office of Gerontological Studies, McMaster University, 57–67.

———— and Neena L. Chappell. 1994. *Voluntary Action by Seniors in Canada*. Victoria, BC: Centre on Aging, University of Victoria.

Robertson, Ann. 1997. 'Beyond Apocalyptic Demography: Towards a Moral Economy of Interdependence', *Ageing and Society* 17: 425–46.

Rosenberg, Mark W., and Eric G. Moore. 1996. 'Transferring the Future of Canada's Aging Population', in Federation of Canadian Demographers, *Towards the XXIst Century: Emerging Socio-Demographic Trends and Policy in Canada*. Ottawa: Canadian Federation of Demographers, 35–41.

Rosenbluth, Gideon. 1996. 'The Debt and Canada's Social Programs', in Osberg and Fortin (1996a: 90–111).

Rosenthal, Carolyn J. 1994. 'Long-term Care Reform and "Family" Care: A Worrisome Combination', *Canadian Journal of Aging* 13: 419–27.

Statistics Canada. 1998. *The Daily*. http://www.statcan.ca/Daily/English/980512/ d980512.pdf

Thompson, Kenneth. 1998. *Moral Panics*. London: Routledge.

US Department of Commerce. 1993. *An Aging World II*. Washington: Government Printing Office; International Population Report Series P-95 (Feb.).

Van Audenrode, Marc. 1996. 'Some Myths about Monetary Policy', in Osberg and Fortin (1996a: 112–23).

Wolfson, M.C., G. Rowe, X. Lin, and S.F. Gribble. 1998. 'Historical Generational Accounting with Heterogeneous Populations', in M. Corak, ed., *Government Finances and Generational Equity*. Ottawa: Statistics Canada Catalogue No. 68–513–XPB, 107–25.

2 | The Impact of Population Aging and Hospital Days
Will There Be a Problem?

Yves Carrière

Whenever a social policy or fiscal measure has been under reform in the past decade or so, the list of reasons raised as justification for change has usually included fiscal responsibility, deficit reduction, economic globalization, and, more and more, population aging. The population aging argument is primarily based on the dependency ratio. It is argued that an increasing proportion of the population is over the age of 65, placing more demands on the working-age population and employers with regard to contribution rates for public pension schemes, income security programs, and, of course, health-care services.

Similar to other reasons used to justify major reform of social policy, population aging is portrayed as a determinist factor that will have unbearable consequences on the welfare state (Burke, 1991; Chawla, 1991; Kettle, 1981; OECD, 1988). Once demography is viewed deterministically, a point is reached where we stop questioning the premise that lies behind the feared consequences and try to find alternative solutions. But often, the premise is basically wrong and the alternatives that are promoted carry the seeds of greater problems.

With most media attention focusing on the apocalyptic aspect of population aging, popular belief tends to embrace the premise that demography is destiny.[1] For that reason, a large proportion of younger people in Canada feel that public pension schemes and universal health-care services might not be available when they reach old age. They feel that they will have to bear the economic burden of providing for aging baby boomers and that they will be forced to provide for themselves when they retire. It is hard to blame the younger generation for taking this scenario for granted considering all the media attention that has promoted this perception. The focus has been on the numbers and proportion of elderly people, while ignoring the possible impact of changing socio-economic and demographic characteristics of the elderly population and the changing institutional environment.

Even though popular belief has it that population aging has already had a significant effect on the health-care system, several Canadian studies show that this has not been the case in the recent past (Barer et al., 1995; Black et al., 1995) and that it will not necessarily be the case in the future (Boulet and Grenier, 1978; Lefebvre et al., 1979). Rochon (1997) shows that the impact of population aging on the costs related to population aging is not as straightforward as often presented and must be examined in the light of many factors. As far as the overall impact of population aging on social programs, numerous studies indicate that although the effect will not be negligible, it should be manageable (Denton et al., 1998; Fellegi, 1988; Wolfson, 1991).

The focus of the present study is on hospital morbidity (i.e., days in hospital). Even though this is only one component of the health-care system, it accounts for a great deal of the total resources directed towards health care. This chapter presents projections of the total number of acute-care hospital days in Canada between 2001 and 2041. In examining these, we will see if anxiety over the possible impact of population aging on hospital morbidity is warranted.

In a similar study, Lefebvre et al. (1979) projected that the number of hospital patient-days would range between 58 and 90 million in the year 2031. In their 'most likely' scenario, the projected number is close to 85 million, a little less than twice the actual number in 1975. In another study for the Canadian Royal Commission on Health Services (the Hall Commission), projections were made of the number of hospital beds needed to respond to the needs of the population in 1991. While the actual number in 1991 was approximately 160,000 beds, the projected number was 235,000, an overestimation of close to 50 per cent over a 25-year period (Government of Canada, 1964, cited in Angus et al., 1995). Why such a large discrepancy?

Projections of hospital days can be a useful tool for planning future resources. However, earlier attempts seem to indicate that these projections have consistently overestimated future needs. As in the case above, overestimation mainly results from assumptions of constant rates of use over a long period of time. Although projections are not predictions and should not be taken at face value, they should indicate a range of possible outcomes based on 'realistic' demographic scenarios and 'plausible' rates of use of hospital beds. One of the main problems with using long-term projections is that we tend to forget that policies change over time and that they affect the use of health-care services. Also, trends in life expectancy and healthy life expectancy will affect measures of hospital morbidity. If healthy life expectancy improves, all things being equal, it will probably reduce the need for hospital beds. The purpose of projections is to indicate what could be the possible outcome if the assumptions that underlie the projections are correct. The validity of the assumptions should be considered before drawing any conclusions from the projections.

By exploring past trends in hospital morbidity, we will make projections on the number of hospital separations, length of hospital stays, and total hospitalization days for the period 2001 to 2041. Different assumptions in the patterns of use of health-care services will be considered and we will discuss the implications of our findings in the context of population aging. These projections do not take into account long-term care facilities; they are restricted to acute care hospitals.

Table 2.1: Summary of the Main Component Assumptions for
the Low-Growth and High-Growth Demographic Scenarios

Assumptions Component	High	Low
Fertility (total fertility rate by 2016)	1.9	1.5
Mortality (life expectancy by 2016)	81.0 M / 86.0 F	77.0 M / 83.0 F
Immigration (level by 2016)	330,000	150,000

The data used for this chapter are taken from annual publications on hospital morbidity and from population projections published by Statistics Canada. These publications report separations from a hospital, length of stay, the disease, and the age and sex of the patient (information on the type of disease is not used here). Records are submitted by each province and represent the hospital experience of all residents of each province (Statistics Canada, 1991). Since some hospitalized cases are not included (mental hospitals, for example), the volume of hospital care is actually slightly higher than what is published. It is also important to note that the statistics on hospital separations refer to the incidence of events (separations), rather than the incidence of disorders suffered by individuals. For the purposes here, and as defined by Statistics Canada, a separation represents the termination of one continuous stay in hospital as an in-patient. The termination can be either a discharge or a death. For each year, hospitalization rates are calculated using population estimates by age and sex for that year.

The projections of acute-care hospital days are based on observed hospital separation rates and average length of hospital stays by age and sex from 1971 to 1991. Different assumptions regarding the future trends of these rates will be applied to population projections for the period 2001–41. Five scenarios of hospital morbidity are presented, and they are matched with two different demographic scenarios. The latter correspond to high and low population growth rates projected by Statistics Canada (George et al., 1994). A summary of component assumptions is shown in Table 2.1. Compared to the low population growth scenario, the high population growth rate is based on higher total fertility, higher life expectancy, and higher immigration. We will briefly explore the effect of these assumptions on the total population and its age structure in the next section.

The first three scenarios assume constant separation rates and average length of stay for the entire period. They are based on the data observed in 1971, 1981, and 1991, respectively. These scenarios do not take into consideration possible changes in hospital morbidity linked to changing population health or to changing policies regarding hospital use.[2] The last two scenarios are based on trends of separation rates and average length of stay between 1971 and 1991. For the first case we have extrapolated the observed trend; as for the last scenario—the lower boundary scenario—we have used either the 1971–91 trend or the 1971 rates, depending on which is the lower. As previously mentioned, projections of hospital days will be

Figure 2.1: Population Projections for Canada, by Age Group, Low- and High-Growth Scenarios

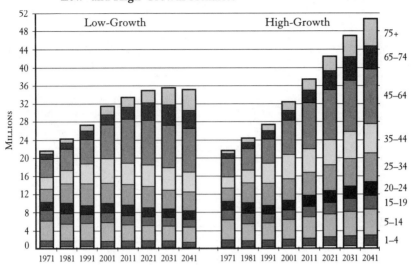

Source: George et al. (1994).

made by matching hospital separation rates and the average length of stay to the projected population by age and sex.

Population Projections and Past Trends in Hospital Morbidity

We will initially introduce our two demographic scenarios for the period 2001–41, after which we will examine trends in hospital morbidity between 1971 and 1991 (separation rates, average length of hospital stay, and number of hospitalization days). These trends will lead to our five scenarios for future separation rates and average length of hospital stay.

Population Projections

As stated earlier, we are using the low and high population growth scenarios from Statistics Canada for the period 1991 to 2041. Figure 2.1 shows that the low scenario projects an increase in the total population from 27.3 million in 1991 to around 35 million in 2041. The number of elderly people would almost triple in a span of 50 years, increasing from 3.2 million to 8.6 million. At the end of the period, seniors would represent 24.6 per cent of the total population compared to 11.6 per cent in 1991. (It is interesting to note that the low-growth scenario projects a decrease in the total population between 2031 and 2041.)

The high-growth scenario shows a rather constant increase in the total population up to 50.6 million in 2041, and still growing. The population of elderly

Figure 2.2: Separation Rates by Age Group, Males, Canada, 1971–1991

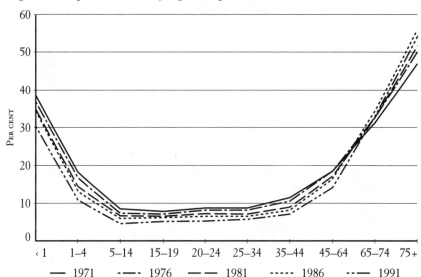

Source: Statistics Canada, *Hospital Morbidity,* various years.

people in 2041 is 11 million, compared to 8.6 million in the low-growth scenario. It is important to note that even though the number of elderly people would be 28 per cent higher in the high-growth scenario, their share of the total population would be less than 22 per cent, whereas the low-growth scenario predicts a proportion of elderly close to 25 per cent. Since an aging population is defined by the proportion of the population that is aged 65 and over, the low-growth scenario shows an older population than the other scenario. However, if we are interested in studying the number of hospital days in the future, numbers might have a greater impact than proportions. This issue will be revisited later.

Hospital Morbidity

Trends in Separation Rates

Separation rates, which reflect the total number of releases from hospital added to the number of people who died in hospital within a specific age group as a percentage of the total population of that age group in a given year, vary greatly according to age and sex. The pattern of separation rates for males has remained quite constant between 1971 and 1991 (Figure 2.2). The rates are high for newborns and then decrease sharply in the first five years of life (from around 35 per cent to less than 10 per cent). The separation rate is relatively stable up to the 35–44 age group, and it finally increases steadily up to around 50 per cent for those 75 years and over. Except for newborns, hospitalization rates are positively related with age.

Also of interest is the trend in the separation rates of each age group from 1971 to 1991. For age groups under the age of 65, separation rates have decreased

Figure 2.3: Separation Rates by Age Group, Females, Canada, 1971–1991

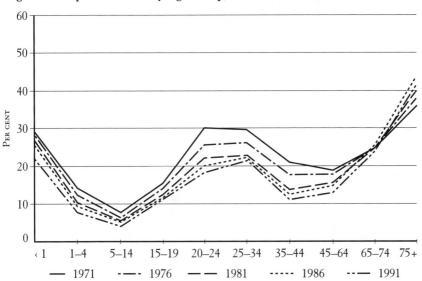

Source: Statistics Canada, *Hospital Morbidity,* various years.

from one year to the next. The drop is the most significant for children under the age of 5; up to age 65 the drop is very similar across age groups; for the 65–74 age group, there is a slight increase in separation rates, with higher rates in 1991; for the oldest age group, the rate increases steadily from 46.7 to 55.7 per cent between 1971 and 1986, and then decreases to 54 per cent in 1991.

The trend for females is similar to that for males, although the overall pattern of the hospitalization rate is quite different according to age (Figure 2.3). The main difference is that women experience a higher separation rate between the ages of 15 and 45, which can primarily be explained by pregnancy-related hospitalization. Over the age of 65, men show higher separation rates than women. When looking at the trend for given age groups, again we notice that between 1971 and 1991 the rates drop at every age except for the 65 and over population. At ages 65–74 the rate remains stable at around 24 per cent. In the oldest age group, there is an increase from 36 per cent in 1971 to 43.4 per cent in 1986. This increase is followed by a small drop in 1991 to 41.5 per cent.

Trends in Length of Hospital Stay

Rates of hospital separation are only one component of hospitalization days. We also have to look at the length of each hospital stay to get a better understanding of the changing nature of hospital morbidity in recent years. Figures 2.4 and 2.5 show, for males and females respectively, the trend in length of hospital stay by age group between 1971 and 1991. For both males and females the average length increases with age, particularly after the age of 45. The length of stay is

Figure 2.4: Average Length of Hospital Stays by Age Group,
Males, Canada, 1971–1991

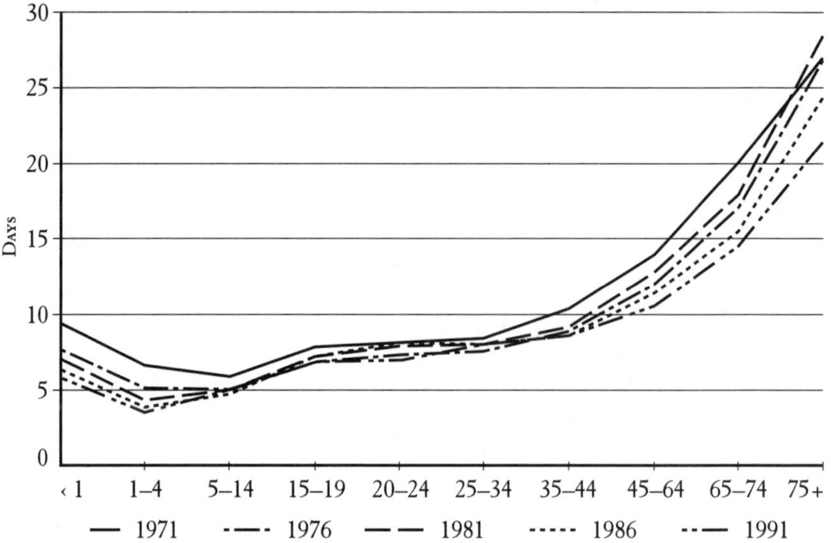

Source: Statistics Canada, *Hospital Morbidity,* various years.

consistently higher for women than for men in the older age groups. At age 75
and over, the average stay is about 40 per cent higher for women.

When looking at trends by age groups, we notice that for nearly every age
group the average length of hospital stay is the lowest in 1991. For both men and
women aged 65 years and over, a downward trend starts in 1981. Between 1981
and 1991, it decreased from 39 to 30 days for women aged over 75, and from 28
to 22 days for men of the same age group.

Trends in Hospitalization Days
The previous discussion demonstrates that separation rates and average length
of hospital stays decreased between 1971 and 1991 for those under the age of 65.
For the 65–74 age group, separation rates were relatively stable while the
average hospital stay decreased. Finally, the oldest age group saw their separation rates increase and their average length of hospital stay decrease over this
period. By matching these separation rates and average length of hospital stays,
we can analyse the trend in the number of hospitalization days for a given age
group. To avoid comparisons between age groups that would be affected by the
number of individuals in each group, we will look at the number of hospitalization days for 1,000 persons within each age group.

For both males and females, the combination of separation rates and average
length of stay by age group results in a curve that shows a sharp increase in hospitalization days after age 64. Between the ages of 5 and 64, males spend an

Figure 2.5: Average Length of Hospital Stays by Age Group, Females, Canada, 1971–1991

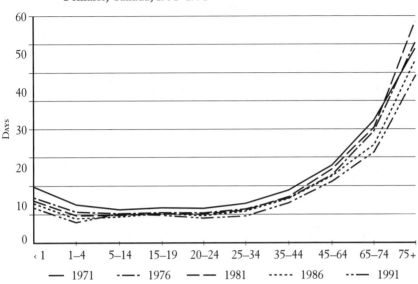

Source: Statistics Canada, *Hospital Morbidity,* various years.

average of less than 2.5 days a year in hospital. For the 65–74 age group, the yearly average number of days increases to approximately 5, and then to nearly 12 days for those 75 years and over. For females the pattern is very similar. These figures show that hospital morbidity, as expected, is strongly related to age. What is interesting to observe is that between 1971 and 1981, the average number of hospitalization days for men aged 75 years and over increased from around 12.5 days to 15 days. Then, between 1981 and 1991, the number of days dropped to 12. A similar trend can be observed for women.

Figures 2.6 and 2.7 show the main source of the anxiety created by an aging population regarding possible consequences for our health-care system. The strong correlation between age and the annual average number of hospitalization days is seen as evidence that the increase in the number of elderly people in the next 50 years will have unbearable consequences on the number of hospitalization days and on the health-care system in general. But the changes we have seen between 1971 and 1991 highlight the need to take into account changing patterns of hospital morbidity before making any projection based solely on the number of individuals in a given age group.

Projected Number of Hospital Days

As already stated, we are using two demographic scenarios and five possible patterns of hospital morbidity for our projections. The purpose of using two demographic scenarios is to show the effect of demographic trends alone on

Figure 2.6: Yearly Hospitalization Days per 1,000 Males by Age Group, Canada, 1971–1991

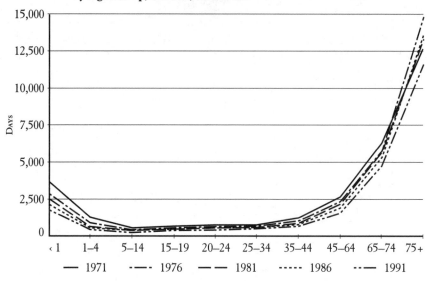

Source: Statistics Canada, *Hospital Morbidity,* various years.

Figure 2.7: Yearly Hospitalization Days per 1,000 Females by Age Group, Canada, 1971–1991

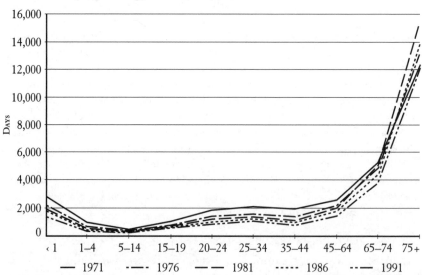

Source: Statistics Canada, *Hospital Morbidity,* various years.

Table 2.2: Assumptions for Separation Rates (%) and
Average Length of Hospital Stays (days) by Age Group
and Sex, Population 65 Years and Over, Canada 1971–2041

		1991	2001	2021	2041
1. Constant rates: 1971					
separation rates	M 65–74/75+	30.9/46.7			
	F 65–74/75+	24.8/36.0			
Average length	M 65–74/75+	19.9/26.9			
	F 65–74/75+	21.5/34.3			
2. Constant rates: 1981					
separation rates	M 65–74/75+	32.6/51.9			
	F 65–74/75+	24.6/39.7			
Average length	M 65–74/75+	17.9/28.3			
	F 65–74/75+	20.3/39.2			
3. Constant rates: 1991					
separation rates	M 65–74/75+	32.4/54.1			
	F 65–74/75+	23.7/41.5			
Average length	M 65–74/75+	14.6/21.5			
	F 65–74/75+	16.0/29.7			
4. Trend of 1971–91					
separation rates	M 65–74/75+	32.4/54.1	33.2/58.2	34.8/67.2	36.5/78.0
	F 65–74/75+	23.7/41.5	23.2/44.5	22.1/51.3	21.1/59.3
Average length	M 65–74/75+	14.6/21.5	12.5/19.2	9.2/15.4	6.7/12.3
	F 65–74/75+	16.0/29.7	13.8/27.6	10.3/23.9	7.6/20.7
5. 'Optimistic' scenario					
separation rates	M 65–74/75+	32.4/54.1	31.9/51.5	30.9/46.7	30.9/46.7
	F 65–74/75+	23.7/41.5	23.2/39.5	22.1/36.0	21.1/36.0
Average length	M 65–74/75+	14.6/21.5	12.5/19.2	9.2/15.4	6.7/12.3
	F 65–74/75+	16.0/29.7	13.8/27.6	10.3/23.9	7.6/20.7

Note: The table shows only the assumptions for age groups over the age of 64, but our
projections are based on assumptions done for every age group (not shown in the table).

hospitalization days. The five scenarios of separation rates and lengths of stay
will help us identify the effect of the pattern of acute-care hospital use on our
projections. The first three scenarios use constant separation rates and lengths of
stay (Table 2.2). By doing so, we want to demonstrate that projecting needs and
costs from data on a specific year is extremely misleading and only fuels an
alarmist view regarding the impact of population aging on hospital morbidity.
The final two scenarios will make use of past trends of separation rates and
length of stay.

Figure 2.8: Projected Relative Increase in the Number of Acute Hospital Days, Low-Growth Demographic, Canada, 1991–2041

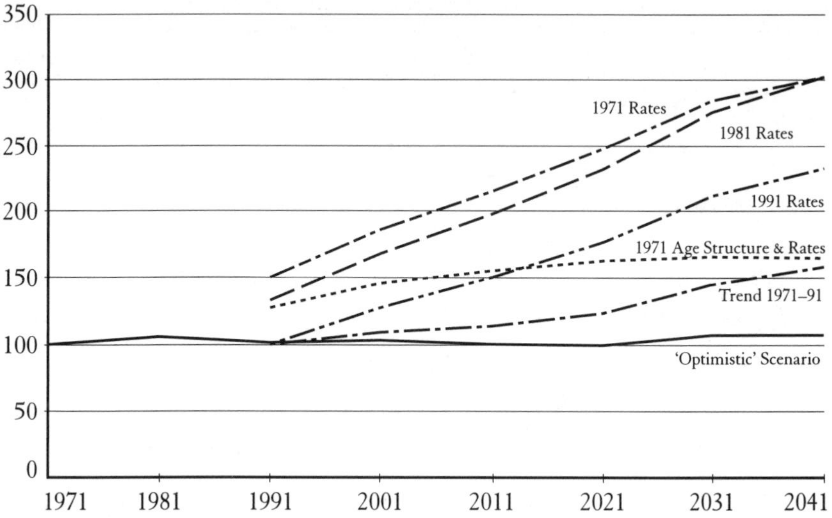

Notes: 1971 = 100; actual data for 1971–91 period.

Projections Based on Constant Patterns of Hospital Morbidity: 1971, 1981, 1991

The first projection shows the impact of both changing age structure and total population between 1971 and 2041. Under the assumptions of the low-growth demographic scenario, hospitalization days are projected to be three times greater at the end the period (Figure 2.8). From 41.3 million hospital days in 1971, we would reach close to 125 million days in 2041. Under the high-growth demographic scenario, hospitalization days would be four times greater than in 1971 (Figure 2.9). To see if this scenario is realistic, we can compare the projected and actual numbers in 1991. The former indicates a total of 62.3 million hospital days when the actual number was 41.4 million days—an overestimation of 50 per cent in a span of 20 years.

The projection based on 1981 rates shows very similar results. When comparing the projected and the actual numbers for 1991, we note an overestimation of 32 per cent in a span of only 10 years. Therefore, using either 1971 or 1981 measures of hospital morbidity produces very unrealistic results—surely not very useful for drawing conclusions on the potential effect of population aging.

The third scenario uses 1991 data on hospital morbidity. As in the previous scenarios, we are maintaining constant rates throughout the projected period. This time, in the low-growth demographic scenario, we get a total of 95.7 million hospital days in 2041, 23 per cent less than in the previous projections but still an overestimate of 131 per cent compared to the actual numbers in 1991. The combination of 1991 hospital morbidity rates and the high-growth demographic

Figure 2.9: Projected Relative Increase in the Number of Acute Hospital Days, High-Growth Demographic, Canada, 1991–2041

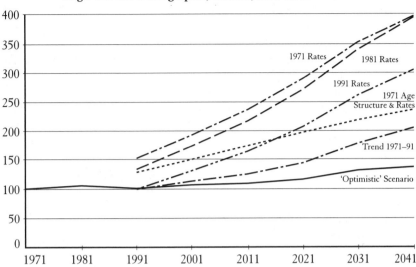

Notes: 1971 = 100; actual data for 1971–91 period.

scenario results in a number of hospital days in 2041 that is similar to the combination of either the 1971 or 1981 rates with the low-growth demographic scenario.

How realistic is this third scenario? The trends of hospital morbidity between 1971 and 1991 suggest that using constant separation rates and average length of hospital stay might not be the best approach. We have seen earlier that for most age groups there is a trend towards lower separation rates and lower average lengths of stay. Only for the 75 years and over age group do we observe an increase in separation rates. The next two scenarios will use these past trends to analyse the potential impact of an aging population on hospital morbidity.

Projections Based on Trends of Hospital Morbidity Observed between 1971 and 1991

Projections using constant measures of hospital morbidity observed at one point in time do not provide realistic projections of hospitalization days. Measures of hospital morbidity have not been constant in the past and there is no reason to think that they will stay at the 1991 level for the next 50 years.

The present scenario is based on the extrapolation of observed separation rates and average lengths of stay between 1971 and 1991. To remain realistic about these projected measures of hospital morbidity, downward trends will be extrapolated based on the assumption that although the trend will continue, it will do so at a slower pace (Table 2.2). This assumption takes into consideration that it might be more difficult in the future to improve on measures already showing levels that are quite low. In the case of measures showing an upward trend, the extrapolation is based on the assumption that this trend will increase its pace (Table 2.2). This assumption takes into account the future increase, both in absolute and relative numbers, in the population over the age of 85. Since the data on hospital morbidity do not provide separate information for those 85 and over, it is possible to assume that measures of hospital morbidity for the population aged 75 and over might go up faster than in the past.

As shown in Figures 2.8 and 2.9, considering past trends in hospital morbidity has a major impact on projected number of hospital days. Matching our measures of hospital morbidity with the low-growth demographic scenario results in a total of 64.8 million hospital days in 2041, an increase of 57 per cent compared to the actual data for either 1971 or 1991 (Figure 2.8). This number of hospital days is lower than the one projected in 2001 using measures of hospital morbidity from either 1971 or 1981 (scenarios 1 and 2). Even though the total population would increase by 63 per cent between 1971 and 2041, with the elderly population multiplying by four during the same period, the number of hospital days would increase by 57 per cent. Using the high-growth demographic scenario, the number of hospital days reaches 83.8 million, twice the number in 1971 (Figure 2.9), which is much smaller than the increases in the total population and the elderly population (134 per cent and 531 per cent, respectively).

The first three scenarios show the impact of an increasing population and a change in its age structure on the number of acute-care hospital days over the first half of the next century. The fourth one demonstrates how this impact could be mitigated by accounting for possible changes in the pattern of hospital morbidity. The final scenario assumes that all measures of hospital morbidity will improve over the next decades for all age groups, contrary to the preceding scenario in which separation rates for older people are assumed to get worse over the years. For this last scenario, extrapolation of past trends is used whenever these trends are downward. In cases where trends are upward, we assume that separation rates and average lengths of stay will slowly return to their 1971 levels and then remain at those levels between 2021 and 2041 (Table 2.2). Before presenting the results of this final scenario, we will look briefly at some research that provides support for these assumptions.

A healthier lifestyle throughout the life course may result in healthy aging, thus delaying hospitalization to older ages. Signs of a healthier lifestyle in the recent past include a decline in smoking, an increase in exercising regularly, healthier diets, etc. On a more theoretical basis, the demographic projections provided by Statistics Canada assume an increase in life expectancy. This increase in life expectancy means lower mortality rates at most ages. If mortality rates go down at a given age, we could also expect hospital morbidity to decrease around that age. Many studies have shown an increase in the use of hospital services in the last two years before death (Felder and Zweifel, 1997; Johansen et al., 1994; McCall, 1984; Roos et al., 1989; Shapiro, 1983). From this relationship we can assume that a drop in the probability of dying at age x will translate into lower hospital morbidity at age x − 1. It is also important to note that health-care costs in the last year of life have been found to be lower as the age of death increases (Mizrahi and Mizrahi, cited in Rochon, 1997).

Even though the relationship between mortality and morbidity is not simple, the drop in disability rates in the elderly population in recent years (Crimmins, 1996; Manton et al., 1998; Robine et al., 1997; Spiers et al., 1996) tends to go against the theory of pandemia (Kramer, 1980) and lends some support to the compression of morbidity theory (Fries, 1980)—healthy life expectancy increasing faster than life expectancy. If this is the case, we have every reason to assume that the onset of disease will be postponed to older ages, reducing measures of hospital morbidity. Past increases in separation rates for the older population might be seen as contradicting this theory, but other studies suggest that these increases might be supply-driven rather than responses to actual need (Barer et al., 1987, 1989). Data collected between 1971 and 1983 for the Manitoba Longitudinal Study on Aging show that a change in morbidity had a very small effect on the increase in service use, which was largely the product of an increase in service intensity (Black et al., 1995).

The results using our more optimistic scenario of a reduction in hospital morbidity, combined with the low-growth demographic scenario, show that the total number of hospital days will remain relatively stable throughout the first half of the next century (Figure 2.8). From 1971 to 2041, this total would increase by just 5 per cent, from 41.3 million to 43.5 million. In the high-growth demographic scenario, the total number of hospital days would reach 56.3 million in 2041, an increase of 36 per cent over a period of 70 years.

Projections using this last scenario emphasize two factors that could have a determining impact on the number of hospital days in the future: improvements in population health; and changes in the way the health-care system provides services. These factors will probably be of greater import on the number of hospitalization days than the impact of population aging. To demonstrate this point, we have projected the number of hospital days matching the measures of 1971 hospital morbidity with both the total population projected from the low- and high-growth demographic scenarios, while keeping constant the 1971 age structure. Figure 2.8 shows that in 2041 the total number of hospital days would then reach 67.5 million—a higher figure than in the last two scenarios we have presented. When using the total population of the high-growth demographic scenario but keeping the 1971 age structure, that total reaches 97.2 million (Figure 2.9). This last exercise shows that the impact of population aging mixed with a changing pattern in hospital morbidity is less significant than the impact of a younger age structure with patterns similar to the ones observed in 1971.

Discussion

Population aging is regularly portrayed as a major obstacle to the solvency of the welfare state. One of the main targets of the apocalyptic discourse has been the impact of population aging on the health-care system. By making projections assuming different scenarios of separation rates and average lengths of stay, we have shown that, at least in the case of hospital morbidity, the apocalyptic discourse is, to say the very least, misleading. This is not to say that population aging will not affect the health-care system.

Even in the most optimistic scenario, the increase in the number of hospital days for the population over the age of 65 would be 2.7 times greater, assuming the low-growth demographic scenario (figure not shown). The elderly population would then account for close to 90 per cent of the total hospital days compared to 36 per cent in 1971. Therefore, in the more optimistic scenario, population aging would not affect the total number of hospital days but it would drastically change the age composition of those being hospitalized. This transition has significant implications for the type of services provided in hospitals and for the training needed for physicians, nurses, and hospital staff.

How can we help to ensure that the optimistic scenarios become reality in the future and make the challenge of population aging manageable? Obviously, it will depend in part on our individual and collective willingness to adjust to this social change. It will not be accomplished without the co-operation of governments, corporations, special interest groups, and individuals.

First, improving the health status of the elderly population will not be achieved without investing more resources in health promotion (OECD, 1996). In the context of the 1990s, it does not seem reasonable to expect governments to increase substantially the financial resources they allocate to health care. More resources towards prevention and health promotion would mean transferring resources at the expense of the medical side of the health-care system, including hospitals. This could hardly be done without some resistance from physicians, who would stand to lose the most. It may also demand that we consider aging to be a normal process that requires an increase in the resources allocated to social services to facilitate 'aging in the community', instead of perceiving aging as a medical challenge—a disease—that requires an unlimited expansion of medical resources.

A broader population health framework requires more than just increasing resources towards health promotion programs. Any policy that affects our social, economic, and physical environment will eventually influence the health of the population and, ultimately, the total costs related to health care (Federal, Provincial, Territorial Advisory Committee on Population Health, 1994). For example, better working conditions, lower unemployment rates, and a more equitable distribution of wealth can positively affect health and lower hospital morbidity.

Finally, as individuals we have to question some of our expectations with regard to what is medically reasonable or possible. Should we expect physicians to have the primary responsibility for our health? Should we expect physicians to make absolutely every attempt to extend life? If so, we should not be surprised or outraged if physicians and other medical professionals are opposed to the reallocation of resources mentioned above.

Earlier, we outlined some factors that support the most optimistic scenarios regarding hospital morbidity. There is one other factor to consider. We have a tendency to disregard our capacity to adapt to major social changes. Optimistic scenarios are then perceived as too idealistic. A lesson can be learned from a study by Lefebvre et al. (1979) on the issue of hospital morbidity. Their most optimistic scenario projected the number of hospital days to be 44.3 million in 1991; their bleak scenario reached a total of 53.9 million hospital days; their most likely scenario projected 51.5 million days.[3] The actual number of hospital days for 1991 was 41.4 million—lower than their most optimistic scenario. Recent data on hospital morbidity support an optimistic scenario; for example, in 1995–6 the rate of hospitalization in Canada reached an all-time low (Statistics Canada, 1998).

Conclusion

Instead of looking at population aging as another reason to dismantle what remains of our welfare state, it should be envisioned as an opportunity to transform those social programs that are ill-equipped to respond to the challenge. In concluding that population aging will not have a catastrophic impact on hospital morbidity, we cannot ignore the impact that it might have on the need for home-care services, especially if we want to alleviate the burden resting on the shoulders of the informal support network, mainly comprised of women. This will be even more of a challenge in the future when the baby boomers reach old age with fewer children to provide the assistance they might need. The biggest challenge that our health-care system will face in the future will probably be the reallocation of its financial resources so that we have the capacity to respond to this need.

One of the major problems with making projections on one specific aspect of population aging is that the outcome is presented as an absolute measure. Taken out of context, these figures may be easily presented as indicating a threat to the health-care system. For example, extrapolation of the trends observed between 1971 and 1991 in separation rates and average length of hospital stays leads to an increase of 57 per cent in acute-care hospital days for the period 1991–2041. Per capita, this translates to an increase from 1.52 acute hospital days in 1991 to 1.84 days in 2041. Even though this represents an increase, the rate would still be lower than it was in 1971 (1.92 acute hospital days per person). A more complete picture would take into account future trends in economic productivity. An annual growth rate of 1.5 per cent would eliminate any negative impact that an increase in public costs related to hospital morbidity would have on the 'financial burden' of the working-age population.

Some, mostly politicians and economists, would be quick to say that we have taken a turn in a positive direction with the closure in recent years of many hospitals in most provinces. We should not confuse what is euphemistically called rationalization of services or administrative restructuring with the reallocation of resources. Closing down hospitals without providing resources for the needs created by the closures only exacerbates the challenge of population aging. The demands that we would make on the family will only serve to increase the private costs related to health care and to widen the gap between rich and poor. When taking into account that economic productivity should more than compensate for the impact of population aging on hospital morbidity, we should make available the resources to respond to the increasing need for home-care services. It is also important to note that reducing the burden on the informal support network should be seen as an opportunity to improve intergenerational relations. To sustain the trend observed between 1971 and 1991 in hospitalization days without generating a major increase in the use of long-term care facilities or without increasing the burden of the informal support network, home-care services will have to be integrated into our health-care system. Redistribution of health-care resources from medical services to social services should be a major objective of health-care policy in the context of population aging. The policy changes that will have to be made to respond to the challenge of population aging should not respond to false assumptions about its consequences on the health-care system (or other social programs). Population aging is a slow process and we have time to adjust. The sooner we tackle the real problems, the smoother the transition will be.

Notes

1. The popularity of the book written by D.K. Foot with D. Stoffman, *Boom, Bust, and Echo: How to Profit from the Coming Demographic Shift* (1996), shows just how much this perception is entrenched in common beliefs.
2. Changing policies may include a retreat from universal access to medical services, changing attitudes of physicians regarding hospitalization of elderly patients, establishment of alternative solutions (e.g., home-care policies), or any other changes that could modify the pattern of hospitalization.
3. The projected number of hospital days was based on a small underestimation of the total population. The overestimation of hospital days obviously resulted from their hypothesis on separation rates and average length of hospital stay.

References

Angus, D.E., L. Auer, J. Cloutier, and T. Albert. 1995. *Sustainable Health Care for Canada*. Ottawa: Queen's-University of Ottawa Economic Projects.

Barer, M.L., R.G. Evans, C. Hertzman, and J. Lomas. 1987. 'Aging and Health Care Utilization: New Evidence on Old Fallacies', *Social Science and Medicine* 24, 10: 851–62.

———, ———, and ———. 1995. 'Avalanche or Glacier?: Health Care and the Demographic Rhetoric', *Canadian Journal on Aging* 14, 2: 193–224.

———, I.R. Pulcins, R.G. Evans, C. Hertzman, J. Lomas, and G.M. Anderson. 1989. 'Trends in Use of Medical Services by the Elderly in British Columbia', *Canadian Medical Association Journal* 141: 39–45.

Black, C., N.P. Roos, B. Havens, and L. MacWilliam. 1995. 'Rising Use of Physician Services by the Elderly: The Contribution of Morbidity', *Canadian Journal on Aging* 14, 2: 225–44.

Boulet, J.-A., and G. Grenier. 1978. *Health Expenditures in Canada and the Impact of Demographic Changes on Future Government Health Insurance Program Expenditures.* Economic Council of Canada. Ottawa: Minister of Supply and Services.

Burke, M.A. 1991. 'Implications of Population Aging', *Canadian Social Trends*, Statistics Canada, Spring: 6–8.

Chawla, R. 1991. 'Dependency Ratios', *Canadian Social Trends*, Statistics Canada, Spring: 3–5.

Crimmins, E.M. 1996. 'Mixed Trends in Population Health Among Older Adults', *Journal of Gerontology* 51B: S223–5.

Denton, F.T., C.H. Feaver, and B.G. Spencer. 1998. 'The Future Population of Canada, Its Age Distribution and Dependency Relations', *Canadian Journal on Aging* 17, 1: 83–109.

Federal, Provincial, Territorial Advisory Committee on Population Health. 1994. *Strategies for Population Health: Investing in the Health of Canadians.* Ottawa: Health Canada, Minister of Supply and Services.

Felder, S., and P. Zweifel. 1997. 'Vieillissement démographique et dépenses de santé; une interprétation erronée', *CIGDOC, Les fiches documentaires*, Centre interfacultaire de gérontologie, Université de Genève, no. 5.

Fellegi, I.P. 1988. 'Can We Afford an Aging Society?', *Canadian Economic Observer* (Oct.): 4.1–4.34.

Fries, J.F. 1980. 'Aging, Natural Death, and the Compression of Morbidity', *New England Journal of Medicine* 303: 130–5.

George, M.V., M.J. Norris, F. Nault, S. Loh, and S.Y. Dai. 1994. *Population Projections for Canada, Provinces and Territories, 1993–2016.* Ottawa: Statistics Canada, Demography Division, Minister of Industry, Science and Technology.

Johansen, H., C. Nair, and J. Bond. 1994. 'Who Goes to the Hospital? An Investigation of High Users of Hospital Days', *Health Reports*, Statistics Canada, 6, 2: 253–69.

Kettle, J. 1981. 'The Big Generation: What's Ahead for the Baby Boomers?', *The Futurist* (Feb.): 3–13.

Kramer, M. 1980. 'The Rising Pandemic of Mental Disorders and Associated Chronic Diseases and Disabilities', *Acta Psychiatrica Scandinavica* 62: 282–97.

Lefebvre, L.A., Z. Zsigmond, and M.S. Devereaux. 1979. *A Prognosis for Hospitals: The Effects of Population Change on the Need for Hospital Space, 1967–2031.* Ottawa: Statistics Canada, Health Division, Minister of Supply and Services.

McCall, N. 1984. 'Utilization and Costs of Medicare Services by Beneficiaries in Their Last Year of Life', *Medical Care* 22, 4: 329–42.

Manton, K.G., E. Stallard, and L.S. Corder. 1998. 'The Dynamics of Dimensions of Age-Related Disability: 1982 to 1994 in the U.S. Elderly Population',

Journal of Gerontology 53A, 1: B59–70.

OECD. 1988. *Ageing Populations: The Social Policy Implications*. Paris: OECD.

———. 1996. *Aging in OECD Countries: A Critical Policy Challenge*. Paris: OECD.

Robine, J.-M., P. Mormiche, and C. Sermet. 1997. 'Examination of the Causes and Mechanisms of the Increase in Disability-Free Life Expectancy', *Journal of Aging and Health* 10, 2: 171–91.

Rochon, M. 1997. 'Vieillissement démographique, état de santé et financement des dépenses publiques de santé et de services sociaux', Ph.D. dissertation, Université de Montréal.

Roos, N.P., E. Shapiro, and R.D. Tate. 1989. 'Does a Small Minority of Elderly Account for a Majority of Health Care Expenditures? A Sixteen-Year Perspective', *Milbank Quarterly* 67: 347–69.

Shapiro, E. 1983. 'Impending Death and the Use of Hospitals by the Elderly', *Journal of American Geriatrics Society* 31, 6: 348–51.

Spiers, N., C. Jagger, and M. Clarke. 1996. 'Physical Function and Perceived Health: Cohort Differences and Interrelationships in Older People', *Journal of Gerontology* 51B: S226–33.

Statistics Canada. 1991. *Hospital Morbidity*. Ottawa: Minister of Supply and Services.

———. 1998. 'Hospital Utilization, 1995–96', *The Daily*, 5 June 1998. Ottawa: Minister of Supply and Services.

Wolfson, M.C. 1991. 'International Perspectives on the Economics of Aging', *Canadian Economic Observer* (Aug.): 3.1–3.16

3 | Aging Families
Have Current Changes and Challenges Been 'Oversold'?

Carolyn J. Rosenthal

Introduction

Apocalyptic demography is typically invoked in relation to state-supported pension and health-care programs. Is there also an apocalyptic demography of the family, or what one might call apocalyptic thinking about the family? How is population aging reflected at the level of the family? What aspects of these demographic and associated changes have been 'oversold'? Once we have identified how families are changing, we may then ask whether these changes are indeed apocalyptic and, further, what the real challenges are.

Most, though not all, of the major changes in contemporary families, as compared to families in the past, are related to demographic changes. Over the course of this century, there have been significant changes in family structure, patterns of marriage and divorce, the occurrence and timing of various family life-course events, and women's paid labour force participation. Increases in life expectancy have resulted in families typically including elderly members. The dynamic aspect of this is a much increased overlap of lives between familial generations. During the past century, widowhood became a typical experience for women—a normative life event. Divorce began to increase when Canadian laws were liberalized in the late 1960s. Female employment began to rise sharply in the early 1970s, with a resultant trend to dual-earner families replacing the traditional male breadwinner/female homemaker family as the normative pattern in husband-wife families.

Apocalyptic thinking about these changes in families has focused mainly on caregiving—either the increased likelihood that middle-aged adults will be faced with an older parent who requires care or the increased likelihood that older people who need care will not have family to whom to turn. In various places in this chapter I will argue that empirical research fails to support such apocalyptic thinking and its related claims. At the same time, I will frequently offer the reminder—and plea—that there is more to family life than caregiving and that we very much need research that goes beyond caregiving in studying what these changes mean to families and family life.

Table 3.1: Percentage of Canadians with Parent/s Alive, by Age and Gender

Age	35–9		40–4		45–9		50–4		55–9		60–4	
Number of Parents	Women	Men	Women	Men	Women	Men	Women	Men	Women	Men	Women	Men
0	8.9	7.5	14.7	14.6	20.7	26.4	46.6	41.0	60.6	62.3	79.4	82.0
1	35.8	36.1	46.2	41.4	52.2	46.7	39.3	46.2	34.6	33.4	17.6	16.8
2	55.3	56.4	39.1	44.0	27.1	26.8	14.1	12.8	4.8	4.3	2.7	1.2
Age of mother (x)	64.2	65.1	69.8	69.3	74.4	73.3	77.5	78.2	82.0	82.8	85.8	86.4
Age of father (x)	66.8	67.7	72.4	72.0	75.6	76.8	79.0	79.3	82.5	84.1	85.9	86.0

Source: General Social Survey of Canada, 1990.

The Changing Structure of Families

How has the structure of families changed? What are the challenges associated with these changes? Have these challenges been overstated? Identifying changes in family structure is not simply a matter of academic interest. Policy-makers and the general public are very interested in the implications of these changes. Anne Martin-Matthews and I (1993) have used the term 'structural potential' to denote how family structure creates the potential for experiencing various types of family role demands. This is distinguished from actually facing demands and providing help or care, an issue to which I will turn later in this chapter.

The Increasing Likelihood of Having an Older Parent Alive

Almost all young adult Canadians have living parents (Table 3.1). A majority have a living parent until ages 55–9, when about 4 in 10 are still in the adult child role. At ages 60–4, only 2 in 10 still occupy this role. It is also important to note that from age 45 onward, a majority of men and women who do have a parent alive have only one parent, a situation that potentially increases responsibility on adult children. If one is ultimately interested in the potential burden placed on adult children by having older parents, it is important to consider the structural feature of having a living parent in the context of that parent's age. Table 3.1 shows that among those in their late thirties and early forties, the average age of parents is relatively young. If we take age 75 and older as the time when health downturns typically occur (Marshall et al., 1983), then we may expect Canadian men and women in their thirties and early forties to have healthy parents who do not require help. Even in their late forties, children are unlikely to have mothers whose age suggests the need for help. Fathers are in a vulnerable age group by this time in their children's lives, but, typically, these fathers will still have their wives to provide such help as is needed. Adult children in their early fifties have parents nearing age 80 and very substantial minorities have only one parent. And by age 55 and over, a majority have only one parent alive and that parent is typically over age 80. In other words, by age 50 and more clearly by age 55, we might speculate that the structural potential for needing to help parents may well translate into actual help provision.

The Increasing 'Generational Overlap' of Lives

To this point I have presented cross-sectional data on the likelihood of having a parent alive at different ages, a likelihood that has increased over the course of this century. This is clearly seen when we examine the increase in the likelihood of a middle-aged adult having a surviving parent. Gee (1990) compares the proportion of three Canadian birth cohorts having a surviving parent at age 50 and age 60. Among Canadians born in 1910, only 33 per cent of individuals at age 50 had a surviving parent. This rose to 49 per cent of those born in 1930 and is expected to rise to 60 per cent of those born in 1960. The likelihood of having a surviving parent at age 60 has increased from 8 per cent of those born in 1910 to 16 per cent for those born in 1930 and is predicted to rise to 23 per cent for those born in 1960. It has thus become the majority pattern to have a surviving parent at age 50 and it is becoming more common to have one even at age 60. A related phenomenon is the growing likelihood that young adults still have a grandparent alive. These are, in my view, very positive changes. Unfortunately, we too often dwell on the negative impact of population aging. For example, with respect to the family, we seem to focus mainly on the increased likelihood of adult children having to provide care to older parents, rather than on the benefits within families of this new generational overlap of lives. Oddly enough, we know relatively little about the consequences, positive or negative, of this demographic change. A point I want to make here, which I will reiterate several times in this chapter, is that while existing research enables us to identify many changes, little research examines and elucidates the effects of these changes. Indeed, most discussion of such effects consists of speculation. Thus, we might well speculate that the increased generational overlap of lives entails both new rewards and new challenges; to a great extent, however, the nature of these rewards and challenges remains under-researched. The longer duration of grandparents' presence in a family ought to create benefits in terms of family cohesion and continuity. It certainly creates the opportunity to be an adult grandchild and for grandparents to have relationships with their grandchildren that extend into the latter's adulthood. Yet research on adult grandchildren is extremely limited. What are the challenges of having older family members? The one challenge that has received extensive research attention is caregiving— the burden on middle generations imposed by older family members with chronic illness or disability who require care. This is an important issue, but surely caregiving is only one aspect of a broad spectrum of family relations.

Changing Patterns of Marriage, Widowhood, and Divorce

Table 3.2 presents data on marital status at different ages for three cohorts of women in order to provide an indication of changing patterns. Among today's

Table 3.2: Marital Status Trends, Women, 1961–1991:
Percentage Distributions by Cohort and Marital Status

Marital Status	1971	1981	1991	Cohort
Married:				
Age in 1991				
65–74	48.9	51.1	53.9	Born 1917–26
55–64	69.9	72.8	71.8	Born 1927–36
45–54	83.8	83.1	77.2	Born 1937–46
Widowed:				
Age in 1991				
65–74	39.6	37.8	34.8	Born 1917–26
55–64	18.6	17.1	14.6	Born 1927–36
45–54	6.9	5.9	4.7	Born 1937–46
Divorced:				
Age in 1991				
65–74	0.9	2.1	4.0	Born 1917–26
55–64	1.6	3.5	7.1	Born 1927–36
45–54	1.9	5.1	9.2	Born 1937–46

Source:Statistics Canada, *The Nation* (1993), Catalogue No. 93–310, p. 33.

elderly women, widowhood is an expectable life event (Martin-Matthews, 1987), while the normative marital status among older men is married (Table 3.2). Divorce was almost unknown among older women who were aged 65–74 in 1991. Similar patterns are seen in the following cohort (women aged 55–64 in 1991), although members of this cohort are somewhat less likely to be widowed as they enter old age, largely due to the declines in mortality rates of males in mid-life. Among those outside of marriage, however, women in this cohort are somewhat less likely to be widowed and more likely to be divorced compared to the previous cohort (Rosenthal et al., forthcoming).

Since the liberalization of Canadian divorce laws in the late 1960s, divorce rates have increased markedly. Divorce has an impact on older families in two ways—directly (i.e., the individual has experienced divorce) and indirectly (i.e., one's children have experienced divorce). Divorce in the adult child generation may increase needs for support from older parents, particularly for the parents of the custodial child (Gladstone, 1988). Conversely, for others, maintaining contact with grandchildren may become problematic. Some grandparents face serious barriers to maintaining relationships with grandchildren following middle-generation divorce, and indeed we read quite a bit about this situation in articles about the grandparent rights movement. We also read (especially in the US press and literature) about grandparents who become surrogate parents, for example, when the adult child is a drug addict. Between these two extremes, however, is what I speculate is the majority of grandparents, who join in the struggle that is part of the aftermath of divorce—trying to help adult children through the difficult divorce transition, trying to provide continuity and stability for grandchildren, trying to maintain relationships in non-custodial situations, in short, trying to muddle through.

Divorce may also be experienced directly, not simply as a parent or grandparent. Having the marital status of 'divorced' is rare among today's elderly but will be somewhat more common in the cohort about to enter old age. It is difficult to predict precisely the proportion of women in the future who will enter old age as divorced persons because some of today's divorced women will remarry.

What impact will these changes have on older people? Divorce legally severs some kin relationships; for example, daughters-in-law become ex-daughters-in-law. Remarriage, on the other hand, creates new relatives; for example, the remarriage of a daughter brings not only a new son-in-law but perhaps step-grandchildren. One's own remarriage may bring not only a new spouse but stepchildren. We do not know very much, though, about the extent to which such relationships become attenuated following the dissolution of marriage through death or divorce. Nor do we know much about the extent to which kin acquired later in the life course, that is in mid-life or later life, are supportive and/or remain so following the death of the 'linking' person. (For example, if a woman remarries in her fifties and is married for 15 years before her 'new' spouse dies, what relationship would be maintained between her and her stepchildren after she is widowed?) Riley and Riley (1993) refer to a 'latent matrix of kin relationships', created by increasing longevity and increasing prevalence of divorce and remarriage. Matilda Riley (1983: 451) argues that the 'kinship structure has become more extensive and complex, the temporal and spatial boundaries of the family have been altered, and the opportunities for close family relationships have proliferated'. Riley's concept of a latent matrix is similar to the concept of 'structural potential' that I referred to earlier (Martin-Matthews and Rosenthal, 1993). Uhlenberg (1993), however, argues that although divorce may lead to a larger web of relationships, research suggests that divorce weakens many types of family relationships. Therefore, although there may be notable exceptions, in the general case the expansion of relationships in reconstituted families does not translate into increased support for older people. Having said this, however, I think we need a lot more research on what happens to kin relationships following divorce or death of the 'linking' individual. For example, we need research beyond that which simply tells us that this type of relative provides less support than another type of relative (e.g., blood kin).

The 'Shrinking' Supply of Children

We hear regularly that the birth rate has fallen and that the average family size (i.e., number of children) has decreased. But what does this mean with respect to actual families, who are not 'averages', and to potential support for older people? Uhlenberg (1993: 225) points out that while it is true that over the long

**Table 3.3: Number of Children Ever Born to Ever-Married Women,
by Age Group, Canada, 1991 (percentage distributions)**

Birth Cohort	Age in 1991	Number of Children							Mean
		0	1	2	3	4	5	6+	
1922–6	65–9	9.9	10.6	21.4	19.3	13.9	8.7	15.8	3.36
1927–36	55–64	8.3	9.0	21.8	21.9	15.9	9.4	13.5	3.31
1937–46	45–54	8.7	11.4	33.9	24.6	11.9	4.9	4.3	2.56
1947–56	35–44*	11.8	15.5	43.0	20.9	6.1	1.5	0.8	2.02

* For this age group, fertility is not yet complete. Therefore, figures presented here are somewhat lower than completed fertility figures will be.

Source: Statistics Canada, *Fertility* (Ottawa: Industry Science and Technology Canada, 1993); 1991 *Census of Canada,* Catalogue No. 93–221, p. 7.

term the demographic transition means a reduced average number of children for the elderly, 'assertions about the future supply of children for the elderly can be misleading unless two important questions are addressed: What changes in family size make a significant difference? What is the timing of changes in the family size of the elderly?' Uhlenberg argues that:

> Although total support received from children is positively related to number of children, the marginal benefits from each additional child beyond the second or third is small. The most critical distinction regarding family size is between having none versus some, and the second-most important distinction is between having one compared with having two or more. Thus, interest in changing family size should pay less attention to changes in mean number and more attention to proportion with zero or only one child. (Ibid.)

US data show that among women aged 85 and older in 1990, fully 25 per cent had no children. The proportion of very old childless women will decline for several decades (down to 10 per cent of those aged 85 and over in 2020) and will again increase in the more distant future as the baby-boom cohorts reach very old age. However, even looking as far ahead as 2050, the proportion of very old women who will be childless will never be as high as it was in 1990 (Chen and Morgan, 1991). The proportion of very old women who have only one child follows the same trend as the proportion of those who are childless.

Canadian data indicate a similar story (Table 3.3). Connidis (1996) identifies the key trends in family size over the 30-year period from 1961 to 1991. The first trend is a decline in the percentage of women having 0, 1, and 5 or more children. In fact, Gee (1995) indicates that for those aged 55 and over, the key decline is actually in the proportion having 6 or more children. The second trend is an increase in the proportion of women having 2 or 3 children, and the third is the surprisingly substantial proportion of families who are continuing to have as many as 4 or more children. Among women aged 45–54 in 1991, these general patterns are quite dramatic: the modal number of children is 2, followed by 3, childlessness is least likely, followed by 5 or more children and then one child. 'Thus, in terms of a family profile, the majority of ever-married people will continue to have at least two . . . or more . . . children for some time' (Connidis, 1996: 6).

Gee (1995) argues that, in old age, it is the number of surviving children, not the number of children ever born, that is critical. The 1990 Canadian General Social Survey showed that 21 per cent of all men and 24 per cent of all women aged 75 and over have no surviving children (remarkably similar to the US figure for childlessness among women aged 85 and over cited above). The trends described here indicate that upcoming cohorts of old and middle-aged adults, particularly the parents of the baby boom, will be more likely than their predecessors to be able to draw upon support from children. The challenges engendered by changes in fertility rates need to be viewed in historical perspective (many are not new) and linked to cohort analysis. It is fair to say that alarm calls about the shrinking supply of children are an overstatement—if not a distortion of reality.

The Changing Structure of Multi-generational Families

All of the changes discussed so far combine to produce changes in the generational structure of families. For at least 20 years, social scientists have described the generational structure of families as becoming 'long and thin'. Bengtson et al. (1990) use the term 'beanpole' family to describe a family form that contains several generations—four or even five—but relatively few people in each generation. This structure implies a heavy burden on middle generations to care for younger and older generation members, with the prospect of someone in old age caring for someone in very old age. This structure is said to have become increasingly common and, indeed, to be the prototypical family form.

Other forms may be less typical, but are important because they represent substantial minorities of the population. The 'age-condensed' form results from several successive generations following patterns of early childbearing, with consequent narrow age differences between generations. This pattern is found in some segments of the African-American population; in these subpopulations, teenage pregnancy is common and women become grandmothers in their thirties (Burton and Bengtson, 1985). The 'age-gapped' pattern occurs when several successive generations have a late childbearing pattern, resulting in large age differences between generations. The 'truncated' family pattern occurs when the youngest generation remains childless. Finally, the 'reconstituted' family is one formed by remarriage and involves one or more children from a previous marriage. George and Gold (1991: 77) refer to an 'unprecedented increase' in the proportion of this type of family.

While these family structure types may indeed be found somewhere in the population, their actual rate of occurrence remains an empirical question. Scholars have not been careful about identifying just how much change is actually occurring; indeed, with respect to some of these types, scholars may have overstated the case (Uhlenberg, 1993). Take the 'reconstituted' family type, for example. While it seems clear that, because of divorce and remarriage, the proportion of elderly who will fit the 'reconstituted' family type will increase over the next few decades, the prevalence may not exceed that of the nineteenth century when reconstituted families followed the death of a spouse rather than divorce. As for the 'truncated' family type, as was pointed out earlier, current levels of childlessness are not historically unprecedented, nor will the percentages of childless elderly in the future be higher than previously experienced (ibid.).

What about the beanpole family type? Uhlenberg asks 'how accurate is the often repeated assertion that four- and five-generation families are becoming increasingly common as a result of increased longevity?' He points out that no estimates for the population based on representative samples exist to back up this claim. Rossi and Rossi (1990), based on their study of 1,400 adults in Boston, contend that popular beliefs about the prevalence of multi-generational families are exaggerated. Data from the National Survey of Families and Households in the United States (Winsborough et al., 1991) suggest that about one-third of adults aged 45–64 are members of four-generation families. All indications are that very few individuals are or ever will be part of a five-generation family. Moreover, Uhlenberg concludes that the four-generation family will not be the dominant lineage type. Therefore, while the beanpole family, in the sense of generational depth, is probably more common than in the past, we need to be cautious about making sweeping statements about its prevalence.

Another pitfall, in which I have fallen, lies in assuming there are or will be few family members within any particular generation. I have often stated, 'In the future, there will be more family members in senior generations and fewer middle-generation members to provide care to them if care is needed', as though this assertion was indisputable. This kind of statement, however, is not very meaningful unless we bring to it the lens of cohort analysis. The cohorts who will turn age 85 over the first two decades of the twenty-first century are the parents of the baby boom. These older adults, in the age group where need for care is most likely, are going to have more, not fewer, children on whom to rely than do those who are currently in very old age. If we want to examine the availability of children to cohorts in the more distant future, we need to examine data for the number of children ever born to those cohorts—as we did earlier.

Finally, even when we identify the prevalence of these various family structure types in the population, we are left to ask what it means to be in one type or another. What is the nature of the experience of living in each of these different types of families, and what are the differences and similarities of these experiences as they vary by family type? Linda Burton's research (e.g., Burton and Bengtson, 1985) demonstrates to some degree what it means to be in a family with an age-condensed structure. With most other structural types, however, we have been relying on speculations. And for every negative implication we can speculate might occur, we can probably counter with a positive one. For example, where there are fewer children more may be required of each child (fewer children among whom to spread care responsibilities). However, parents with few (one or two) children may have much more intimate relationships with those children than is characteristic in larger families. This may place later-life caregiving in an entirely different light: the tangible and intangible 'rewards' to the child throughout the life course and in the parent's later life may be more substantial compared to those to children in larger families.

The Scattering of the Family

Another component of apocalyptic thinking at the level of family change is that, should older people require care, their children will be too far away to provide it. This view encompasses assumptions about both living arrangements and wider geographic dispersion.

Considering living arrangements first, since about 1960 there has been a trend for older Canadians to live either as a married couple or alone. This trend in living alone is especially pronounced among women (Connidis, 1989; Wister, 1985). Between 1961 and 1991, the proportion of women aged 65 and over living alone more than doubled, from 16 per cent to 34 per cent. Among widowed women, the proportion living alone is close to 80 per cent (Martin-Matthews, 1991: 79). In my view, this is a positive rather than a negative change, one that reflects not only changing norms but, more fundamentally, the opening up of options to women in that Old Age Security and subsidized housing make independent living possible. 'One woman, one kitchen' seems to be a strong cultural preference in North America. We have enough evidence that older people like to see their children regularly but do not want to share the same household that we can put to rest arguments promoting shared living between older parents and adult children as an optimal arrangement for most older people.

The trend to independent living does have implications for family care in that, should an older parent need care, separate residence makes care provision more complicated. We know that as the need for care intensifies, some adult children have a parent move in with them, although we are very short of good data on this issue. One study (CARNET, n.d.) suggests that establishing co-residence as a strategy to accommodate caregiving responsibilities is very uncommon in Canada. In that study, which examined the experiences of 250 employed Canadians who were providing a significant amount of assistance to older relatives, only 3–7 per cent of care recipients moved in with a caregiver over a two-year period.

The fact that most older people do not live in the same household as their children, however, does not necessarily mean that they do not live near their children. Assumptions and statements about the decreasing proximity of older parents and adult children because of increased rates of geographic mobility have perhaps been more common in the US than in Canada, but these statements are not rare in Canada. Proximity is an important issue because it is strongly related to contact and the exchange of help (although much less related to emotional closeness and support). Uhlenberg (1993) shows that mobility rates in the United States were considerably lower in the 1970s and 1980s than they were in the 1950s and 1960s. The data, therefore, do not show a trend that would produce greater dispersion of kin over time. Moreover, the 1987–8 National Survey of Families and Households found that about three-quarters of older people who have an adult child have a child living within 25 miles. This is almost identical to the percentage of older parents with a child living nearby that was reported by Ethel Shanas in 1968 and—to add some Canadian data—very similar to the percentages Victor Marshall, Jane Synge, and I found in our Hamilton study in 1980 (Rosenthal, 1987). We found that, among people aged 70 and over who had children, about two-thirds lived either in the same household or the same city as a child, and just about 90 per cent lived within an hour and one-half travel time of a child.

This is not to say that older people do not have a child who lives at some distance from them. Most studies only examine the proximity of the nearest child; this obscures the reality that, when people have more than one child, they may have some children close by and others more distant. In the Hamilton study, among respondents aged 70 and over who had children, only 11 per cent had no children living within one and one-half hours' travel time. Of the remainder, excluding those who still had dependent children living at home or who had only one child, 42 per cent said that all their adult children lived within one and one-half hours' travel time, while 58 per cent said some children lived within this distance and some farther away. In other words, total family dispersion is very unusual, no dispersion beyond one and one-half hours' travel time is characteristic of a large minority of older families, and—importantly—partial dispersion is the most common pattern. We also need to be aware that proximity is something we typically measure at one point in time. In real life, however, proximity is fluid. Adult children may move to another city, only to move back to their city of origin later on. Older parents may make a retirement move to another city. Or, they may move at retirement or later on to be closer to a child. In sum, the geographic dispersion issue seems to have been oversold. My intention here is not to underrate the experience of geographically distant children and parents, particularly when the parents need care; it is simply to emphasize that this is far from the typical experience and it is not on a sharp rise.

Increased Participation of Women in the Paid Labour Force

A well-known trend that must be considered when discussing changing families is the trend towards increased female labour force participation. Consider, for example, women's labour force participation at ages 45–54. Among women who were aged 45–54 in 1991, 72 per cent were in the paid labour force, up from 56 per cent among women of those ages in 1981 and 44 per cent in 1971. Especially noteworthy are the increases in paid employment among married women and women with children at home. These trends mean that combining work and family roles has become much more common than in the past. By 1994, dual-earner families made up 60 per cent of all husband-wife families, compared with 33 per cent in 1967 (Statistics Canada, 1996). Rosenthal and colleagues (1997) investigated the prevalence of dual-earner families in three age cohorts of currently married women—those aged 65–74 in 1991, those aged 55–64, and those aged 45–54. Using a fairly broad set of employment criteria (a woman who had worked in the paid labour force for any period of time after age 35, either full-time or part-time, was considered to have been employed and therefore part of a dual-earner couple), 67 per cent of married women in the oldest age group had been part of dual-earner families. This percentage rose to 73 per cent in the middle age group (55–64) and to 85 per cent in the youngest age group (45–54). The question remains as to what these changes in women's labour force partici-pation imply for the care of older parents. Apocalyptic thinking would focus on the projected inability of employed women to provide care, an issue to which I return later.

To this point, I have been discussing changes in family structure. Three struc-tural changes that have been clearly oversold are the so-called shrinking supply of children, the beanpole family structure, and the geographic scattering of fam-ilies. With respect to marital status, we saw that widowhood is declining some-what, related to increased longevity of men as well as to the growing numbers of women who will enter old age as divorced persons. I highlighted the issue of the expanded latent matrix of kin associated with reconstituted families and argued that we know relatively little about what happens to these relationships in later life. I also mentioned the dramatic increase in women's labour force participa-tion, leaving until later the question of the extent to which this has altered care provision to older parents. One major change that has not been overstated with regard to its occurrence is the increased likelihood that adult Canadians will have a parent alive and the related increased generational overlap of lives. These changes create the structural potential for experiencing care-related needs from older parents, but to what degree does this structural potential translate into actually experiencing such demands? Has the extent to which this potential translates into actual demands been oversold? I address this question in the next section.

The Overselling of the Dependency Burden on Families

We saw earlier that the structural potential to have aging parents who require help exists for a large percentage of Canadian women. Much media attention is currently given to the potential burden of old family members on those in middle generations. A particularly difficult version of this is the burden and conflict experienced by middle-generation adults who have care responsibilities for family members in both older and younger generations.

While the care-related needs of older parents may present a daunting challenge for families, empirical research suggests that issues of prevalence and burden have been overstated. While the chances are we will all experience the death of our parents, there is great variability in the need for and extent of involvement of adult children, and in the duration of care. We will not all become primary caregivers, many of us will provide only a little or no care to our parents, some of us will be involved in assisting parents for a number of months or years, while others will have intense involvement for a very short period of time and still others will have intermittent periods of involvement as parents move in and out of health crises.

The Extent of Provision of Help to Parents

There has been an enormous amount of research on caregiving over the past two decades, but it is important to note that much of this research uses non-representative samples and focuses only on primary caregivers, and only on elders who need substantial amounts of care. This does not give us much of a perspective on how much help adult children typically provide to older parents. Data from the 1990 Canadian General Social Survey (Rosenthal et al., 1996) show that only small proportions of adult Canadian sons and daughters actually help parents once a month or more. Respondents were asked about five kinds of help: housework, transportation, personal care, financial support, and outside work/household maintenance. Across five-year age categories from age 35 to age 64, from 11 to 22 per cent of daughters and 7 to 12 per cent of sons provided at least one of these types of help monthly or more often. Based on these data, we may say that only small minorities of adult children can be considered to be 'active' helpers.

Personal care is arguably the most important type of help to examine, both because it may signify that the parent is highly dependent and because it is the most demanding and intensive type of care. Very small percentages of daughters provided personal care monthly or more often, although the percentages increased with age; at ages 35–49, between 1.2 and 2.0 per cent of daughters provided personal care. This rose to 5.6 per cent at ages 50–4 and 7 per cent at ages 55–9, then dropped to 0 per cent at ages 60–4. Among sons, a high of 1 per cent provided personal care at least monthly.

When we talk about dependency and need for help in the family context, we are usually referring to informal care. An additional type of dependency, however, is the need for financial assistance. There is certainly speculation these days about how the erosion of universal health care —not to mention the increased need for types of long-term care that have never been covered by state-based health insurance—may place an increasing financial burden on adult children in meeting the needs of their older parents. This would fly in the face of a well-documented pattern (Hogan et al., 1993; Rosenthal, 1987; Shanas et al., 1968) in which financial assistance flows much more commonly from older to younger generations. Data from the General Social Survey indicate that very small percentages of Canadian daughters or sons provide financial assistance to parents: the highest proportion in any age group to provide financial support monthly or more was 2 per cent of daughters and 3 per cent of sons. The percentages who had provided financial support in the past year were not much higher—4 per cent of daughters and 5 per cent of sons. Whatever increases we might see in the future, this type of help is very uncommon at present, and speculation about the future must be placed in this context. For example, even if the percentages giving this type of help doubled, small proportions of adult children would be involved.

The 'Sandwich Generation'

The particular manifestation of the need to help older parents that has caught the public imagination is the woman facing care demands from parents and children—popularly termed the 'sandwich generation'. David Foot (1996), in his best-selling book, *Boom, Bust, and Echo*, devotes a chapter to how demographics can affect family life, but the only issue specifically related to older family members is the sandwich generation—the increased likelihood that one will have an aged parent in declining health and in need of assistance, occurring in the context of being 'sandwiched' or pulled between the needs of one's parents and children. When people read Foot's book—and many Canadians have read it—the message about aging families they receive is that more and more women are being sandwiched. However, Foot makes the leap from the demographic fact that women have the family structure that makes multiple and conflicting demands potentially possible to the assumption that they actually experience such demands.

It is ironic that Foot highlights the sandwich generation issue as emblematic of the impact of demographic change on older families, since it is becoming well established that this is one aspect of demographic change that has been overstated (Rosenthal et al., 1996; Spitze and Logan, 1990; Uhlenberg, 1993). In looking at the sandwich generation, we must first specify what characteristics entitle a person to claim membership in that group, which is less straightforward than it might at first seem. One obviously needs a parent alive—and a child, but does this mean any child regardless of age? Do we restrict the child component to a young child? To a child in the household, therefore including teenaged children? Do we also require that a person hold a paid job? The definitional criteria are very important because they greatly affect the percentage of the population that will be estimated to be sandwiched. Further, as has been emphasized earlier, we need to distinguish between the structural potential to be sandwiched (e.g., having a parent alive and a child in the household) and having a parent who requires help and actually receives help from the child in question. In our analysis of 1990 General Social Survey data, Anne Martin-Matthews, Sarah Matthews, and I (Rosenthal et al., 1996) found that the proportion of women with the structural potential to be sandwiched between the roles of adult child and parent of a dependent child (defined as a child in the household) dropped from 71 per cent among women aged 35–9 to 51 per cent among women aged 45–9 and to 24 per cent among women aged 50–4. The most difficult combination of roles is paid worker, adult child, and parent of a dependent child. This role configuration holds the greatest structural potential for competing demands, should an older parent need care. This combination dropped from 42 per cent in the 40–4 age group to 35 per cent for women in their later forties and to very small proportions after that.

Among women with the structural potential to be sandwiched, what proportion actually provides tangible help to parents? Among daughters who had a parent alive and a child at home, the highest percentage in any age group who helped a parent at least monthly was 13 per cent. In the potentially most problematic group, those who had a living parent, a child at home, and a paid job, the highest percentage in any age group who helped a parent at least monthly was 7 per cent.

Being truly 'sandwiched' or 'caught in the middle' is therefore very uncommon among Canadian women. Among daughters, active help to parents is more common at older ages when there are fewer potentially conflicting roles. Thus, for example, while 18 per cent of daughters aged 55–9 provided active help to parents, these daughters no longer had a child in the household and most were not in the paid labour force. In sum, the highest proportions of daughters who help parents are not in the configurations denoting multiple roles.

Our analysis has a number of limitations, but it serves to indicate that relatively small proportions of adult children provide tangible, regular help to older parents, and even smaller proportions are in a situation that fits the popular portrayal of the sandwich generation. We should, therefore, avoid very broad assertions that caregiving by middle-aged women to older parents is common. Similarly, we should avoid placing undue emphasis on the sandwich generation phenomenon.

I do not mean to diminish the difficult situations faced by women who do carry these responsibilities—these women need more than our sympathy; they need a range of choices and supports that currently are rare, inadequate, or non-existent. The point here is that the sandwich generation is more a popular construction than a typical experience. Indeed, parent care by adult children, regardless of other role responsibilities, seems to be quite an uncommon occurrence when we measure it cross-sectionally and limit it to tangible help. The apocalyptic spectre of adult children being overwhelmed by the care needs of their aged parents is not apparent in the real world when we assess rhetoric with empirical data.

The fact that few adult children seem to be providing assistance at any one point in time does not mean the family is a great untapped resource that can provide much more free labour so that society can save money on the formal health-care system. Creating this impression is one of the dangers of presenting this kind of data (although, clearly, I have had other purposes in mind). I do worry that these data could be misused. Let us assume that with more people living to old age and very old age, there will be more people living with chronic illness and limitations. Let us further assume that this will mean an increased need for help. That is where the assumptions end, in my view. We need to ask:

How much help? How do older people prefer to meet their care needs? Who ought to provide this help? What are the pitfalls in relegating care of parents to adult children? We should not assume that, because adult children are not providing much tangible help, they have lots of extra time and money that the state can expect them to devote to parents. This is, unfortunately, what seems to be happening. Governments expect families to fill the gaps in care that arise as a result of the shift to community care and of earlier discharges from acute care.

Women's Labour Force Participation and the 'Caregiving Crunch'

The trend to female employment has led to the concern that women will no longer be available to fulfil their traditional roles of family caregivers to older parents, based on the seemingly logical speculation that employment reduces availability of women to provide family care. Myles (1991) uses the term 'caregiving crunch' to refer to the crisis stemming from the decreased supply of informal caregivers as a result of women's increased employment outside the home. Myles refers to a crisis in caregiving, the result of the 'dramatic decline in the amount of unpaid working time available to the women who have traditionally performed these tasks'. Myles sees this caregiving crunch as the next crisis of the welfare state, one that we are already experiencing. A caregiving crunch is very familiar to women who combine employment with family responsibilities, whether those are for older or younger family members. Research has documented the strains on such women, including the impact of care responsibilities on employment careers (Martin-Matthews and Rosenthal, 1993). It is important to recognize, however, that most employed women whose parents require care continue in paid employment. Further, they appear to provide as much help to parents as their non-employed peers. In other words, the 'crunch' does not seem to result in a decreased amount of care to older people. In an analysis of 1996 General Social Survey data (Rosenthal et al., 1999), there were minimal differences between employed and non-employed women in the type of help provided to parents and in the amount of time spent helping parents. This issue needs more examination, and I am not implying that everything is fine because employed women seem to provide care despite their job responsibilities. The point is that the so-called 'caregiving crunch', to the extent that it exists, is not yet a crisis for the state; it may well be a crisis, however, for those women faced with these multiple demands. The question becomes one of appropriate policy directions. While policies that provide workplace flexibility and support for employed caregivers are important, it is equally or more important to provide policies that create options to family-provided care.

Conclusion

While family structure is changing, some aspects of these changes have been oversold—namely, the shrinking supply of children, the beanpole family, and geographic dispersion. On the other hand, families are more likely to have senior-generation members alive. We have tended to accept speculations about the implications of these changes—implications about the growing dependency burden on families—without testing them against empirical data. In examining three of these assumptions—that most adult children are swamped by the need to help parents, that the sandwich generation is a common predicament, and that women's employment is having a profound impact on care provision—we can see they have been oversold. Demographic change in families is not leading us into the apocalypse. It is important to maintain this perspective, in part because it means government programs to assist people who are in these situations are not likely to face massive hordes of caregivers but rather a comparatively small but highly needy segment of the population at any one point in time.

How do we counteract the tendency towards thinking apocalyptically about changes in older families? First of all, we need to identify carefully what is really happening and to pay attention to cohorts and trends over time. Second, we need to investigate the implications of these trends, rather than simply speculating about what they might be. Third, we need to look beyond averages, a point that is well demonstrated by examining the data on numbers of children ever born to different cohorts of women. To the extent that we have been able to address these issues, the apocalyptic position appears greatly overstated and indeed unsupportable. This is not to say that families are not changing, for they are changing significantly. The point is rather that they are not changing in ways that set kin relations adrift.

In the public discourse on state-provided health care and income security, apocalyptic demography is used to justify the retreat from the welfare state, that is, to legitimate an ideology and policy direction that are quite separate from demographic data (Walker, 1993). This same ideology would place care of the elderly firmly in the private/personal sphere, on the shoulders of families, in reality on the shoulders of wives, daughters, and daughters-in-law. I have argued in this chapter that there is also an apocalyptic demography of the aging family, but that its purposes (if one can attribute purpose to it) are probably quite different. It may be that the apocalyptic demography of the family has been heralded by well-meaning people (gerontologists, for example) who are genuinely worried that the family will not be able to bear the burdens of caring for older members. By arguing against some of these dire predictions, I emphatically do not want to suggest that we should all relax and allocate responsibility for the care of the elderly to the family. Nor do I mean to gloss over the burdens experienced by those who are faced with heavy care demands from older family members.

It is important to uncover the realities of social organization and social life, and for this reason we need to understand how the family is changing and what the implications of those changes are. However, there is a real danger that findings may be wrongly interpreted and/or used in support of policies that would not be good for families. I recognize that in much of my own work, for example, work that asks what the changes in family structure mean for support to older people, the implicit or explicit dependent variable is family support. This is a perfectly legitimate and important question. However, it is vital that our questions do not stop there. Whether families are or will be capable of providing needed support to older relatives must take second place to the question of who should be responsible for the care of older people. My position, one that is growing stronger over the years as I continue to learn more about older families, is that the care of the elderly is a public, not a private, issue and that responsibility lies with the state. Within that framework, we may then examine the role families might play if they are able and willing.

References

Bengtson, Vern L., Carolyn J. Rosenthal, and Linda Burton. 1990. 'Families and Aging: Diversity and Heterogeneity', in Robert H. Binstock and Linda K. George, eds, *Handbook of Aging and the Social Sciences*. New York: Academic Press, 263–87.

Burton, Linda, and Vern L. Bengtson. 1985. 'Black Grandmothers: Issues of Timing and Continuity of Roles', in Vern L. Bengtson and Joan Robertson, eds, *Grandparenthood*. Beverly Hills: Sage, 61–77.

CARNET (Canadian Aging Research Network). n.d. 'Work and Eldercare Survey', unpublished data. Guelph, Ont.: University of Guelph.

Chen, R., and S.P. Morgan. 1991. 'Recent Trends in the Timing of First Births in the United States', *Demography* 28: 513–33.

Connidis, Ingrid. 1989. *Family Ties and Aging*. Toronto: Butterworths.

————. 1996. 'Family Ties and Aging: Continuity and Change Over Three Decades', paper presented at the International Colloquium 'Le vieillissement des populations revisite/Revisiting the Aging Process', Montreal, 2–4 Oct.

Foot, David K., with Daniel Stoffman. 1996. *Boom, Bust, and Echo: How to Profit from the Coming Demographic Shift*. Toronto: Macfarlane Walter and Ross.

Gee, Ellen M. 1990. 'Demographic Change and Intergenerational Relations in Canadian Families: Findings and Social Policy Implications', *Canadian Public Policy* 16, 2: 191–9.

————. 1995. 'Families in Later Life', in Roderic Beaujot, Gee, Fernando Rajulton, and Zenaida Ravanera, *Family Over the Life Course: Current Demographic Analysis*, Ottawa: Statistics Canada Demography Division, 77–113.

George, Linda K., and Deborah Gold. 1991. 'Life Course Perspectives on Intergenerational and Generational Connections', *Marriage and Family Review* 16: 67–88.

Gladstone, James. 1988. 'Perceived Changes in Grandmother-Grandchild Relations Following a Child's Separation or Divorce', *The Gerontologist* 28, 1: 66–72.

Hogan, Dennis P., David J. Eggebeen, and Clifford C. Clogg. 1993. 'The Structure of Intergenerational Exchanges in American Families', *American Journal of Sociology* 98, 6: 1428–58.

Marshall, Victor W., Carolyn J. Rosenthal, and Jane Synge. 1983. 'Concerns About Parental Health', in Elizabeth W. Markson, ed., *Older Women*. Lexington, Mass.: Lexington Books, 253–73.

Martin-Matthews, Anne. 1987. 'Widowhood as an Expectable Life Event', in Victor W. Marshall, ed., *Aging in Canada: Social Perspectives*, 2nd edn. Markham, Ont.: Fitzhenry and Whiteside, 343–66.

———. 1991. *Widowhood in Later Life*. Toronto: Butterworths.

——— and Carolyn J. Rosenthal. 1993. 'Balancing Work and Family in an Aging Society: The Canadian Experience', in George Maddox and M. Powell Lawton, eds, *Annual Review of Gerontology and Geriatrics, vol. 13*. New York: Springer, 96–119.

Myles, John. 1991. 'Women, the Welfare State and Caregiving', *Canadian Journal on Aging* 10, 2: 82–5.

Riley, Matilda W. 1983. 'The Family in an Aging Society: A Matrix of Latent Relationships', *Journal of Family Issues* 4: 439–54.

——— and John W. Riley. 1993. 'Connections: Kin and Cohorts', in Vern L. Bengtson and W. Andrew Achenbaum, eds, *The Changing Contract Across Generations*. New York: Aldine de Gruyter.

Rosenthal, Carolyn J. 1987. 'Aging and Intergenerational Relations in Canada', in Victor W. Marshall, ed., *Aging in Canada: Social Perspectives,* 2nd edn. Markham, Ont.: Fitzhenry & Whiteside, 311–42.

———, Anne Martin-Matthews, and Sarah Matthews. 1996. 'Caught in the Middle? Occupancy in Multiple Roles and Help to Parents in a National Probability Sample of Canadian Adults', *Journal of Gerontology: Social Sciences* 51B, 6: S274–83.

———, Laura Hurd, Margaret Denton, Susan French, Anne Martin-Matthews, Demetrio LaBella, and Jason Lian. 1997. 'Dual-Earner Families: Characteristics and Relevance for Tomorrow's Older Population', paper presented at the annual meeting of the Canadian Association on Gerontology, Calgary, Oct.

———, Anne Martin-Matthews, Lynda Hayward, and Margaret Denton. 1999. 'Women's Multiple Roles: How Constraining Is Employment on the Provision of Parent Care?', paper presented at the 52nd Annual Scientific Meeting of the Gerontological Society of America, San Francisco, 19–23 Nov.

———, Margaret Denton, Anne Martin-Matthews, and Susan French. Forthcoming. 'Changes in Work and Family Over the Life Course: Implications for Economic Security of Today's and Tomorrow's Older Women', in Frank Denton, Deborah Fretz, and Byron Spencer, eds, *Independence and Economic Security in Old Age*. Vancouver: University of British Columbia Press.

Rossi, Alice S., and Peter H. Rossi. 1990. *Of Human Bonding: Parent-Child Relations Across the Life Course*. New York: Aldine de Gruyter.

Shanas, Ethel, Peter Townsend, Dorothy Wedderburn, Henning Friis, Poul Milhoj, and Jan Stehouwer. 1968. *Old People in Three Industrial Societies*. New York: Atherton Press.

Spitze, Glenna, and John R. Logan. 1990. 'More Evidence on Women (and Men) in the Middle', *Research on Aging* 12: 182–98.

Statistics Canada. 1996. *Characteristics of Dual-Earner Families 1994*. Ottawa: Minister of Industry, Catalogue No. 13–215–XPB.

Uhlenberg, Peter. 1993. 'Demographic Change and Kin Relationships in Later Life', in George Maddox and M. Powell Lawton, eds, *Annual Review of Gerontology and Geriatrics*, vol. 13. New York: Springer, 219–38.

Walker, Alan. 1993. 'Intergenerational Relations and Welfare Restructuring: The Social Construction of an Intergenerational Problem', in Vern L. Bengtson and W. Andrew Achenbaum, eds, *The Changing Contract Across Generations*. New York: Aldine de Gruyter, 141–65.

Winsborough, H., L. Bumpass, and W. Aguilino. 1991. *The Death of Parents and the Transitions to Old Age*. National Survey of Families and Households Working Paper No. 39. Madison: University of Wisconsin.

Wister, Andrew. 1985. 'Living Arrangement Choices Among the Elderly', *Canadian Journal on Aging* 4, 3: 127–44.

4 | Intergenerational Caregiving

How Apocalyptic and Dominant Demographies Frame the Questions and Shape the Answers

ANNE MARTIN-MATTHEWS

Introduction

In the previous chapter, Carolyn Rosenthal noted that apocalyptic thinking about family change has focused primarily on issues of caregiving, in terms of either the increased likelihood of being faced with intergenerational caregiving or the likelihood that older people needing care may not have family members available to them. While Rosenthal ably refutes the concept that will not die—'the sandwich generation'—and documents the realities masked by the rhetoric of family decline and elders being abandoned by their families, other aspects of the rhetoric of caregiving remain outside of the analysis she presented. These include overgeneralizations as to what caregiving actually is and how the dominant renditions of intergenerational caregiving, building on apocalyptic demography, frame our research questions and shape our answers. Some important realities of the caregiving experience get left out in the process.

Elsewhere (Martin-Matthews and Keefe, 1995), I have noted that frequently the most compelling and memorable 'data' on intergenerational caregiving come not from the welter of facts and figures generated by researchers, policymakers, and service providers but from the stories and voices of those who provide care and, more rarely heard, of those who receive care.

In this vein, I will anchor my discussion of the apocalyptic rhetoric of intergenerational caregiving by presenting two vignettes that involve members of families caring for one another.

> Maureen is 45 years old and employed part-time as a physiotherapist. She and Mike have one child, a daughter Erin, aged 22, who is in second-year university about two hours' drive from her parents' home. Mother and daughter are especially close. Erin phones her mother at least every second day, and they talk at length about concerns they both have, but most especially about Erin's social life and how she is doing in her courses. Maureen regularly sends money to Erin. Because Erin has chronic asthma problems, Maureen occasionally travels the two hours to help care for her daughter if she has a particularly bad attack, or if she is

too unwell to travel home on her own. Helping Erin in this way helps Maureen through the periods of 'feeling blue' that have plagued her all her life.

Janet is a 32-year-old part-time art teacher and freelance artist. Recently married, she lives about a five-minute drive from the home of her parents, Martin and Thelma, both in their early seventies. A sister lives nearby and a brother in a city about three hours away. Janet, the youngest child in the family, is close to both her parents, especially so since their recent health problems. Thelma has severe arthritis and suffered a mild heart attack about three years ago; in the past two years Martin has suffered a series of mild strokes. Martin and Thelma are limited in their mobility, and Janet helps out, running errands for them, especially in the winters when the driving is treacherous, taking them to lunch regularly to help get them out of the house, even augmenting their meagre pensions whenever she gets extra cash from an art sale. Her brother as well helps his parents financially and, when he visits, with house and yard maintenance. Janet and her parents exchange telephone calls almost daily. In appreciation for Janet's help, Thelma sews items, like draperies and quilts, to decorate the newlyweds' home.

Each of these vignettes tells of intergenerational ties. Although the specifics vary, each portrays strong family bonds across households, across generations, a primarily (but not exclusively) unidirectional flow of task-based assistance and what appear to be emotionally close and emotionally reciprocal relationships. In each vignette, there is evidence of the kinds of intergenerational linkages that social scientists have assiduously identified and analysed: attachment (Bowlby, 1980); filial piety and obligation (Wolfson et al., 1993); and various forms of solidarity, including associational, affectual, and functional solidarity (Bengtson et al., 1985).

However, there is an important way in which the second of these vignettes differs substantially from the first. The second depicts the relationship between an adult child and her elderly parents. In the language of social science, social practice, and social policy today, with few exceptions (Matthews and Heidorn, 1998), the words used above would not be used to characterize the second of these two vignettes. Despite their relevance, words like solidarity, attachment, filial piety, and reciprocity would not typically frame the dominant paradigm for discussion of such issues within social gerontology today.

In the last decade, quite another word has come to dominate the study of intergenerational relations involving adult (especially mid-life) children and their aging or elderly parents; that word is 'caregiving'. In Chapter 8, Susan McDaniel poses the questions, 'When did we begin to talk about ourselves as baby boomers and how did that phrase come to affect the ways we think about ourselves, and with what consequences?' These are the same questions we should be asking in relation to the term 'caregiving'. Most persons who attend gerontology conferences on a regular basis can identify the time a dozen or so years ago when 'caregiving' seemed suddenly to appear everywhere in conference programs and then came to dominate the literature. At first the term was applied quite specifically, and often quite appropriately, to family members helping relatives with Alzheimer's disease and other dementias; today, however, its use is far more widespread and encompasses almost any helping behaviour, especially across generations.

When I first became a student of social gerontology over 25 years ago, among the most influential works in the field was *Old People in Three Industrial Societies* by Shanas et al. (1968). I recently examined that work, and several others that appeared later, such as Shanas and Sussman's *Family, Bureaucracy and the Elderly*, as well as others well used in my early teaching career, such as *Aging: Stability and Change in Families* (Fogel et al., 1981). All of these volumes discussed important issues of the structure of the family, the household and family relations of old people, and health and incapacity in later life, and dealt conceptually with many of the same elements of intergenerational exchange and assistance that we continue to examine today. The word 'caregiving' simply did not appear in that literature as a descriptor of the intergenerational relationship. Nor were the roles of 'caregiver' and 'care recipient' described as notable features of intergenerational family relationships either within or between households. The question remains, why the rise of 'caregiving', and with what consequences?

This chapter argues that there are indeed consequences to the widespread use of the term 'caregiving' as a way of characterizing our understanding of intergenerational relationships. Problems with this terminology relate to both the nature of the relationship portrayed and the breadth of the activities and behaviours encapsulated. As well, how we define what caregiving is, and who does it, relates to dominant renditions of caregiving roles and relationships.

The Rhetoric of Apocalyptic Demography: The Rise of 'Caregiving' and 'Eldercare'

Susan McDaniel (Chapter 8) notes the intersection of family, work, and society. As we focus our attention on issues of work and family balance within the context of the 'intergenerational challenge', we see the extension of the mindset that views family relationships almost exclusively in terms of caregiving through the emergence of the odious term 'eldercare'. At one time in my career I easily adopted the term 'eldercare' as an effective shorthand for the research in which I was involved on how employees balance responsibilities between their paid labour and their responsibilities for care of elderly relatives (see Gottlieb et al.,1994; Martin-Matthews and Rosenthal, 1993). The project was known to team members as the 'Work and Eldercare' research program, with the design of the studies lending themselves to comparisons between child care and eldercare. With subsequent immersion in the data and with attention not only to the words of the participants in the study but also to the ways the research findings were received and reported, I came to see the dangers of this shorthand. The conceptualization of assistance to elderly people in terms of eldercare promotes and reinforces an image of older people as inherently dependent. The obvious referent or parallel category, against which it is juxtaposed, is child care. Eldercare metaphorically connotes 'care' as parallel to that given to children (Campbell and Martin-Matthews, 1998). The continued and widespread use of this term promotes and reinforces an image of elderly people only as *recipients* of care, and, in terms of the basic necessities of food, clothing, and shelter, as *dependent* as are children on the care provided to them.

The terms 'caregiving' and 'eldercare' imply burden, and in doing so they support and sustain the rhetoric of apocalyptic demography. With the sweeping, broad-brush approach implied in such terminology, an extremely wide range of behaviours and relationships is encapsulated. A recurring question that confounds researchers and policy-makers alike is: what are caregiving and eldercare anyway? Do these terms imply close, proximate, or even co-residence situations? Do they include emotional support as well as more direct aid? Are they descriptive of and applicable only to certain kinds of assistance given under particular conditions?

Most importantly and fundamentally, how are caregiving and eldercare distinct from normative family life, from the reciprocal give and take of aid and support that characterizes many family relationships throughout life? Are they generic terms that include the full spectrum of intergenerational interaction and exchange? What purpose is served in so inclusive a definition? Whose purpose? Why should it be that, as reflected in the vignettes, the relationship between Janet and her parents would be defined as caregiving while that between Erin and her parents would not? The kinds of assistance provided by each are in many ways parallel; what differs are the ages and generational status of those who appear to be receiving somewhat more assistance than they are providing.

British researchers Arber and Ginn (1990) distinguish between 'caring' and 'normal' family care by considering qualitative differences in the support and assistance provided by carers and helpers. In discussing intergenerational assistance, however, rarely is the relationship conceptualized in terms of a continuum along which family members move back and forth over time, from reciprocal exchanges of help to the provision of modest levels of assistance (and even episodically back again) and, then, more rarely, to situations requiring intensive levels of care for a highly dependent elderly person. In the blanket use of the terms 'eldercare' and 'caregiving', all types of intergenerational assistance oriented 'upward' to the older generation and a wide variety of relationships are considered together, or are focused on only one point on the continuum. So pervasive has this language become that in some studies of elderly persons admitted to hospital, individuals identified in the admission records as the 'contact' persons are subsequently referred to as 'caregivers', even though nothing was known about the nature of their relationships to the elderly persons and the parameters of the assistance provided prior to admission.

Such usage is problematic for a number of reasons. For one, and this is an issue to which we will return later, such terminology ignores the prevalence of reciprocal exchanges between elderly people and members of their kin and friendship networks. In my research, even that quite specifically focused on the nature of the tasks that employed persons 'perform' for their elderly family members, unsolicited descriptions of the assistance received in turn from elderly kin were frequently given by study participants. 'Caregivers' constantly reminded us of what they received from their elderly relatives in return, either tangibly in the present or in terms of reciprocal 'credentials' from the past.

It is also important to recognize that social scientists and policy-makers apply the 'caregiving' label to actions and behaviours that are not necessarily defined as caregiving by the people engaging in them; we also label as 'caregivers' people who do not and would not describe themselves in that way.

O'Connor (1999a, 1999b) describes the experiences of elderly individuals living with a memory-impaired spouse—a process she characterizes as '(re)cognizing the experience'. She found that all of the participants in her study grounded their caring activities in the idea that caring was a natural extension of their marital relationship. In other words, for many participants in her research, the provision of such care was a matter of 'what a wife does'. For some, this belief went without question, an extension of their marriage vows (i.e., 'in sickness and in health'). O'Connor contrasts these women's views of their labour of care as a 'private contribution' with 'caring as a public contribution'. The latter applies to the process of coming to define oneself as a caregiver. O'Connor emphasizes that not all of her participants identified with the 'caregiver' label. Although these are the very kinds of situations in which we would typically apply that label, it is not one readily or casually applied by the people actually providing assistance. These observations are as relevant to our discussions of intergenerational relations as to O'Connor's consideration of spousal ties.

Analyses that seek to understand 'the discourses, or story-lines, that influenced how spouses positioned their response to their partners' increasing dependency' (O'Connor, 1999a: 2) are far removed from the apocalyptic demography of intergenerational relations and yet are highly relevant to our challenge of it. We can ask the same question of how, in an intergenerational context, family members, friends, and neighbours position their responses to the changing frailty and dependency of an elderly relative or friend. Asking such questions enables us to stand outside the rhetoric of apocalyptic demography, outside the language of caregiving and eldercare, and to question the saliency and appropriateness of this all-too-easy application of terminology.

Eldercare and Child Care: Polar Opposites, Not Parallels

The term 'eldercare' has particular currency in the human resources field because of its assumed parallels with child care and all that it connotes in terms of issues, programs, and benefits to assist employees with family responsibilities. The term has become widely used, especially in North America, in discussions of the 'business' of aging. Various national 'eldercare' institutes have been established in the

US. The term 'corporate eldercare' is widely used to describe the provision by employers of programs, benefits, and/or services designed to assist employees in caring for elderly family members. It is ironic that the widespread use of a concept that perpetuates images of older people in dependent roles and non-reciprocal relationships should come at a time when, despite cutbacks to many services and programs, the ability of older people to live independently into advanced old age is greater than it has ever been.

The parallels between child care and eldercare are, in fact, few. Elsewhere (Martin-Matthews, 1996) I have identified some of these comparisons and contrasts; however, because they so well illustrate specifics of the rhetoric of apocalyptic demography in relation to caregiving, I will elaborate and discuss them further here.

The trajectory of the relationship is far more heterogeneous and unpredictable in the case of eldercare than it is for child care. In cases where the development of the child follows a 'normal' and healthy pattern, the provision of child care is highly regularized in terms of the sequence of responsibilities of the caregiver and the anticipated duration of the caregiving role. So much is this the case that society has enacted rules and regulations as to the appropriate ages at which children may legally be left alone without parental supervision and the ages at which children can legally assume responsibility for the care of younger children. As a society we fully understand that caring for a child of six, in typical circumstances, has far different implications than caring for a child of 13. The likely duration of particular types of care can be anticipated and predicted as part of one's 'life plan' as a parent even though, as Barbara Mitchell shows in Chapter 5, active participation in the parenting role may continue intermittently for many years beyond its anticipated duration. Thus, in the human resources and personnel fields, and for those in the 'work and family' field, the knowledge that an employee has a dependent child of a particular age in and of itself conveys some information about the nature of the child care role and related responsibilities; certain assumptions can be made on the basis of simply knowing the ages of the children.

This is not at all the case for eldercare. For those who assist elderly family members or friends, responsibilities may wax and wane in relation to the health or other transitions in the life of the elderly person. The knowledge that an employee or colleague has an elderly parent or other relative conveys nothing whatsoever about that person's eldercare role. Even the knowledge that last month an employee averaged four hours of assistance per week to an elderly relative conveys no information at all that is predictive of what her or his likely level of involvement in eldercare will be in the weeks ahead. Similarly, the anticipated duration of involvement in providing assistance usually cannot be predicted in any way. Nevertheless, assumptions of linearity pervade the empirical literature on caregivers, with efforts to measure caregiving on the basis of average numbers of hours per week or per month over, for example, a six-month period.

There are also differences between child care and eldercare in the number of 'helpers' involved. Ten years ago Connidis (1989: 88) decried the 'predominant reliance on data about the one child who provides the most care, often termed the primary caregiver'. Although today more studies do focus on 'secondary' caregivers, the literature nevertheless is still characterized by a predominant 'one child' focus. The narrow focus of the lens of caregiving has implications for the rhetoric of apocalyptic demography. The observation a decade ago that 'This focus on specific relationships within the family, rather than on the whole family unit, artificially inflates the apparent burden on families of caring for an older member' (ibid.) is still very much true today. While the provision of assistance to an older person may be restricted to one primary provider of care, it may also involve a broader network of kin and friends, each helping in unique or complementary ways or in providing assistance at intervals or sequentially. In the case of child care, on the other hand, responsibility usually resides with one or both parents.

Child care and eldercare also vary in their crisis episodes. Illness episodes in children frequently follow a regularized course so that even if the onset of illness cannot be predicted, the 'courses and sequelae' (Avison et al., 1993) will typically be experienced as a matter of days rather than weeks or months. Recovery from illness or injury is typically a lengthy and more complicated process in later life. Reflecting this reality, employees who assist elderly family members are far more likely than those providing child care to require longer periods of time away from paid employment in order to deal with such episodes (Martin-Matthews and Rosenthal, 1993). Nevertheless, there remains an imperative within some sectors of the human resources field to find the magic formula of a particular number of days per year of family leave to address eldercare issues.

Child care and eldercare also vary in the extent to which the person being 'cared for' has, and is acknowledged to have, rights in decisions concerning that care. As a society, we increasingly recognize the rights of older persons as autonomous decision makers in relation to the care they receive. Long- or short-term arrangements that may be best suited to the needs of older persons may not be compatible with the needs of the family members or friends who are assisting them. The location, timing, duration, and nature of the supportive services that best meet the elder's need may exacerbate stress and strains on other family members. What an elderly person will 'accept' may not be consistent or compatible with what best suits the needs of the spouse or adult child. Children typically have no comparable role in determining the care they will receive and accept. In this respect, one disturbing aspect of the apocalyptic demography of caregiving is the extent to which its rhetoric silences the voices of elderly persons themselves. Where they emerge at all is as the source of the 'problem' to be 'managed' by caregiving.

Typically, elderly persons are portrayed in the gerontological literature as 'acted upon' (often as victims in positions of dependency) rather than as 'actors' in their own life stories. By the very nature of their status as 'receivers' of care, elderly persons are assumed to be almost exclusively without agency. The rhetoric of caregiving does not recognize the extent to which the vast majority of elderly persons live in their own homes in the community, drawing little or not at all on the limited formal support systems society provides and, as the material presented by Rosenthal (Chapter 3) illustrates, overall relying little on family members outside their households for any form of support.

Child care and eldercare have both parallels and points of divergence with regard to the involvement of community-based services in the provision of care. The term 'child care' implies both direct, hands-on responsibilities for care of one's child(ren) and also time-limited (usually daytime only) care provided by trained personnel in agencies. The caregiving provided to elderly persons, however, does not necessarily involve direct, hands-on assistance; family members may help to 'manage' or orchestrate the care the older person receives through formal service providers. This may involve negotiating for, and making arrangements on behalf of, an older family member (often working collaboratively with the older person), monitoring service use, and supplementing or bridging between services. The availability and accessibility of community services in the provision of care are important to both child care and eldercare but have particular salience for the care of older persons.

The availability and accessibility of community services relates also to the rhetoric of apocalyptic demography, which assumes that intergenerational care is now, and will increasingly become, inherently burdensome. However, as other authors have well documented, the extent of the felt 'burden' of caregiving on the part of individual family members or of society as a whole is not due to the aging of the population *per se*. Rather, it derives from how we as a society choose to respond, by focusing, for example, on hospital and medical services (Barer et al., 1995), or by providing a broad base of community support services (Chappell, 1994, 1997), or by regarding the care of older persons to be primarily the responsibility of family members (McDaniel, 1993; Rosenthal and Neysmith, 1990).

What Is Caregiving? Prevalence, Patterns, and Misconceptions

Neysmith (1999) has noted that researchers and policy-makers are contributors to the rhetoric of apocalyptic demography. We have a role and a stake in these developments within our fields of inquiry and we must acknowledge our role in so doing. I have, unwittingly, played such a role.

For five years I was the Research Group Leader for the Work and Eldercare Research Group of CARNET (Canadian Aging Research Network). From 1990 through 1995, we surveyed some 8,500 Canadian employees and their managers and supervisors in regard to a host of familial, workplace, and community support issues involved in the provision of assistance to elderly family members.

Several years ago, after having contributed some information from our project for a national television report on 'You and Your Aging Parents', I noted their reference to 47 per cent of all Canadian employees having responsibility for eldercare. This figure was also cited recently in a report in *Family Connections,* which noted that '47 percent of working adults have some level of responsibilities for aging relatives' (MacLachlan, 1996). In both of these media usages of data from a research project with which I had been strongly identified and intimately involved, it was evident that the CARNET research findings fed spectacularly into the rhetoric of apocalyptic demography. There, for all to see, were 'the facts': fully 47 per cent of Canadian employees report that they are caregivers to one or more elderly parents! Nearly one-half! This is an extremely compelling figure in the context of issues of work-family balance. But there is a problem; it is not true.

The issue for me then became one of how our data had been misinterpreted and the role that we had played in the misinterpretation, and perhaps even misrepresentation, of our own data. Data were collected on 18 tasks with which these employees may have helped an elderly relative at least once in the six months preceding data collection. These included what are typically known as the Activities of Daily Living (ADLs), which include bathing, feeding, toileting, and dressing; the Instrumental Activities of Daily Living (IADLs), which include shopping, transportation, household chores, meal preparation, home maintenance and yard work, laundry, banking, and filling out forms; as well as other activities relating to the 'emotion work' (MacRae, 1998) of caregiving, such as helping with mood swings and memory problems (see Figure 4.1). It is also important to acknowledge that we had oversampled those aged 35 years and over in order to access more employees with the 'structural potential' for provision of care to an elderly parent (see Rosenthal, Chapter 3).

If an individual indicated that help had been provided with *any one of these activities in the preceding six months*, then he or she was loosely categorized into the group of 'caregivers'. Using this criterion, we estimated that approximately 47 per cent of the employees surveyed had some level of involvement in providing such assistance to an elderly family member. It is worth emphasizing that this is 47 per cent of a non-random and age-stratified sample, so the findings should never be reported as a percentage of *all* employees. What we believed our data showed was that 47 per cent of a sample of employees over the age of 35 had said that they had helped with at least one of these types of assistance in the six months preceding the study. Some helped Mom with her income taxes, some took Dad to the grocery store on Thursdays; this did not make these people caregivers in their own minds, let alone in that of the researchers. To our credit, we did note that for most employees, the levels of assistance provided were 'modest to moderate' and that only 'for about 12 percent of the employees . . . their responsibilities included more potentially burdensome responsibilities for personal care' (Martin-Matthews, 1999b).

But even with these caveats, the damage had been done. Innocently, but emphatically, we had fed into the rhetoric of apocalyptic demography in our heady declaration that 47 per cent of employees were engaged in activities related to caregiving. Because of the typically low levels of involvement by the majority of these sons and daughters in the care of their elderly relatives, we

Figure 4.1: Types of Assistance Provided

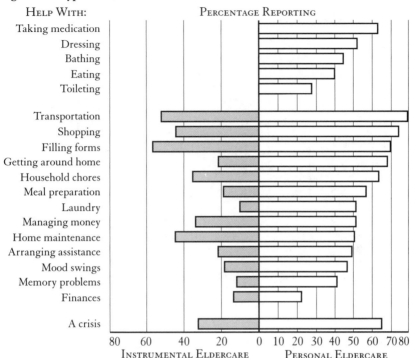

Source: Work and Eldercare Research Group, CARNET: Canadian Aging Research Network, 1994.

subsequently went on to refine our measurement and to categorize as caregivers those who had assisted with one ADL or two IADLs in the preceding six months.

Using the criteria we employed, however, Janet, the character in the vignette, would most assuredly be categorized as a caregiver, even though the care she provides is defined by her as part of her filial responsibilities as a daughter, even though she does not think of herself as a caregiver, and even though such terminology simply does not represent the context of meaning for her in her interactions with her parents. In fact, by these criteria, even her long-distance brother would qualify as a caregiver. In neither case, however, would they ascribe to the label of 'caregiver'.

By any standards, assisting one's parent to fill out an income tax form does not make one a caregiver. Even taking a parent shopping once a month in addition to helping her fill out the income tax form does not make one a caregiver. Certainly, what the CARNET data found was that 47 per cent of the people surveyed were involved in some way in the provision of assistance to an elderly relative. A substantially smaller proportion were engaged in activities that *might* be deemed caregiving if we had a rigorous definition of what caregiving is.

Figure 4.2: Global Stress Measure

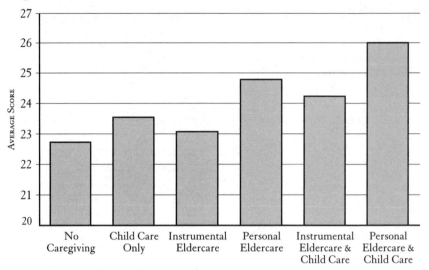

Scores can range from 0 to 56.
(N=5,496)
Source: Work and Eldercare Research Group, CARNET: Canadian Aging Research Network, 1994.

It is important to acknowledge that caregiving has been and is loosely defined in much of the research in social gerontology. It is also important to recognize the damage done by these overestimates of prevalence, by the mislabelling of patterns of intergenerational familial assistance. Other conceptual and methodological practices also overstate the consequences and impacts of these caregiving behaviours. The CARNET project was very careful to avoid these. In comparisons of the different caregiving groups, the group of respondents who reported 'no caregiving' activities, either for children or for elderly family members, was included.

Figure 4.2 depicts the different levels reported by the different caregiver groups on a global measure of stress. In this analysis, and in others, the 'no caregiving' group served an important function as a baseline category; instead of assuming the reference point on any variable as 'zero' or 'unknown' and comparing caregivers against that reference, the 'no caregiving' group provided insights that otherwise would have been lost. As this illustration of the stress measure indicates, the 'no caregiving' group reported levels of stress not significantly different from the caregiving groups; in fact, only those persons combining responsibilities for children with the more demanding 'personal' (ADL) care of elderly relatives reported significantly higher stress levels.

Had data only been collected and reported on caregivers, the interpretation of the research findings would have been less sensitive to the generally stressful nature of life in general and the extent to which other responsibilities may not add that much to daily strains and hassles. The inclusion of the control group, rarely done in caregiving research, proved especially important in preventing the research team from overstating the consequences and impacts of caregiving behaviours and thereby buying into another aspect of the rhetoric of apocalyptic demography.

These observations should in no way be taken as denial of the issues faced by individuals engaged in providing care—and occasionally, quite significant levels of care—to elderly relatives and friends. There are well-documented indications of the very real consequences for many of these people in terms of stresses and strains, burden, burnout, and difficulties balancing all of their responsibilities. However, the lack of rigour in our definitions of caregiving, our lack of precision in separating the ebb and flow—the give and take—of family and social relationships, the failure to look at the linkages and supportive behaviours within and across generations and households—contribute to an overstating of caregiving and eldercare in terms of prevalence and impact.

Does overstating the prevalence of elder caregiving matter? Lynn McDonald, in Chapter 7, speaks of the problem of overdramatizing issues. It is rather hard to overdramatize the kind of 'caring' depicted by Susan McDaniel in Chapter 8 when she reports return visits to hospital every six hours of patients still attached to IV tubes. But the issue here is something considerably further removed along the continuum of care (and we must be far more precise in thinking about it as a continuum). When researchers and policy-makers include in discussions of eldercare and caregiving the activities of people who take their mothers shopping and help fill out their income tax forms, we trivialize the hard labour and ongoing everyday challenges of individuals who provide demanding, continuous, and laborious care to frail spouses, parents, siblings, and children. It takes the focus away from a genuine and targeted effort to develop systematic and well-funded community care.

Who, then, stands to gain from the rhetoric of apocalyptic demography in relation to caregiving? An examination of recent newspaper reports well illustrates the drama of the rhetoric, and the extent to which it fuels the apparent need for an arsenal of specialists to tackle the 'problem'. Examples include: 'Eldercare is a bigger issue than child care ever was or will be'; 'Employers struggle to cope with the looming crisis of eldercare'; and 'Eldercare is the workplace challenge of the 90's'. However, far from promoting corporate interest in and support for workplace-based initiatives signalling an understanding of employees' needs to balance their work and home responsibilities, these kinds of statements make systematic change less likely. They create among human resources people a concern that the floodgates will open if workplaces begin to offer benefits or extend programs to assist individuals struggling to balance employment and care for elderly family members. The research in which I have been involved for several years strongly indicates that many employees, even those providing quite significant levels of care, for some, the equivalent of an extra day of 'work' per week, do not ask for much in the way of workplace-based assistance. What most desire and welcome is often little more than the understanding and support of a manager or supervisor who has been trained to understand the issues of work-family balance in the context of aging. For others, some options for leaves of absence or flex-time or job-sharing are more appropriate. But the scare tactics of apocalyptic demography have the possible danger of stifling much-needed initiatives in this area.

Apocalyptic Demography: What's Missing from the Rhetoric?

It is also important to acknowledge what gets left out of the rhetoric of apocalyptic demography. One dimension that is omitted is any notion of reciprocity— that individuals who provide assistance may themselves be assisted. Respondents in the CARNET surveys told us this repeatedly. But considerations of reciprocity—the ways in which older persons contribute to and facilitate the employment activities and labour force participation of their children – are hardly consistent with apocalyptic demography. Other authors in this book note the issue of commodification, i.e., of treating intergenerational linkages and transfers as commodities to be exchanged. It is part of the 'accounting and counting' approach that Susan McDaniel, in particular, notes in Chapter 8. Reciprocity is often difficult to quantify; especially hard to quantify are what I have referred to here as 'reciprocal credentials' from the past. The motivations expressed by the people we interview ('I do it because she is my mom and not because I am a 'caregiver') speak far more of reciprocity and attachment and the affectual solidarity noted by Bengtson and colleagues (1985) than they do of caregiving; in that sense they stand outside the dominant discourse of our studies of intergenerational relations today.

We speak of dominant discourses in our fields of inquiry, but there is also a 'dominant demography' of which we must be wary. This term refers to the fact that our renditions of the 'problem' or the 'issue' often focus on the demographically most typical or most pressing of situations: the largest groups or those who are the most visible. Too often, 'demographic determinism' colours the ways in which gerontologists and policy-makers approach issues. As an example, we focus much of the discussion of marital status issues in later life on the transition to widowhood, when in fact we are coming to understand the quite unique deprivations and challenges faced by aging and elderly women who are separated and divorced.

Another illustration involves the place of gender in studies of caregiving. As Lopata (1995) has noted, the existence of gender identity as a category in the social structure has led social scientists to use it as a variable in quantitative analyses. The conversion of gender variation into a single variable flattens women and men into a single dimension that ignores their heterogeneity and views them only in contrast to the other gender. Because of the well-documented fact that most providers of care and assistance to elderly family members are women, care by men has, until quite recently, been virtually ignored. Thus, where men appear at all in studies of caregiving, it is to compare and contrast their actions, behaviours, and motives with those of women. This approach perpetuates the 'two-sphere' ideology of much of research in social gerontology (Lopata, 1995).

There are different *kinds* of men and different *kinds* of women; yet these differences are masked in broad-brush discussions of gender typically found in studies of families and aging. For example, a recent study of sons who provide assistance to elderly parents found important *differences among men* in the provision of care, with sibling status being a key factor; men who are only children (having no siblings) and those with only male siblings are more likely to be involved in these roles (Campbell, 1997; Campbell and Martin-Matthews, 1997, 1998). Likewise, there were many *similarities between men and women* in their experiences of providing care, especially when it involved elderly relatives with substantial needs for care.

Another issue relates to the understanding of what gender comparisons and contrasts mean in the context of studies of families and aging. For the most part, gender is used as an independent or control variable in many studies of caregiving, often with little or no examination of any gender differences observed or even without recognizing that in many areas of investigation, no gender differences appear to exist (Miller and Cafasso, cited in Bengtson et al., 1996). Published articles tend to emphasize statistically significant gender differences and ignore findings of no gender differences.

It is noteworthy that *men's* experiences stand largely outside dominant renditions of the apocalyptic demography of caregiving (Martin-Matthews, 1999a). It is no accident that the vignettes that began this chapter both involved daughters; one explanation is the now recognized 'lack of visibility of men' in aging families (Bengtson et al., 1996: 267). In many studies, for example, sample sizes are simply not large enough to provide enough men for meaningful analyses of gender differences, controlling for kin relationships. The same holds for research on widowhood (my own included). Widowhood research focuses almost exclusively on women, not only because women are four times more likely than men to be widowed, but also because widowed men are hard to find; thus we tend not to ask the questions that would include them. Lynn McDonald, in Chapter 7, makes a similar point; studies of poverty in old age focus almost entirely on older women because women are far more likely than men to be poor. The demography that we challenge here is thus not only apocalyptic but also dominant demography, which, as this chapter attests, drives the caregiving discourse by the way in which it frames questions and thereby shapes answers.

References

Arber, S., and J. Ginn. 1990. 'The Meaning of Informal Care: Gender and the Contribution of Elderly People', *Ageing and Society* 10: 429–54.

Avison, W.R., R.J. Turner, S. Noh, and K. Nixon Speechley. 1993. 'The Impact of Caregiving: Comparisons of Different Family Contexts and Experiences', in S.H. Zarit, L.I. Pearlin, and K.W. Schaie, eds, *Caregiving Systems: Formal and Informal Helpers*. New York: Lawrence Erlbaum Associates, 75–106.

Barer, M., et al. 1995. 'Avalanche or Glacier? Health Care and the Demographic Rhetoric', *Canadian Journal on Aging* 14, 2: 193–224.

Bengtson, V.L., N.E. Cutler, D.J. Mangen, and V.W. Marshall. 1985. 'Generations, Cohorts and Relations Between Age Groups', in R.H. Binstock and E. Shanas, eds, *Handbook of Aging and the Social Sciences*, 2nd edn. New York: Academic Press, 304–38.

———, C.J. Rosenthal, and L. Burton. 1996. 'Paradoxes of Families and Aging', in R.H. Binstock and L.K. George, eds, *Handbook of Aging and the Social Sciences*, 4th edn. New York: Academic Press, 253–82.

Bowlby, J. 1980. *Attachment and Loss, Volume III: Loss, Sadness and Depression*. New York: Basic Books.

Campbell, L.D. 1997. 'Sons Who Care: Exploring Men's Involvement in Filial Care', Ph.D. dissertation, University of Guelph.

——— and A. Martin-Matthews. 1997. 'Examining Men's Filial Care Within a Gendered Context of Caregiving', paper presented at annual meeting of the Canadian Association on Gerontology, Calgary, Oct.

——— and ———. 1998. 'The Importance of Co-residence and Being Primary Provider of Care on Men's Filial Lives', paper presented at the annual meeting of the Canadian Association on Gerontology, Halifax, Oct.

Chappell, N.L. 1994. 'Health Care Reform: Will It Be Better or Worse for Families?', plenary address at the annual meeting of the Canadian Association on Gerontology, Winnipeg, Oct.

———. 1997. 'Health Care Reform: Implications for Seniors', *Journal of Aging Studies* 11, 3: 171–258.

Connidis, I.A. 1989. *Family Ties and Aging*. Toronto: Butterworths.

Fogel, R.W., E. Hatfield, S.B. Kiesler, and E. Shanas, eds. 1981. *Aging: Stability and Change in the Family*. New York: Academic Press.

Gottlieb, B.H., E.K. Kelloway, and M. Fraboni. 1994. 'Aspects of Eldercare that Place Employees at Risk', *The Gerontologist* 34, 6: 815–21.

Lopata, H.Z. 1995. 'Feminist Perspectives on Social Gerontology', in R. Bleiszner and V.H. Bedford, eds, *Handbook of Aging and the Family*. Westport, Conn.: Greenwood Press, 114–31.

McDaniel, S.A. 1993. 'Caring and Sharing: Demographic Aging, Family and the State', in J. Hendricks and C.J. Rosenthal, eds, *The Remainder of Their Days: Domestic Policy and Older Families in the United States and Canada*. New York: Garland, 121–43.

MacLachlan, M. 1996. 'Wake Up Corporate Canada! Eldercare Is Here', *Family Connections* (Fall): 36–7.

MacRae, H. 1998. 'Managing Feelings: Caregiving as Emotion Work', *Research on Aging* 20, 1: 137–60.

Martin-Matthews, A.1996. 'Why I Dislike the Term "Eldercare"', *Transition* 26, 3: 16. Ottawa: Vanier Institute of the Family.

————. 1999a. 'Widowhood: Dominant Renditions, Changing Demography and Variable Meaning', in S. Neysmith, ed., *Critical Issues in Social Work with Elderly Persons*. New York: Columbia University Press.

————.1999b. 'Managing Employment and Care of the Frail Elderly', in V. Lechner and M.B. Neal, ed., *Working and Caring for the Elderly: An International Perspective*. New York: Taylor and Francis.

———— and J.M. Keefe. 1995. 'Work and Care of Elderly People: A Canadian Perspective', in J. Phillips, ed., *Working Carers: International Perspectives on Working and Caring for Older People*. Aldershot, UK: Avebury, 116–38.

———— and C.J. Rosenthal. 1993. 'Balancing Work and Family in an Aging Society: The Canadian Experience', in G.L. Maddox and M.P. Lawton, eds, *Annual Review of Gerontology and Geriatrics: Focus on Kinship, Aging and Social Change*. New York: Springer, 96–119.

Matthews, S.H., and J. Heidorn. 1998. 'Meeting Filial Responsibilities in Brothers-Only Sibling Groups', *Journal of Gerontology: Social Sciences* 53B, 5: S278–86.

Neysmith, S.M. 1999. *Critical Issues in Social Work with Elderly Persons*. New York: Columbia University Press.

O'Connor, D.L. 1999a. 'Constructing Community Care: (Re)Storying Support', in Neysmith (1999).

————. 1999b. 'Living with a Memory-Impaired Spouse: Re(Cognizing) the Experience', *Canadian Journal on Aging*. 18, 2: 211–35.

Rosenthal, C.J., and S.M. Neysmith. 1990. 'Informal Support to Older People: Conclusions, Forecasts, Recommendations and Policy Descriptions in Recent Policy Deliberations', unpublished report prepared for Statistics Canada.

Shanas, E., P. Townsend, D. Wedderburn, H. Friis, P. Milhoj, and J. Stehouwer. 1968. *Old People in Three Industrial Societies*. New York: Atherton Press.

———— and M.B. Sussman.1977. *Family, Bureaucracy and the Elderly*. Durham, NC: Duke University Press.

Wolfson, C., R. Handfield-Jones, K.C. Glass, J. McClaran, and E. Keyserlingk. 1993. 'Adult Children's Perceptions of Their Responsibility to Provide Care for Dependent Elderly Parents', *The Gerontologist* 33, 3: 315–23.

5 | The Refilled 'Nest'

Debunking the Myth of Families in Crisis

Barbara A. Mitchell

Introduction

Recently, researchers and the popular press have paid increasing attention to the changing organization of family-related life-course transitions. One notable development has been the dramatic shift in the nature and direction of inter-generational obligations and socio-economic support. At the beginning of the twentieth century, responsibilities for the financial and residential needs of impoverished aging parents rested squarely on the shoulders of their offspring (Goldscheider, 1997). According to Caldwell (1976), wealth and support of this kind flowed up the 'generational ladder'. By this century's end, however, the direction of responsibility and living arrangement patterns had reversed. Grown adult children are now the primary beneficiaries of parental economic assistance and housing support (Goldscheider, 1997). This has created new intergenerational challenges because of the extension of the transition to adulthood and, concurrently, continued day-to-day 'in-house' parenting for many Canadian families.

It is now commonly understood that mid-life parenthood often comprises prolonged periods of co-residence with grown young adults. These adult children have either remained in the parental home until later ages or have returned home following an initial departure to refill the parental 'nest'. Although considerable research has accumulated on the phenomenon of parent-adult child co-residence in Canada and the United States (e.g., Boyd and Pryor, 1989; White, 1994), very little is known about home-returning in Canada, with the exception of a Vancouver study (Gee et al., 1995). In part, this is because middle-generation family development has been a neglected area of research in studies of aging families (McDaniel, 1996). But also, Statistics Canada did not collect information on the home-returning experiences of Canadian young people until the mid-1990s.

The topic of home-returning deserves separate attention from delayed home-leaving because this behaviour reflects a distinct set of circumstances that have unique implications for family roles and intergenerational relations over the life course. Moreover, we need to analyse critically the popular perception propagated by many social scientists and media outlets that the increasing demographic trend of co-residence, in particular, home-returning, represents something 'pathological' in individual or family functioning (Weinick, 1995), and therefore presents a 'crisis' for middle-generation families. For example, social scientists have offered conceptualizations fraught with negative connotations of inter-generational co-residence, such as the 'incompletely launched young adult phenomenon' or the 'returning young adult syndrome' (Schnaiberg and Gold-enberg, 1989). Indeed, it is not uncommon for researchers to assume that when young adults return home 'everybody loses' (Bibby and Posterski, 1992: 221; Clemens and Axelson, 1985).

In addition, media images of 'boomerang kid' families tend to be sympathetic to a middle-aged, middle-class readership. Parents are often portrayed as victims of greedy or lazy children (Hartung and Sweeney, 1991) afflicted with what has been termed 'The Peter Pan Syndrome' (Goldscheider, 1997) . Young men, in particular, are depicted by the media as immature adults who are unable or unwilling to let go of 'the apron strings' (Gross, 1991). One article, for instance, urges parents to 'cut the cord' before sharing the parental home once again (Ten-nant, 1992). Taken together, since young adults are depicted as being reluctant to grow up and because they are represented as feeling entitled to continued sup-port (Hartung and Sweeney, 1991), it is typically assumed that a return to the parental home can only present serious problems for the mid-life family.

It should be emphasized that many of these stereotypes or ideas have been formulated in the absence of careful research or have been propagated by sensa-tionalistic media accounts based on anecdotal evidence. It is the objective of this chapter to evaluate these images of family crisis and demographic apocalypse. This will be accomplished by a comprehensive analysis of relevant theoretical, conceptual, and research material on the subject, which will be supplemented with new data drawn from a large Canadian national study. The specific goals of this chapter include: (1) an examination of co-residence and the prevalence of returning to the parental household in Canada; (2) a critical review of explana-tions for home-returning; (3) elaboration of the nature and direction of inter-generational exchanges in refilled 'nests'; (4) investigation of the extent to which 'boomerang kid' living arrangements affect intergenerational well-being; and (5) discussion of social policy issues.

Theoretical Perspective

A life-course theoretical perspective provides both a developmental and histori-cal framework for the study of intergenerational relations (Elder, 1977, 1985; Hareven, 1996). It focuses on 'age-related transitions that are socially created, socially recognized, and shared' (Hagestad and Neugarten, 1985: 35–6). More-over, this perspective offers a theoretical understanding of the connections among historical time, family time, and individual time (Elder, 1994; Hareven, 1996). This notion of 'timing' takes into consideration the family-historical context defining current socio-cultural and economic conditions that subsequently affect opportunity structures and kin interactions.

Applied to family change over the life course, this approach focuses on 'linked lives' or the interdependence of family members' life histories (Elder, 1994). A central tenet of this perspective is that interactions between life careers occur across generations, so that the transitions of one family member create changes for others in the family (Hagestad, 1981). A young adult's decision to return home, for example, can move parents, voluntarily or not, out of the empty nest phase and back into the launching phase of the family life course (Aquilino, 1996). Thus, this chapter focuses on how family-related transitions and intergenerational relations are best understood within a historical, socio-demographic, and economic context. Furthermore, consideration will be given to how intergenerational relations are influenced by the behaviour and developmental life trajectories of individual family members.

Methods

Two data sets are used to address the research goals outlined above: the 1995 General Social Survey (GSS), Cycle 10, and a local Vancouver study conducted in 1993–4, originally entitled the 'Cluttered Nest Project' (CNP).

The 1995 General Social Survey, Cycle 10

This data set concentrates on the topic of family life and measures major changes in demographics, social characteristics, and family conditions of Canadians. The target population of the 1995 GSS consisted of all persons aged 15 and over living in a private household in a Canadian province. Data were collected over a 12-month period from January to December 1995 using a computer-assisted telephone interview system. Interviews were completed by 10,749 respondents, for a response rate of 81.1 per cent (Statistics Canada, 1995).

The sub-sample used in this analysis is comprised of 3,328 young adults aged 19–34. This group is further divided into one of three groups: those who have never left home or the 'home-stayers' (n = 745), those who have left home and never returned for four months or more, termed the 'home-leavers' (n = 1,844), and home-returners (n = 709). Home-returners are those who had left and later returned to live at home (either in the past or currently) for at least four months.

The 1993–4 Cluttered Nest Project

This study involved telephone interviews with a random sample of 420 families in which both a parent and a child (from the same family) were interviewed separately, in late 1993 and early 1994. Based on the adult child's history of living arrangements, a sub-sample of 218 families with a returnee or 'boomerang' child was identified. This sub-sample consists of families in which a returnee adult child resided at home for at least one period of six months after leaving home for at least six months within the past five years. Children were required to be between 19 and 35 years of age and parents were required to be between 35 and 60 years of age. These final two criteria were introduced in order to reduce the number of age cohorts of the study population (Gee et al., 1995).

The sampling pool was comprised of household numbers listed in the Greater Vancouver telephone directory. Trained interviewers made contacts using the technique known as random digit dialling. Approximately 10 per cent of the sample were recruited through snowball sampling and through replies to advertisements placed in local newspapers. We calculated a response rate of about 50 per cent (of all contacted eligible households). Of the 218 'boomerang families', 120 (55 per cent) are current returners, while 98 (45 per cent) are families in which the return occurred in the past five years. The average age of the parent respondent is 53.1, and the average age of children at first return is 21.2 years.

The telephone interviews were between 30–45 minutes, on average, for each family member. Families were queried about the timing of, and factors contributing to, leaving and returning home, aspects of their intergenerational relationships, and perceptions of instrumental and emotional task exchanges, as well as the role of a variety of economic, employment, educational, and housing factors in making living arrangement decisions.

Co-residence and the Prevalence of Home-returning in Canada

As previously noted, social scientists and the popular press have increasingly presented home-returning or co-residence more generally as something aberrant or abnormal. However, it is important to appreciate that, within a historical or cross-cultural context, parent-adult child co-residence (as distinct from multigenerational living arrangements) is not something 'new'. For example, high rates of co-residence between an aging parent and unmarried adult child were observed in earlier parts of this century in North America, particularly during recessionary periods (White, 1994). It was also quite common for unmarried children to contribute substantial amounts of their earnings to their parents for room and board (Baker, 1989). In the following section, attention is paid to presenting co-resident living arrangements and home-returning patterns within a historical context. Differences in co-resident living arrangements between younger and older (i.e., senior) generations are also noted.

Co-residence between parents and their adult children decreased most dramatically between 1971 and 1981, paralleling a twentieth century trend towards non-familial living arrangements. These types of households have been termed 'primary individual households' (Kobrin, 1976). Over the last two decades, however, census data show a reversal in this trend, such that Glenn (1987) and others have identified this as a relatively rare 'profamilistic' pattern. Parent-adult child co-residence increased modestly during the 1980s, particularly during the recession of the early 1980s. Overall, there has been an increase of about 10 per cent in parent-adult child co-residence since the 1970s (Boyd and Norris, 1995).

In contemporary society, it has also been rare for young adults to contribute to the family household (Goldscheider and Goldscheider, 1993). Compulsory education, increased affluence, and the creation of public welfare (e.g., pensions, disability payments) are among the main reasons for this trend. This has freed many families from reliance on the labour of 'dependants' for additional income. Overall, although intergenerational doubling-up is relatively common from a historical perspective, what has changed is how these living arrangements are formed as well as the nature of parent-child support and obligations during co-residence.

Notably, a co-resident living arrangement may be created as the result of a young adult returning to the parental home. What is the likelihood that young adult children will return after leaving home? As previously noted, until recently, this question was unanswerable because Statistics Canada did not collect information on the home-returning behaviour of Canadian young adults. However, in the 1995 GSS, young adults were asked how many times they left home to live on their own. If they had left more than once and they had returned home for at least one period of four months or more, they were classified as home-returners. According to the 1995 GSS, returning to the parental home is surprisingly common; 27 per cent of all young adults aged 19–35 interviewed reported that they had left home and had returned for four months or more. As previously noted, this estimate combines both recent and current returners.

Given that home-returning or parent-adult child co-residence more generally is relatively commonplace, how does this compare to the living arrangements of elderly persons? It is clear that intergenerational doubling-up is more frequent between mid-life parents and their grown children than between mid-life parents and at least one elderly parent. For example, Boyd, using data from the 1991 Canadian census, finds that half of the single young adult population aged 20–34 were residing with their parents. Surprisingly, between two and three out of ten 'older' young adults (aged 32–4) were living at home (Boyd, 1998). This compares with between 3 and 8 per cent of senior parents who live with an adult child (Statistics Canada, 1994, 1995), depending on the age group selected.

Why Are Young Adults Flocking Back to the Nest?

As discussed at the beginning of this chapter, a common perception exists that the inability to leave home 'on time' and 'for good' indicates a marker of personal or family failure. In this section, focus is placed on why adult children are returning to the parental household. The primary question considered is: Are young adults returning home because they have 'failed' to achieve full adult status?

The 1995 General Social Survey

GSS respondents were asked to indicate their main reason(s) for returning home from the following list of reasons: 'job ended', 'relationship ended', 'financial reasons', 'obtained degree or left school', 'end of school term/year', or 'other

Figure 5.1: Reasons for Returning Home, 1995

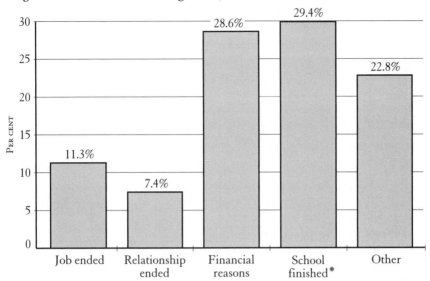

Total = 487 (recent returners only)
* Includes: left school, got degree, term ended
Source: General Social Survey.

reasons'. From this list, they were asked to identify the primary or main reason for returning home. Results from this question are presented in Figure 5.1.

We can see that the most common primary reason for returning, accounting for 29.9 per cent of all answers, was school-related. This category combines all school-related reasons (returning because the young adult obtained a degree, left school, or because school had finished). This is followed by: returning for financial reasons (28.6 per cent), for other reasons (22.8 per cent), because a job ended (11.3 per cent), and because a relationship ended (7.4 per cent).

Additional preliminary multivariate analyses also show several predictors of home-returning in Canada. Results of a proportional hazards model analysis reveal that young adults are more likely to return home if: their fathers have higher education, they left home for particular reasons (i.e., to seek independence rather than for school-related reasons), they are male, they left home at early ages, and they have few siblings. There also appear to be important cultural variations, as measured by mother tongue, in the propensity to return home. However, further analysis is also required on this topic (Mitchell et al., forthcoming).

Unfortunately, regional or urban/rural area differences in returning home cannot be examined using the 1995 GSS because previous returners were not asked the region/place of residence in which they lived during their return home. However, results of the CNP shed some light on why young adults return

Figure 5.2: Economic Reasons for Returning Home, 1993–1994

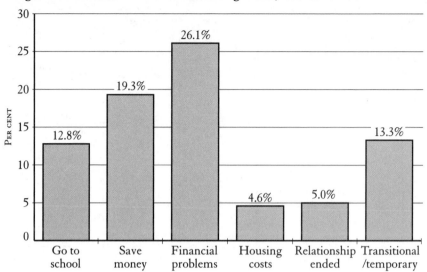

Subtotal = 177 (81.2% of sample)
Source: Cluttered Nest Project, Vancouver.

home in a large urban area—the Greater Vancouver Region—during approximately the same time period (Mitchell and Gee, 1996a). These data also offer more detail on the motivating factors affecting home-returning decisions.

The 1993–4 Cluttered Nest Project

Figure 5.2 presents the distribution of the main reasons for the respondents' last return home. Similar to the results of the 1995 GSS, it is clear that economic reasons take precedence over non-economic reasons. Economic reasons account for 81.2 per cent of all reasons for returning. Of these economic reasons, 26.1 per cent stated that they had returned because of financial problems, 19.3 per cent returned to save money, 12.8 per cent 'boomeranged' because of school-related reasons (i.e., to attend university), 4.6 per cent due to high housing costs, 5 per cent because a relationship ended, and 13.3 per cent for transitional/temporary reasons.

It is interesting to note that many of the 19 per cent of the sample who stated that they lived at home to save money indicated that they could actually afford to live on their own. However, they were willing to sacrifice some independence in order to live at their parents' standard of living. This phenomenon has been called an 'intergenerational taste effect', whereby the luxuries of one generation become the necessity of the next generation (Crimmins et al., 1991).

Regarding non-economic reasons for returning (Figure 5.3), 9 per cent returned for psychological reasons. For example, many of these young adults

Figure 5.3: Non-Economic Reasons for Returning Home, 1993–1994

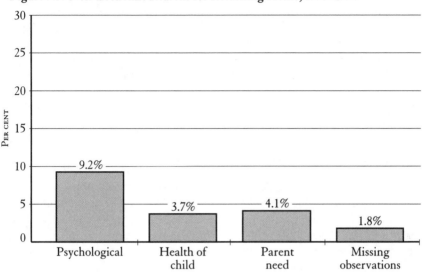

Subtotal = 37 (17.1% of sample)
Source: Cluttered Nest Project, Vancouver.

had left home at very early ages and did not feel psychologically prepared or mature enough to live independently of their parents. Young adults also returned because their parents required assistance (4.1 per cent). Another 3.7 per cent reported that the most important reason for moving back home was because of their own health problems, for example, because of disability or due to an accident.

Multivariate analysis techniques were also used to examine the factors contributing to the likelihood of returning home (Gee et al., 1995). Child characteristics were found to be more important than parental characteristics as important predictors of co-residence. Never-married, unemployed, and those who have a step-parent at the time of the survey were more likely to return. Also, among those who left home at later ages, those who initially left for employment or other reasons were less likely to return home.

In summary, these data do not support the view that young adults (or their families, for that matter) should be held totally responsible for their so-called 'failure' to secure and maintain permanent residential independence. Current economic conditions and diminished opportunity structures play an important role in the increased tendency of young adults to return home. For example, it is clear that some young adults attended post-secondary institutions, attained degrees, but were still unable to find secure employment or to afford independent households. However, it is overly simplistic to focus only on economic factors. It is also important to appreciate that broad socio-demographic changes such as delayed marriage and family formation, educational inflation, the desire to save money, psychological factors (Mitchell and Gee, 1996a), and shifting cultural norms regarding the social acceptability of this living arrangement (Alwin, 1996) all contribute to increasing numbers of refilled nests. In summary, these data indicate that the parental home is sometimes used as a 'safety net', implying some kind of 'slip'. However, it is apparent that for others the refilled nest is more of a 'home base', denoting a 'normal' base of operation, for example, during transitional periods (DaVanzo and Goldscheider, 1990), or it is simply a lifestyle choice.

Intergenerational Exchanges and Perceptions of Support

Research on parent-adult child co-residence often highlights how such living arrangements are formed for the child's benefit. As two researchers comment, 'Co-residence more commonly involves children residing in parental households for reasons that reflect prolonged child dependence on parental resources' (Ward and Spitze, 1992: 559). Similarly, the popular perception regarding home-returns—propagated by the mass media—is that the parental household is something akin to a 'boomerang motel'. That is, there is a common image of the parental home as a refuge or haven where children have unlimited access to goods and services during a return home. This would include such things as free rent, home-cooked meals, laundry services, cable TV, use of the family car and so on. In other words, intergenerational support is assumed to be unidirectional, with the child the clear 'beneficiary of the parent's largesse' (Hartung and Sweeney, 1991). However, virtually no research has examined patterns and perceptions of intergenerational support during home-returns.

The CNP study, by examining two central issues, takes a first step towards uncovering whether intergenerational relations during a return are largely asymmetrical (Veevers and Mitchell, 1998). The first set of research questions relates to levels of support: to what extent do mid-life parents and their grown children actually engage in and exchange helping behaviours (instrumental support) and affective types of informal support in these family living arrangements. Do 'boomerang kids' revert back to pre-departure behaviours, whereby parents provide a disproportionate amount of helping? Or do young adults contribute help in relatively equal amounts as their parents because they are now considered adult-like in status?

A second important issue is the degree to which parents and their children perceive receiving and giving assistance. Do receivers of helping behaviours perceive this exchange in a similar manner as the giver, and vice versa? This question is important in that perceptions of support may have significant implications for feelings of entitlement, fairness, obligations, and reciprocity, as well as for future expectations regarding helping behaviour.

Several measures of social support were available in the CNP for analysis. The parent respondent was asked: 'What kinds of assistance and how often do (did)

Table 5.1: Perceptions of Support Flowing to Child: Percentage of Respondents Reporting Providing Support Daily or Weekly

	Type of Support				
Respondent	Meal Preparation	Grocery Shopping	Transportation	Laundry	Emotional
Parent	74.9	69.5	36.8	32.4	73.9
Child	72.6	65.2	31.4	37.3	70.1

Table 5.2: Perceptions of Support Flowing to Parent: Percentage of Respondents Reporting Providing Support Daily or Weekly

	Type of Support					
Respondent	Meal Preparation	Grocery Shopping	Transportation	Laundry	Cleaning	Emotional
Parent	51.1	20.8	22.2	50.2	49.5	51.8
Child	62.2	29.2	16.7	32.4	48.1	30.9

you provide help to your returnee child with the following tasks in or around the home?' The following list of tasks was provided: meal preparation, grocery shopping, transportation, laundry, and emotional support. The amount of help provided was ascertained by the respondent stating whether it was: 1 = daily, 2 = at least once/week, 3 = at least once/month, 4 = less than once/month, 5 = never, or 9 = not applicable. They were also asked to estimate how much help their spouse provided. Children were asked the same questions (including the additional task of household cleaning), and were asked to give separate responses for each parent. Parent respondents and children were also asked the type and how much assistance they received from the other generation.

As shown in Table 5.1, from the parent's perspective, the most frequently occurring type of support provided to the child (received daily or once per week) is meal preparation (74.9 per cent), followed by emotional support (73.9 per cent) and grocery shopping (69.5 per cent). Less support was provided to children in the areas of transportation (36.8 per cent) and help with laundry (32.4 per cent). Children reported receiving these types of support in roughly similar proportions as parents. However, there is a tendency for children to acknowledge receiving slightly less help for four out of the five types of support with the exception of help with laundry.

In Table 5.2, we examine level of support flowing to the parents for six types of help (house cleaning is added). Parents report that the most frequently occurring types of help received (daily or once per week) are emotional support (51.8 per cent), meal preparation (51.1 per cent), laundry (50.2 per cent), and house-cleaning (49.5 per cent). One finding that stands out is the tendency for parents to report receiving more emotional help on a daily or weekly basis than children report providing to parents (51.8 per cent compared to 30.9 per cent). In our study, parents typically interpreted emotional support in the form of day-to-day companionship or friendship.

Our study of financial exchanges revealed a similar pattern, although many of the parents did not want any kind of significant monetary contribution in exchange for household assistance. In fact, roughly one-half of parents did not 'charge' their children rent or room and board and the other one-half asked for only a nominal amount (e.g., $150 per month). Instead, they appeared to prefer that their adult children help out in other ways (e.g., by helping around the house) and save their money for the future.

In summary, these results reveal that intergenerational exchange relations during a home-return are not unidirectional. The fact that children engage in relatively frequent exchange behaviours suggests that they attempt to maintain reciprocity in situational contexts that generally favour parental giving of support. This does not diminish the fact, however, that returnee children receive more frequent instrumental and affective support from parents than parents receive in return. Another important finding is that parents and children share similar perceptions on these exchanges. However, this can depend on the type of assistance being provided, especially for emotional support, which parents report receiving in fairly high levels.

Consequences of the Refilled Nest for Intergenerational Well-being

Some researchers argue that the presence of 'boomerang kids' in the household is problematic and can create intrafamilial conflict and tension (Clemens and Axelson, 1985; Schnaiberg and Goldenberg, 1989; Umberson, 1992). Mid-life parents, faced with the day-to-day presence of returnee children, are speculated to experience disruption and to think that this situation reflects badly on their child-rearing skills (Aldous, 1996). As a result, stress associated with a parental mindset of 'where did I go wrong?', combined with the extra dependency and responsibility, is assumed to create a host of negative side-effects for family functioning and well-being.

In this section, the outcomes of home-returning for intergenerational relations are examined. Living arrangement satisfaction, and the positive/negative aspects experienced during a return home are explored, using the 1993–4 CNP data.

The Parental Perspective
Similar to recent American research (e.g., Aquilino, 1996), the CNP finds that sharing a home with a 'boomerang kid' does not lead inevitably to a troublesome or conflict-ridden living environment (Mitchell, 1998). In fact, a majority of the parents surveyed reported that their 'boomerang' living arrangement was

working out 'very well'. Fewer than one in 10 (8.8 per cent) reported that it was working out only 'somewhat well' or 'very poorly'.

What do parents like and dislike about this living arrangement? When parents were asked this question, few had difficulty in offering both positive and negative aspects associated with co-residence, although negative aspects tend to be weighed against the positive ones in order to arrive at overall evaluations of the living arrangement. Among mothers, 72.5 per cent stated that they enjoyed their adult child's companionship/friendship, 17.4 per cent reported that they liked having the family together, 4.7 per cent liked their child's emotional/instrumental support, and 5.4 per cent stated 'other' reasons. For fathers, 47.5 per cent enjoyed their children's companionship/friendship, 36.1 per cent liked having the family together, 6.6 per cent stated that they liked the child's help/emotional support, and 9.8 per cent stated 'other' reasons.

From the mother's point of view, the following negative aspects were cited: lack of privacy/independence (24.5 per cent); child was messy/did not help out (11.9 per cent); child's lifestyle (10.6 per cent); child's dependence (9 per cent); conflict (6.6 per cent); and 'other' reasons (8.6 per cent). It should be noted that 19.2 per cent of mothers did not provide a response, partly because they 'liked everything'. Regarding negative appraisals from fathers, the following aspects were reported: lack of privacy and independence (17.7 per cent), the child's personality/attitude (16.1 per cent), the child's lifestyle (8.1 per cent), child's messiness/lack of help (6.5 per cent), conflict (6.5 per cent), child's dependence (1.6 per cent), and 'other' reasons (11.3 per cent). A higher percentage of fathers (32.3 per cent) than mothers provided no answer to this question.

Multivariate analyses were performed to determine the predictors of how well the living arrangement was working out (Mitchell, 1998). The most persistent relationships with parental living arrangement satisfaction relate to positive and negative dimensions of intergenerational sharing and exchanges of support. Help with housework and positive interpersonal interactions, such as fewer hostile arguments and more enjoyable activities spent together are significant predictors of how well the living arrangement is working out. However, the single strongest finding is that parents are more likely to report being satisfied with the living arrangement if the young adult has or is occupying a role that appears to lead to full independence. That is, parents tend to be more satisfied if the young adult initially left home for school than if he/she left to achieve independence or if the child is working full-time during co-residence. In summary, parental satisfaction is greater when children reciprocate exchanges of support, are more autonomous, and are closer to the completion of adult roles. These findings are similar to those in American research on this topic (e.g., Aquilino, 1996).

Verbatim accounts from the CNP further elaborate and illustrate these findings. As one mother stated, 'She's a very nice person. I'm being selfish. I like her and enjoy having her around.' Another father, who claimed that the living arrangement was working out only 'moderately well', stated:

> [What I like about having my daughter at home] is being involved in her life—
> the social activities that we do together and the intellectual discussions. [What I
> don't like about her living at home] is that she had trouble adjusting to our
> rules—we had disagreements. She was already independent, having lived on her
> own for awhile. . . . Yes [I sometimes feel taken advantage of] sometimes she
> didn't do her share of the housework.

A financially well-off homemaker stated that although she enjoyed her unemployed 31-year-old son's company, she often felt frustrated and annoyed with
his presence. She further maintained that her son had become too dependent, was
messy, and felt that his parents 'owed' him a lavish lifestyle. She told the interviewer: 'He's good company—easy to have around. [But] I would like him to be
independent. He smokes and piles up beer cans at home. . . . Life is too comfort-
able for him at home. . . . Yes, he could be taking advantage of the situation.'

The Child Perspective

Research has also begun to examine living arrangement satisfaction from the
perspective of young adults (see Wister et al., 1997). Are young adults happy
living back at the parental homestead? Or do they feel disappointed and frustrated because they were unable to maintain residential independence? Based on
the CNP, we are able to estimate how satisfied young adults are with their
'boomerang' living arrangement. Similar to parental assessments, the majority
(78 per cent) of young adults report being 'very satisfied' or 'somewhat satisfied'
with this living arrangement. Multivariate analyses indicate that several vari-
ables are statistically significant predictors of living arrangement satisfaction.
Specifically, the odds of being satisfied (versus dissatisfied) with co-residence are
lower: when co-residing with higher-income parents (with household incomes
of $80,000); if living with a step-parent compared to a biological parent; and if
co-residing with a parent who attends religious services once per week compared to never/rarely. Multiple returners (those returning three or more times)
are less satisfied than those returning only once, and those reporting higher personal incomes ($20,000+) are more satisfied than those earning less.

What do young adults like and dislike about living at home once they return?
In rank order, the aspects that young adults like about living at home are: the
financial benefits (34 per cent), companionship/friendship (31 per cent), the
'comforts of home' (21 per cent), safety and security (10 per cent), and 'other'
aspects (4 per cent). Again, the positive aspects were weighed against the negative ones to arrive at an overall appraisal of the situation. For example, although
a 23-year-old woman experienced what she called 'big-time guilt' on a daily
basis because she had returned home twice, she was able to report largely positive outcomes:

> This situation is ideal! I get to see my parents daily—I can't ask for anything
> more. No rent, no responsibilities, the location is great; no restrictions, it's heaven.

I have very liberal parents. I'm allowed to have my boyfriend here. My parents are my best friends.

Another 27-year-old man who returned home after completing university because he was unable to find work that would allow him to live on his own stated: 'I can save money and there are lots of amenities—great TV, stereo, large home, nice neighbourhood, use of their car. I also like their dog.'

Similar to parents, young adults predominantly dislike their lack of privacy and independence (60 per cent). They also dislike conflicts and stress (12 per cent), parental rules and regulations (10.5 per cent), and having to subject themselves to the parental dictum: 'As long as you're under my roof you'll do what I say.' Only a minority disliked their dependency (8.5 per cent), while 9 per cent disliked living at home for 'other' reasons. For example, a 26-year-old mother of a nine-month-old returned because she needed the companionship of her parents and could not find a job. However, she disliked living at home for several reasons. She told the interviewer that 'my mom is always telling me what to do and she treats me like a child. There is a lack of privacy and she is always telling me how to raise my child. I also don't feel like an adult because I live at home.' A young male, aged 20, had left home to live with his girlfriend for six months, but the relationship ended. He reported:

I was not given full freedom. I had to comply with house rules. After being on my own it was hard to fit into being told what to do . . . there was a lack of communication with my stepmother at times. . . . My father also didn't know how to respond to me at my age level.

In conclusion, recent research does not support the view that the refilled nest presents serious problems for most families experiencing this living arrangement. Recent studies, based on representative samples, have revealed a picture at odds with this popular perception. Both American studies (e.g., Aquilino, 1991, 1996; Aquilino and Supple, 1991) and results of the CNP (Mitchell, 1998; Mitchell and Gee, 1996b) find generally positive experiences associated with the presence of co-residing and/or returning adult children. Research on 'boomerang kids' and mid-life marital satisfaction also reveals that the majority of marital relationships are seemingly unaffected by the presence of a returning young adult (Mitchell and Gee, 1996b). Returning young adults also appear to be relatively satisfied with co-residence (Wister et al., 1997).

Overall, many parents report that they enjoy day-to-day interaction with their adult children, while adult children appear to view co-residence as a practical and positive solution to the challenges they face at this stage in their lives. The striking pattern of positive appraisals of co-residence is contrary to the image portrayed in the media that these living situations are fraught with intergenerational conflict and tension. Finally, these findings also highlight a central tenet of the life-course perspective—that is, how generations can profoundly affect one another. Notably, the parental life course is inextricably tied to the developmental stages and trajectories of their children.

Social Policy Issues

In recognition of recent and continuing government cutbacks, policy-makers and legislators need to consider fully the consequences of shifting more responsibility for the care of young adults from public to private sources, or back onto the shoulders of families. With ongoing cuts in social spending, educational inflation so that the same degree or diploma is worth less today than it once was, the high cost of living, and high youth unemployment, it is convenient for the state to leave the problems surrounding youth transitions to the older generation. However, not all parents have the resources to facilitate a return home, and not all young adults have the option to return in the first place. For example, young adults residing in rural areas who want to live at home while attending college or university simply cannot do this because of the geographical location of these institutions (Mitchell and Gee, 1996a). Also, young adults with poor or unsupportive family relationships are unlikely to return.

An important implication is that the potential for inequality may be widening under current and future patterns. For example, many of those who return home are able to reap a number of short- and long-term benefits compared to those who do not have this same option. This can occur in a variety of social, economic, and psychological arenas, for example, with regard to education, labour market opportunities, psychological well-being, and possibly increased intergenerational solidarity (Mitchell and Gee, 1996a).

Therefore, we need to consider carefully policies that highlight ties across generations (Pampel, 1998) and that do not assume a linear model of family development over the life course. Specifically, policy makers need to devise policies that reflect the fact that contemporary society has experienced what has been termed 'age inflation' (Vobejda, 1991) for many family-related transitions. For example, under the 1998 BC Family Bonus Program (administered by the Ministry of Finance), the maximum monthly payment is $103 per child (up to five children per family) under the age of 18. However, this policy is based on an outdated premise that once children reach the age of 18 they are no longer financially dependent on parental support. Perhaps the government needs to acknowledge the present diversity of caring or supportive relationships by considering tax provisions or benefits for those housing financially dependent adult children, at least for low-income families.

Additional kinds of legislation and programs require consideration and/or adjustment to meet the needs of mid-life parents and their grown young adults more equitably. Family-friendly work policies, such as flex-time policies (Gee and McDaniel, 1991), would be helpful for those parents, especially women, who are experiencing stress balancing work and family responsibilities. Young adults could also benefit from a variety of policies aimed at reducing poverty and unemployment and at making post-secondary education and housing more affordable. Finally, families could be further strengthened by increasing awareness and access to community-based organizations that offer resources and support (Mitchell and Gee, 1996a).

Conclusion

These findings challenge a common perception that the demographic trend of the refilled nest, as a distinct form of intergenerational co-residence, presents a 'crisis' for middle-generation families. Families are flexible and adaptive and only a minority who opt for this living arrangement exhibit signs of serious generational 'combat'. It is also important to appreciate that from a historical and cross-cultural standpoint, intergenerational doubling-up has often been an effective means to maximize the social-psychological and financial welfare of family members. This research also highlights how interdependent the generations are with regard to the unfolding of their life courses and their developmental trajectories (Aquilino, 1996).

Moreover, an analysis of intergenerational exchanges of support does not support the tendency in gerontological research to characterize routine relations between grown adult children and their parents as dependent and unidirectional (Logan and Spitze, 1996). Although young adults return home primarily because of their own needs for housing and other kinds of support, intergenerational exchange relations tend to be characterized by mutual sharing and reciprocity rather than generational self-interest. Middle-generation parents receive 'payoffs', although not always in the form of tangible goods and services. For example, parents may experience benefits such as companionship or satisfaction derived from facilitating their child's transition to adulthood (Veevers and Mitchell, 1998). These findings also call into question the (contradictory) assumption that aging parents are the demanding, dependent partners in intergenerational relations, as popular and scientific accounts sometimes portray (Logan and Spitze, 1996: 53).

Furthermore, co-operation rather than conflict characterizes most generational relations in the refilled nest. Family members appear to be relatively satisfied with this living arrangement. This does not negate the fact that family members can experience negative side-effects, such as a loss of privacy or independence or the challenges presented by lifestyle or personality differences. However, it is important to remember that returning young adults may be positively selected. Co-residence is more likely to occur when parents and their children already have strong relations (Aquilino, 1996). This selection process can inhibit the formation of 'boomerang' living arrangements among less compatible family members. It is also interesting to note that mothers are generally more satisfied with 'boomerang kid' living arrangements than fathers. Perhaps women have had more experience juggling various family roles in the past and have learned to handle and even derive satisfaction from this balancing act (Spitze et al., 1994).

This does not undermine the fact, however, that some mothers can experience considerable stress with additional family responsibilities.

Finally, these findings underscore the necessity of conducting more studies on intergenerational relationships over longer periods of the life course. We also need to consider a wide array of social policy implications related to home-returning trends. For example, what are the consequences of changes in the nature of intergenerational relations? Will adult child co-residers feel obligated to provide caregiving or a home to a frail parent later on in life? Or will parents expect more assistance in old age from their children because they provided help beyond 'conventional' ages of support provision? And does doubling-up increase intergenerational solidarity to the extent that these families reap a variety of long-term benefits? As the population ages and parent-adult child co-residence becomes an increasingly common household strategy, these and other issues become even more significant.

Acknowledgements

The research presented in this chapter is from work done under a grant funded by the Social Sciences and Humanities Research Council of Canada and also draws on data from the 1995 General Social Survey, Cycle 10. Thanks to Ellen Gee, Andrew Wister, and Doug Talling for their contributions to this research.

References

Aldous, J. 1996. *Family Careers: Rethinking the Developmental Perspective*. Thousand Oaks, Calif.: Sage.

Alwin, D. 1996. 'Coresidence Beliefs in American Society—1973 to 1991', *Journal of Marriage and the Family* 58: 393–403.

Aquilino, W.S. 1991. 'Predicting Parents' Experiences with Coresident Adult Children', *Journal of Family Issues* 12: 323–42.

———. 1996. 'The Returning Adult Child and Parental Experience at Midlife', in C.D. Ryff and M.M. Seltzer, eds, *The Parental Experience in Midlife*. Chicago: University of Chicago Press, 423–58.

——— and K. Supple. 1991. 'Parent-Child Relations and Parents' Satisfaction with Living Arrangements When Adult Children Live at Home', *Journal of Marriage and the Family* 53: 13–27.

Baker, M. 1989. *Families in Canadian Society: An Introduction*. Toronto: McGraw-Hill Ryerson.

Bibby, R.W., and D.C. Posterski. 1992. *Teen Trends: A Nation in Motion*. Toronto: Stoddart.

Boyd, M. 1998. 'Birds of a Feather: Ethnic Variations in Young Adults Living at Home', paper presented at the annual meeting of the Population Association of America, Chicago, Apr.

———— and D. Norris. 1995. 'Leaving the Nest: The Impact of Family Structure',*Canadian Social Trends,* Statistics Canada, Autumn, 14–17.

———— and E.T. Pryor. 1989. 'The Cluttered Nest: The Living Arrangements of Young Canadian Adults', *Canadian Journal of Sociology* 14: 461–77.

Caldwell, J.C. 1976. 'Toward a Restatement of Demographic Transition Theory', *Population and Development Review* 2: 321–66.

Clemens, A.W., and L.J. Axelson. 1985. 'The Not-So-Empty Nest: The Return of the Fledgling Adult', *Family Relations* 34: 259–64.

Crimmins, E.M., R.A. Easterlin, and Y. Saito. 1991. 'Preference Changes among American Youth: Family, Work, and Goods Aspiration, 1976–86', *Population and Development Review* 17: 115–33.

DaVanzo, J., and F.K. Goldscheider. 1990. 'Coming Home Again: Returns to the Parental Home of Young Adults', *Population Studies* 44: 241–55.

Elder, G.H., Jr. 1977. 'Family History and the Life Course', *Journal of Family History* 2: 279–304.

————. 1985. 'Perspectives on the Life Course', in Elder, ed., *Life Course Dynamics.* Ithaca, NY: Cornell University Press, 23–49.

————. 1994. 'Time, Human Agency, and Social Change: Perspectives on the Life Course', *Social Psychology Quarterly* 57: 4–15.

Gee, E.M., and S.A. McDaniel. 1991. 'Social Policy for an Aging Society', in V. Marshall and B. McPherson, eds, *Aging: Canadian Perspectives.* Peterborough, Ont.: Broadview Press, 219–31.

————, B.A. Mitchell, and A.V. Wister. 1995. 'Returning to the Parental "Nest": Exploring a Changing Canadian Life Course', *Canadian Studies in Population* 22: 121–44.

Glenn, N.D. 1987. 'Social Trends in the U.S.', *Public Opinion Quarterly* 51: S109–26.

Goldscheider, F. 1997. 'Recent Changes in U.S. Young Adult Living Arrangements in Comparative Perspective', *Journal of Family Issues* 18: 708–24.

———— and C. Goldscheider. 1993. *Leaving Home Before Marriage: Ethnicity, Familism, and Generational Relationships.* Madison: University of Wisconsin Press.

Gross, J. 1991. 'More Young Men Hang onto Apron Strings', *New York Times,* 16 June, 1, 18.

Hagestad, G.O. 1981. 'Problems and Promises in the Social Psychology of Intergenerational Relations', in R. Fogel, E. Hatfield, S. Kiesler, and E. Shanas, eds, *Aging: Stability and Change in the Family.* New York: Academic Press, 11–46.

———— and B. Neugarten. 1985. 'Age and the Life Course', in E. Shanas and R. Binstock, eds, *Handbook of Aging and the Social Sciences.* New York: Van Nostrand Reinhold, 36–61.

Hareven, T.K. 1996. *Aging and Generational Relations: Life-Course and Cross-Cultural Perspectives.* New York: Aldine de Gruyter.

Hartung, B., and K. Sweeney. 1991. 'Why Adult Children Return Home', *The Social Science Journal* 28: 467–80.

Kobrin, F. 1976. 'The Fall in Household Size and the Rise of the Primary Individual in the United States', *Demography* 13: 127–38.

Logan, J.R., and G. Spitze. 1996. *Family Ties: Enduring Relations Between Parents and Grown Children*. Philadelphia: Temple University Press.

McDaniel, S. 1996. 'The Family Lives of the Middle-Aged and Elderly in Canada', in M. Baker, ed., *Families: Changing Trends in Canada,* 3rd edn. Toronto: McGraw-Hill Ryerson, 195–211.

Mitchell, B.A. 1998. 'Too Close for Comfort? Parental Assessments of "Boomerang Kid" Living Arrangements', *Canadian Journal of Sociology* 32: 21–46.

———— and E.M. Gee. 1996a. 'Young Adults Returning Home: Implications for Social Policy', in B. Galaway and J. Hudson, eds, *Youth in Transition to Adulthood: Research and Policy Implications.* Toronto: Thompson Educational Publishing, 61–71.

———— and ————. 1996b. '"Boomerang Kids" and Mid-Life Parental Marital Satisfaction', *Family Relations* 45: 442–8.

————, A.V. Wister, and E.M. Gee. Forthcoming. 'Culture and Co-residence: An Exploration of English-French Variation in Home Returning', *Canadian Review of Sociology and Anthropology*.

Pampel, F.C. 1998. *Aging, Social Inequality and Public Policy*. Thousand Oaks, Calif.: Pine Forge Press.

Schnaiberg, A., and S. Goldenberg. 1989. 'From Empty Nest to Crowded Nest: The Dynamics of Incompletely-Launched Young Adults', *Social Problems* 36: 251–69.

Spitze, G., J.R. Logan, G. Joseph, and E. Lee. 1994. 'Middle Generation Roles and the Well-Being of Men and Women', *Journal of Gerontology* 49: S107–16.

Statistics Canada.1994. *Families in Canada*. Catalogue No. 96–307E. Scarborough, Ont.: Statistics Canada and Prentice-Hall Canada.

————.1995. *General Social Survey, Cycle 10, Family*. Ottawa: Minister of Supply and Services.

Tennant, P. 1992. 'Cut the Cord Before Sharing the House', *Kitchener-Waterloo Record*, 6 Mar., F1.

Umberson, D. 1992. 'Relationships between Adult Children and Their Parents: Psychological Consequences for Both Generations', *Journal of Marriage and the Family* 50: 1037–47.

Veevers, J.E., and B.A. Mitchell. 1998. 'Intergenerational Exchanges and Perceptions of Support within "Boomerang Kid" Family Environments', *International Journal of Aging and Human Development* 46: 91–108.

Vobejda, B. 1991. 'Declaration of Independence: It's Taking Longer to Become an Adult', *Washington Post Weekly Edition*, 23–9 Sept., 9–10.

Ward, R.A., and G. Spitze. 1992. 'Consequences of Parent-Adult Child Coresidence', *Journal of Family Issues* 13: 553–72.

Weinick, R.M. 1995. 'Sharing a Home: The Experiences of American Women and Their Parents over the Twentieth Century', *Demography* 32: 281–97.

White, L. 1994. 'Coresidence and Leaving Home: Young Adults and Their Parents', *Annual Review of Sociology* 20: 81–102.

Wister, A.V., B.A. Mitchell, and E.M. Gee. 1997. 'Does Money Matter? Parental Income and Living Arrangement Satisfaction among "Boomerang Children" During Coresidence', *Canadian Studies in Population* 24: 124–45.

6 | # Apocalyptic, Opportunistic, and Realistic Demographic Discourse

Retirement Income and Social Policy *or* Chicken Littles, Nest-Eggies, and Humpty Dumpties

Michael J. Prince

'It's very provoking', Humpty Dumpty said after a long silence,—'to be called an egg—*very*!'

Lewis Carroll, *Through the Looking-Glass*

Introduction

Discourse on pensions and population aging can be thought of and analysed as stories and tales. As such, they comprise a mixture of myths, motives, and morals (Featherstone and Hepworth, 1993; Wood and Kroger, 1995). My purpose in this chapter is to outline three images or representations of population aging, seniors, and retirement that are apparent in the mass media, opinion surveys, public talk, and policy documents. The three images are the persistent prophecy of apocalyptic demography (the Chicken Littles), the fairly prominent notion of the golden years of retirement (the Nest-Eggies); and, a far less spoken of image of aging and retirement but one no less a harsh reality for many Canadians, the prospect of falling into poverty (the Humpty Dumpties). By employing these nursery rhyme characters, my intent is not to trivialize issues concerning aging and retirement, but rather to take seriously the images often used and to reflect critically on them and their implications for Canadian social policy. A central theme of this chapter is that neither the dire predictions of population aging nor the rosy pictures of retirement are fully what they are cracked up to be. For many people, it is anemic public policy—not apocalyptic demography—that is causing and will continue to cause problems and dim their retirement prospects. I conclude with some suggestions on action strategies for retirement income policy, especially with respect to the role of public pension programs.

Apocalyptic Demography: The Chicken Littles of Social Policy

Much of the prevailing discourse on aging in Canada, the United States, and Britain, among other countries, entails the apocalyptic demography argument that 'an increasingly dependent older population represents social and fiscal catastrophe' (Robertson, 1997: 426). The scenario relates directly to the baby-boomer generation, in Canada those born between 1946 and 1966, followed by the baby-bust generation of 1967–79. Ellen Gee (1998: A15) notes three components to the general view of the ruinous effects of population aging: that the present and future aged population 'is a major drain on the public purse'; that 'the elderly are getting more than their fair share of public monies'; and that 'this unfair distribution of societal resources is setting the stage for intergenerational conflict.' Eventually, according to this scenario, Generation Xers and younger taxpayers of the future will vigorously resist carrying more and more of the cost of supporting the range of benefits and services for the retired boomers.

The institutional focus of this argument is the welfare state, in particular health-care services and public pension programs. The existing social safety net more generally is viewed to be unsustainable given the shifting ratio between workers-to-seniors in the Canadian population. The view of seniors here is of a passive, burdensome mass of people dependent on, and increasingly demanding of, public services. Population aging is therefore an ominous trend, a public threat to civil politics. The future is regarded with deep concern, if not fear. Demography has joined, if not replaced, economics as the dismal science. The 1998 report by the Office of the Auditor General of Canada, for instance, devotes a chapter to 'Population Aging and Information for Parliament: Understanding the Choices'. In it, the Auditor General warns that our aging population may well have several disturbing consequences: it may put pressure on government spending through higher pension payments and increased demands for health-care services; it may dramatically reduce labour force growth, which in turn would slow economic growth and thus government revenues (Auditor General of Canada, 1998). Underpinning the Auditor General's analysis is the belief that we are heading towards a very unfavourable demographic structure in the next few decades.

At their most extreme, the prophets of demographic doom are like Chicken Little—predicting, on the basis of a real but single factor, like an acorn hitting one's head, that the sky is falling or soon will be, rushing off to warn the King, and along the way whipping others into a state of hysteria.[1] Population aging, because it is perceived as a threat, is used as a political weapon for attacking public social programs, for urging cutbacks in entitlements, and for promoting private-sector methods. It is claimed that the inevitability of population aging in Canada, coupled with economic globalization and deficit reduction, will produce irresistible pressures to constrain the social policy system. This image of population aging, of seniors, and of retirement has been prominent in the media and conservative think-tanks as well as in government reports (Courchene, 1987, 1994).

These apocalyptic messages, amplified by the politics of deficits, have undoubtedly influenced reforms to elderly benefits and public pension programs over the last several years (Prince, 1997). Beginning in 1989, a surtax on Old Age Security (OAS) benefits was phased in over the next three years, representing by 1991 a $300 million annual cutback. In 1994, the Age Credit became income-tested, with 600,000 seniors losing some of this tax reduction and 200,000 more seniors losing the entire tax relief. The 1995 federal budget introduced changes to the tax assistance for Registered Retirement Savings Plans (RRSPs) and Registered Pension Plans (RPPs), reducing contribution limits and freezing them until 2003. In 1996, OAS benefits became income-tested. Benefits are no longer paid to all people aged 65 and over; only benefits net of the surtax are paid. The Canada Pension Plan (CPP) has also been recently revised. Based on a federal-provincial consensus, the revisions involve raising the contribution rates for funding the plan, altering the investment policy to earn higher returns, and trimming some benefits for future pensioners in order to slow the growth of program costs. The reforms agreed to by Ottawa and eight provinces (the British Columbia and Saskatchewan NDP governments dissenting) seek to moderate the impact of costs that would fall on future generations of workers and employers in the form of high contribution rates, while also shielding present seniors from any cuts to their existing benefits. Today's seniors have little to fear from these reforms to the CPP. All retired pensioners or anyone age 65 as of 1997—about 3.6 million people—will not be directly affected. CPP benefits will remain fully indexed to inflation and retirement age will remain the same.

For non-senior groups—near seniors, boomers, and Generation Xers—various benefits under the CPP are being reduced. Retirement pensions will be based on the average of maximum pensionable earnings over the last five working years rather than the last three, having the effect of lowering maximum benefits by $144 a year. The CPP death benefit, a one-time payment to the estate of a deceased CPP contributor, is being reduced from $3,580 to $2,500 and de-indexed as well. The eligibility for and administration of disability benefits are becoming more restrictive. Finally, the yearly basic exemption, which is $3,500 and indexed to wages, is to be frozen at that amount. Currently, contributions are made only on pensionable earnings above the exemption. This move adversely affects low-income and many part-time workers who, over time, will pay disproportionately more of their salaries as contributions to the CPP. While freezing the basic exemption may sound like a minor technical change to the CPP, it is an example of social policy by stealth. No longer indexed to the average industrial wage, the exemption will decline gradually in real terms, even though in nominal terms (current dollars) it would appear to be the same. The result is a steady lowering of the real basic exemption each year, imposing what amounts to a hidden payroll tax increase on low-income earners.

Economic studies and demographic analyses strongly suggest that we can afford to maintain our health and social service systems in an aging society over the next many decades (Canada, 1985; Fellegi, 1988; Denton and Spencer, 1997). Despite this body of evidence, the cries of the Chicken Littles have caught the attention of Canadian governments and journalists. The popularity of this view of population aging may decline over the next number of years as the federal government and many provincial governments are eliminating their budget deficits and generating fiscal surpluses.

Opportunistic Demography: Feathering Your Own Nest Egg

Another widespread perspective on population aging is what may be called entrepreneurial or opportunistic demography. The greying of Canadian society is regarded as a chance to organize investments and manage personal and business decisions for financial advantage. This is not a new idea in financial and marketing circles, but it has been very effectively popularized by demographer-economist David K. Foot with journalist Daniel Stoffman in their hugely successful book, *Boom, Bust, and Echo* (1996). The subtitle captures the main message and appeal of the book—*How to Profit from the Coming Demographic Shift*. This is quite different from the apocalyptic vision that the aging of the population will cost Canadians as citizens and taxpayers, that demography is a menacing threat the public should be greatly concerned about, even if there is little positive action that can be taken. For Foot (and Stoffman), demography is a powerful tool to foretell the future.[2] Understanding and anticipating demographics can help Canadians as individuals make money and feather their own retirement nest eggs. Though we may have to pay more in taxes for an aging populace, we can also profit from the demographic shifts. Within this genre are books on how to take care of your money and build wealth (Chilton, 1989; Costello, 1997); books on how to retire rich and live abroad as 'snowbirds' (Gray, 1997; O'Shaughnessy, 1998); and books on how to prosper from population aging and even the retirement crisis that some claim is coming (Cork and Lightstone, 1996; Turner, 1997).

As Foot and Stoffman (1996: 209–10) explain, there is no inevitable catastrophe associated with population aging:

> Fears are often expressed about how Canada will cope once the large baby-boom generation reaches its retirement years. Before panic sets in, it should be remembered that the Canadian workforce by then will have been reinforced by the large echo generation [the children of the boomers, born between 1980 and 1995]. The combination of the echo and the baby bust [the cohort born from 1967 to 1979] is larger than the baby boomers, so there is little reason to fear a shortage of working-age Canadians during the grey interlude of boomer retirement.

This is a reassuring message for many people, in particular those I call the 'Nest-Eggies'. The stereotypical image of a Nest-Eggie is someone employed with a 'good job'—that is, a job that pays well (better than average earnings), is relatively secure with opportunities for upward mobility, and has an occupational pension plan along with a host of other work-related benefits. Nest-Eggies are predominately male and able-bodied. The apocalyptic view focuses on the overall labour market and worries there will be too few workers in the future. In contrast, the opportunistic perspective concentrates on the well-to-do part of the labour market and wonders how to build a mix of investments in a portfolio that will meet a person's long-term goals and feelings about risk and is balanced for optimum performance. Demographic shifts may be a threat to public pension programs, but there is a belief that golden opportunities exist for financial institutions, investment counsellors, and tax advisers with respect to private retirement planning. Consider the following statement on retirement planning made recently in the *Globe and Mail* ('Report on Your Money', 1998): 'If you daydream occasionally about retirement, you're not alone. For some, it's world travel and cultivating favourite pastimes; for others, it's winters in the sun and summers by the lake. For still others it's some combination of them all. Whatever your dreams, you'll need financial security to achieve them.'

Here, the prospect of retirement is something to contemplate happily in daydreams and also to plan for with the expert advice of financial organizations. The main institutional focus of opportunistic demography is on the economy, especially the stock market. The future is viewed with optimism in light of the effect of compound interest on investments over time and the expectations by many baby boomers of inheritances. The successful Nest-Eggie is portrayed as a homeowner who, as well, has a cottage or cabin. Upon becoming a senior, the Nest-Eggie can continue to enjoy these properties plus travel around the globe and to warmer climates during Canadian winters. These seniors are active and adventuresome, far from the burdensome and passive images of aging in the apocalyptic scenario.

Optimism towards private retirement savings is mixed with a growing pessimism regarding public pension provisions. The cuts announced for the CPP and the targeting of the OAS and old age tax credit shift more of the responsibility for retirement planning onto individuals, families, and workplaces. Commenting on the recent round of cutbacks to government retirement programs, the chief economist of the Royal Bank of Canada stated: 'The message is clear: Higher-income, older Canadians cannot expect any government support in future, either directly or in the form of tax concessions. . . . Ultimately, the most effective way to deal with the retirement uncertainty that lies ahead is to increase your personal savings' (McCallum, 1997: C16).

In pension policy discourse, a nest egg, of course, is money accumulated from savings, investments, inheritances, and other sources, held in reserve after retirement from the paid labour force. Ideally, the nest egg provides the bulk of the funds necessary for retirement living. In fact, the term 'nest egg' originally referred to a real or artificial egg left in a nest to induce a hen to continue laying eggs there. It is useful to adopt this meaning to pension debates, too, and to think of various tax policy measures as devices to induce Canadians to engage in saving for retirement. The federal Income Tax Act is such a nest egg providing incentives in the form of deductions and credits that support, among other retirement income measures, the creation and continuance of work-based pension plans and personal retirement savings plans. Thus, contributions to RPPs, usually made by both employees and employers (up to a specified maximum), are tax deductible, as are contributions individuals make to RRSPs. The investment income earned from both RPPs and RRSPs is also tax exempt. In addition, contributions employers may make on behalf of their employees to a Deferred Profit Sharing Plan are tax deductible. In 1995, the seven-year limit on carrying forward unused RRSP contributions was eliminated to allow people to take advantage of this tax assistance at whatever stage of their work/life course. Payments out of all these plans are taxable, but that normally occurs when the person is partly or totally retired and thus at a lower income tax bracket. In the short to medium term, these measures are tax expenditures, that is, forgone revenue for the federal and provincial governments (Finance Canada, 1998).[3]

Through the 1990s, both the number of Canadians contributing to an RRSP and the overall amount contributed each year to RRSPs have been rising steadily. From approximately $15 billion in 1991, annual contributions reached a record $26.4 billion in 1996 (the latest year figures are available), a 68 per cent increase, though employment income increased by only 7 per cent over the same period; and the number of contributors increased by 28 per cent, from 4.7 million to 6 million Canadians across all provinces and territories. In 1996, the average contributor was 42 years old and the average contribution was $4,398. Statistics Canada (1998: 1) attributes this growth in RRSP contributions and contributors to several factors:

> changes in the Income Tax Act in 1990, which increased RRSP contribution opportunities for most taxfilers, as well as improvements in the economy, notably employment growth since 1993. Growing concerns about the future of the Canada and Quebec Pension Plan and the Old Age/Guaranteed Income Supplement programs also encouraged greater RRSP participation. In addition, . . . growth in group RRSPs [sponsored by employers] likely played a role.

Part of the opportunistic view of population aging is a general optimism that personal retirement savings plans and occupational pensions will steadily and naturally increase in value and coverage. As of 1996, 5.1 million Canadians were members of nearly15,500 registered pension plans at their places of work (Statistics Canada, 1997). A March 1998 survey of 711 Canadian baby boomers found that almost one-half think that savings and investments will be their primary source of income when they retire, while another one-quarter believe that a work-based pension will be their main source of retirement income. Only about 12 per cent think that the CPP will be their main income source as seniors. Among boomers who have commenced saving for retirement, most report they started before they turned 30. In the words of an executive at Angus Reid Group, the polling firm that conducted the survey, 'Canadians are busy as beavers preparing for retirement' (cited in Barnes, 1998).

Visions of a bright retirement for boomers are also fuelled by talk of a huge transfer of wealth from older generations. This vision was perhaps generated by a 1990 *Maclean's* cover story that wrote of a trillion-dollar windfall of wealth— cash, property, businesses, and other assets—baby boomers will inherit over the next 20 years from older generations of Canadians. The article noted that, 'for many members of the baby boom generation using most of their disposable income to pay down their mortgages, inheritances represent their only chance to build the nest egg that they failed to accumulate on their own' (Fennell et al., 1990: 52). Since then, the trillion-dollar figure has been accepted and repeated by journalists, financial advisers, and others. A 1997 Gallup Canada survey of 1,004 adults expecting to inherit some income or wealth found that, among boomers, priorities for using any inheritance are: first, investing in the markets; second, paying for their children's post-secondary education; third, paying debts; followed closely by allocating the monies directly to retirement savings plans. In the next few decades, the survey estimates this trillion-dollar transfer of wealth will entail 8–10 million bequests (Ross, 1997).

Other sources have spoken of even larger inheritance amounts. The Canada Mortgage and Housing Corporation, the federal government's housing agency, estimates that baby boomers will inherit $12.7 billion a year between 1996 and 2006, totalling $1.27 trillion, and that $12.7 billion each year will boost the housing sector in terms of purchases and renovations (McIntosh, 1998). The Community Foundations of Canada was told by one of its members that $3 trillion or more in wealth is shifting to the baby boomers, presenting 'an avalanche of opportunity' for charities and philanthropic foundations (Picard, 1998). This expected intergenerational transfer of wealth is thus seen as offering tremendous benefits for boomers and their children, the post-secondary education system, charities, the housing industry, financial planners, and investment counsellors— not forgetting Revenue Canada.

The profile of opportunistic demography will, I believe, continue to rise over the coming years as government budgets and public accounts improve, as further tax relief is provided to Canadians, and as boomers begin to inherit money, homes, and other assets from their parents and others. The politics of Nest-Eggies involves a strong defence of RRSPs against any further restrictions by the federal government. It is noteworthy that in 1995, RRSPs surpassed RPPs as the main source of retirement savings for Canadians. Pressure continues to be directed at the Minister of Finance by investment industry groups to raise the foreign content limit on RRSPs and RPPs from the present ceiling of 20 per cent to 25 or 30 per cent of non-Canadian equities. There also would likely be sharp reaction against any move to introduce a wealth tax on this anticipated intergenerational transfer of resources. Well before the boomers retire in large numbers with the predicted grey power that will follow, the *current* preferences and practices of boomers, and the financial business interests associated with them, are a significant form of pension politics.

Realistic Demography: Many Will Fall Like Humpty Dumpty

Each of the previous demographic stories conveys important ideas yet also contains exaggerations and gaps. Apocalyptic demography overemphasizes population aging as an explanatory and predictive variable. Generational cohorts are generalized as homogeneous cultural and political social groupings, and seniors are assumed to be non-productive and costly members of the community. If apocalyptic demography is too pessimistic and general in its analysis, opportunistic demography is too optimistic and partial in its analysis. The benefits of population aging are oversold while the challenges are underplayed or ignored. For many Canadian men and women, there is a mismatch between the rosy images of retirement portrayed in the advertisements by financial institutions and their everyday lives and attainable futures.

A third story of population aging and retirement prospects is needed, one mindful that there are problems and possibilities, and winners and losers, from every demographic shift. I call this third approach realistic and pragmatic. It focuses on what is attainable and workable, and on the affairs of state as well as the stock market. Realistic demography addresses the varieties of people's lives and places them in the larger context of social positions and political and economic institutions, to understand differences in the ability to earn a living wage, to save, to invest, to accumulate assets and shelter them from taxes, and to inherit wealth. It is absurd, of course, to think or suggest that all Canadians or even the majority have the same opportunities to do these things or to be able to daydream blissfully about their retirement. Some people will or do have a well-built nest egg for retirement, but for many it is or will be a tumble-down nest.

There is a substantial and possibly expanding segment of the population I call 'Humpty Dumpties', after the character in the Mother Goose nursery rhyme. You will remember that Humpty Dumpty sat on a wall, but eventually had a great fall and could not be put together again. In *Through the Looking-Glass,* Lewis Carroll has Alice meet Humpty Dumpty on her journey and engage in conversation with him. Both Alice and Humpty Dumpty know the rhyme, but Humpty is convinced that there is no chance of his falling, and if he did fall, the King has promised Humpty that he would be picked up and put together again in a minute.

Many Canadians do not share Humpty's belief that no risk of falling exists, or that the King (the state) will be there to catch them or to help even if it ever did happen. Over the last decade or more, polls reveal a contemporary uneasiness about the future of public pension programs and the retirement outlook for a sizable number of citizens. A 1995 *Maclean's*/CBC News poll reported that a large majority of Canadians are expecting serious problems soon for the CPP. Of those surveyed, 27 per cent indicated that they thought the CPP will be bankrupt by the year 2000; 54 per cent felt that the plan would have somewhat worse or significantly worse funding; only 11 per cent believed it will have the same funding; and just 6 per cent thought it will have better funding and benefits. A number of factors lie behind this pension apprehension, which I have discussed elsewhere (Prince, 1996).

Attention to and knowledge of pension matters, as well as confidence in the existing retirement income system, increase with age. A 1996 national survey of 1,200 Canadians concerning pension and retirement issues done for the federal

Department of Finance found that current seniors have the highest levels of faith in the system and the greatest awareness of issues. By contrast, Generation Xers were found to be not as focused on, or aware of, pension programs or related policy issues. Younger Canadians were also fatalistic about having to do more for themselves in preparing for retirement through such devices as RRSPs, and about eventually receiving little if anything from public pension plans (Earnscliffe Research & Communications, 1996). A 1998 survey found that 40 per cent of Canadian boomers are not confident their current financial plan will allow them to enjoy their retirement. Another 1998 survey of a range of Canadian adults found that 59 per cent expect their net worth at retirement to be less than $250,000—a nest egg that will optimistically generate only about $12,500 annually. This net worth figure, however, does not include income from the CPP, an RPP, or any expected inheritance (Barnes, 1998).

Who is most likely to experience a great fall in income in retirement? Lynn McDonald's (1997) research on retired widows highlights gender, family and marital status, race, health, education, and work history. In brief, those at greatest risk of being poor are women, especially women who are unattached and living alone, women of colour, those in poor health, people with lower levels of educational attainment, and those who were in insecure and low-paying jobs and without an occupational pension plan. Among current retired widows, virtually one-half live in what Statistics Canada describes as financially straitened circumstances or what social policy groups call poverty.

The kind and length of participation in the paid labour force deeply shapes retirement prospects. More women than ever are in the labour force (in 1994, 58 per cent overall, and 77 per cent of women aged 25–44), but this does not necessarily mean that far fewer women will have low incomes as seniors. As McDonald (1997: 577) observes: 'Women's work patterns still do not approximate the "standard" male career trajectory upon which the pension system is built. Most Canadian women continue to work in low paying jobs, in nonstandard work in the service sector, which translates into smaller investments and lower contributions to public and private pensions, if they are lucky enough to be covered by a private pension plan.' In addition, women in the paid workforce still face major differences in earnings and income compared to men and still shoulder a disproportionate amount of the unpaid family responsibilities and household work. As a consequence, many women do not have a continuous lifetime of paid work. In dual-earner families, the fact that both partners are in the paid labour market has effectively kept many households out of poverty or maintained their real incomes during the 1980s and 1990s, rather than provided a tidy amount of money for a nest egg. In divorces and separations, it is women who usually suffer most in terms of financial security and economic well-being.

Workplace pensions and registered savings plans both have serious limitations in offering general coverage and security for retirement. The number of working Canadians with occupational pension plans (RPPs) has been declining through the 1990s because of the severe recession earlier in the decade and because of corporate and public-sector downsizing measures. As of 1995, just 34.3 per cent of the labour force was covered by an RPP (35.1 per cent of men and 33.5 per cent of women). Even if we exclude the self-employed, unpaid family workers, and the unemployed, the percentage of paid workers with an occupational pension plan still only rises to 42.4 per cent (Statistics Canada, 1997). Expressed another way, six or seven out of every 10 people in the labour force do not have a workplace pension plan that will provide retirement income.

The picture for RRSPs is no brighter. In 1995, only 35 per cent of eligible taxfilers in Canada made a contribution to an RRSP. While the number of contributors and contribution amounts have been increasing, so, too, have the number and size of pre-retirement withdrawals from RRSPs. Of the $179 billion that Canadians could have theoretically contributed to RRSPs in 1996, only 12 per cent of that amount was used. The size of contribution corresponds with income levels and age. People in older age groups and at higher income levels participate more and thus reap more of the tax benefits associated with RRSPs. Both RPPs and RRSPs, then, are limited policy instruments, particularly for low- and modest-income Canadians. Furthermore, the tax expenditures linked with RRSPs and RPPs disproportionately benefit high-income Canadians. The National Council of Welfare (1996: 44) has concluded sombrely:

> RRSPs do encourage savings for retirement, but primarily by those who have large amounts of discretionary income from year to year. They reward the rich the most, they offer modest encouragement to people with average incomes and they provide very little help to the poor. Given the financial realities facing people in different income groups, there is unlikely to be any change in this pattern in years to come.

What of the supposed $1–3 trillion transfer of wealth to the boomers from their parents? It would be prudent for the boomers not to count their chickens until they've hatched. Most talk of the trillion-dollar transfer of wealth fails to mention that these surveys are based on asking people what they *expect* to inherit from others and what they *plan* to do with the money. The fact that people are living longer in retirement, perhaps 30 or more years (Baxter and Ramlo, 1998), is overlooked, as is the matter of capital gains taxes. If today's seniors have amassed huge amounts of wealth, at least some of it would be apparent in their sources and levels of incomes. Yet, the largest share of income for senior husband-wife families is from public pensions (33.4 per cent in 1995), followed by private pensions (21.6 per cent), employment income (19.5 per cent), and then investments (15.6 per cent) and other sources (9.9 per cent). In addition, the proportion of seniors aged 65 and over who have relatively low incomes was 20.8 per cent in 1996, fractionally less than the child poverty rate so prominent in contemporary policy debates but almost three percentage points higher than the national average rate of low income. A growing number of seniors who are 'house-rich but cash-poor' are borrowing money against the value of their homes through reverse mortgages. Payments on these loans are typically not due until the house is sold. Any inheritances would come after such loans and capital gains taxes were paid. According to a 1997 survey done for the Investors Group, about 45 per cent of Canadians expect to inherit very little—less than $25,000—if anything in the future, and only 20 per cent expect to inherit over $100,000. This is a far cry from the image of a huge windfall cascading from the present generation of seniors to boomers and their children (Ross, 1997; Townson, 1996).

Concluding Observations and Possible Action Strategies

In this age of post-modernism, there are a multiplicity of Humpty Dumpties in Canadian society. They are sitting on walls of different materials, designs, and heights; some will fall sooner than others, some faster and farther than others. Can some of those who fall be put together again? Is the faith Humpty has in the King warranted? What action strategies can be taken in social policy to prevent more people from falling into poverty? Several conclusions can be drawn from the discussion in this chapter.

First, politics and public policies, along with private privileges, determine in large part the material conditions of the elderly population and our mental constructs of demography. Robertson (1997: 442) reminds us that 'We need not believe ourselves to be at the mercy of blind forces, such as demography and economic imperatives, as if they existed outside the realm of public discussion and debate.' Choices are available; programs can be crafted; changes can take place. Accounts of the death of the welfare state due to population aging are greatly exaggerated (Esping-Andersen, 1996). Impacts of demographic shifts depend on, and interact with, a range of factors and circumstances. Foremost among these would be a reaffirmation to a policy of high and stable levels of employment, informed by a strategy of sustainable growth in economic and social capital. We still have time, a decade or more, to plan for what Foot and Stoffman aptly call the 'grey interlude' of boomer retirements and to adjust health and social services, such as home care and pension and taxation policies.

Second, the reduction of poverty among seniors over the past 30 years has been a major achievement of social policy at both the federal and provincial levels. It is a dangerous myth, however, to think that the face of poverty in Canada today is wrinkle-free. Considerable work still needs to be done in tackling poverty among current seniors. Due to government retrenchment and the growing insecurities and inequalities of earnings and opportunities in the paid labour force, gerontologists like McDaniel (1997: 479) caution that 'the much vaunted success of pension policy in alleviating poverty among the elderly may be overstated and inapplicable to future cohorts.' In other terms, more of Canada's future seniors, not fewer of them, may well need the support of public pension programs.

Third, the problems of widespread insecurity and poverty in old age in Canada will not be solved by calls for increasing personal work effort, promoting private thrift, and hoping for family inheritances. The risks of becoming Humpty Dumpties, of falling down in retirement, are rooted in the contradictions of our labour market, inherent limitations in private retirement plans, and the contractions of our public programs. Offloading more of the responsibility for care, pensions, and retirement income onto individuals and the private sector is not a solution. As presently configured, neither the private nor the public level of the retirement income system, nor both in combination, is adequate for meeting the needs of most current and future elderly Canadians.

Fourth, as the fiscal position of the federal government and provinces continues to improve, public pressure will build again to enhance public benefits, including old age benefits and the Canada and Quebec Pension Plans (Prince, 1997, 1998). A second round of intergovernmental discussions needs to take place in the next few years with a view, in light of the low earnings of many working women, to maintaining if not improving survivor benefits. CPP benefits should not be cut any further. Indeed, as the investment policy of the plan establishes a track record of sound financial management and returns, consideration should be given once again to raising CPP retirement benefits to a higher replacement rate, to offering flexible retirement options for older workers, and to unfreezing the yearly basic exemption. With respect to Old Age Security benefits, a fundamental issue is the apparent lack of concern by the Chrétien government about low-income seniors. The last general increase in benefits for low-income seniors was made in 1984 by the Liberal government of Pierre Trudeau. The subsequent 15 years represent the longest period in which old age benefits have not been augmented since the federal government entered the pension policy field in the 1920s. The challenge, then, is not apocalyptic demography but rather anemic public policy and absent political leadership.

Notes

1. For example, Frank McGilly (1998: 5, 266) writes that the long-term implications of the aging of Canada's population is 'drastic, not to say frightening', and emphasizes the 'warnings about the problems Canada will face in the twenty-first century arising from the age composition of the population'.
2. The optimistic work of Foot and Stoffman does share with the apocalyptic approach a form of demographic determinism, overemphasizing population structures and trends at the expense of social values and economic, political, and cultural factors. See Adams (1998).
3. Besides the RRSP and RPP tax expenditures, other retirement income tax expenditures include the non-taxation of Guaranteed Income Supplement benefits, Spousal Allowance benefits, and employer-paid premiums for the Canada and Quebec Pension Plans; the Age Credit; the Pension Income Credit; and the Saskatchewan pension credit. For more details and estimates and projections of the value of these measures, see Finance Canada (1998).

References

Adams, Michael. 1998. *Sex in the Snow: Canadian Social Values at the End of the Millennium.* Toronto: Penguin.

Auditor General of Canada. 1998. *Report.* Ottawa: Supply and Services Canada. Available at: www.oag-bvg.gc.ca/domino/reports

Barnes, Angela. 1998. 'Polls Apart: Surveys Diverge on Retirement Outlook', *Globe and Mail,* 23 Apr.: B6.

Baxter, David, and Andrew Ramlo. 1998. *What Can You Expect? Life Expectancy in Canada, 1921 to 2021.* Vancouver: Urban Futures Institute.

Canada. 1985. Royal Commission on the Economic Union and Development Prospects for Canada, *Report*, vol. 2. Ottawa: Supply and Services Canada.

Chilton, David. 1989. *The Wealthy Barber.* Toronto: Stoddart.

Cork, David and Susan Lightstone. 1996. *The Pig and the Python: How to Prosper from the Aging Baby Boom.* Toronto: Stoddardt.

Costello, Brian. 1997. *Taking Care of Your Money.* Toronto: ECW Press.

Courchene, Thomas J. 1987. *Social Policy in the 1990s: Agenda for Reform.* Toronto: C.D. Howe Institute.

———. 1994. *Social Canada in the Millennium: Reform Imperatives and Restructuring Principles.* Toronto: C.D. Howe Institute.

Denton, Frank T., and Byron G. Spencer. 1997. 'Population Aging and the Maintenance of Social Support Systems', *Canadian Journal on Aging* 16, 3: 485–98.

Earnscliffe Research & Communications. 1996. *A Report to the Department of Finance of Quantitative Research on Pension Issues.* Dec.

Esping-Andersen, Gosta. 1996. *Welfare States in Transition.* London: Sage.

Featherstone, Mike, and Mike Hepworth. 1993, 'Images of Ageing', in John Bond, Peter Coleman, and Sheila Peace, eds, *Ageing in Society: An Introduction to Social Gerontology*, 2nd edn. London: Sage.

Fellegi, Ivan P. 1988. 'Can We Afford an Aging Society?', *Canadian Economic Observer* (Oct.): 4.1–4.43.

Fennell, Tom, with Ann Walmsley and Glen Allen. 1990. 'A Trillion-Dollar Windfall', *Maclean's*, 5 Nov.: 52.

Finance Canada. 1998. *Government of Canada: Tax Expenditures.* Ottawa: Public Works and Government Services Canada.

Foot, David K., with Daniel Stoffman. 1996. *Boom, Bust, and Echo: How to Profit from the Coming Demographic Shift.* Toronto: Macfarlane Walter and Ross.

Gee, Ellen. 1998. 'The Myth of Apocalyptic Demography', *Vancouver Sun,* 5 May: A15.

Gray, Douglas A. 1997. *The Canadian Snowbird Guide: Everything You Need to Know About Living Part-time in the USA and Mexico*, 2nd edn. Toronto: McGraw-Hill Ryerson.

McCallum, John. 1997. 'Will You Be Prepared to Retire in the Next Century?', *Globe and Mail,* 28 Jan.: C16.

McDaniel, Susan A. 1997. 'Serial Employment and Skinny Government: Reforming Caring and Sharing Among Generations', *Canadian Journal on Aging* 16, 3: 465–84.

McDonald, Lynn. 1997. 'The Invisible Poor: Canada's Retired Widows', *Canadian Journal on Aging* 16, 3: 553–83.

McGilly, Frank. 1998. *An Introduction to Canada's Public Social Services: Understanding Income and Health Programs*, 2nd edn. Toronto: Oxford University Press.

McIntosh, Gord. 1998. 'Housing Industry to Get Lift From Inheritances, Agency Says', *Toronto Star*, 23 Aug.: D2.

National Council of Welfare. 1996. *A Pension Primer*. Ottawa: Supply and Services Canada.

O'Shaughnessy, James. 1998. *How to Retire Rich*. New York: Broadway Books.

Picard, André. 1998. 'Charities Told to Change to Cash in on New Wealth', *Globe and Mail*, 25 May: A3.

Prince, Michael J. 1996. 'Public Apprehension Over the CPP: How Real Is It?', *Perception* 20, 1: 3–4.

————. 1997. 'Lowering the Boom on the Boomers: Replacing Old Age Security with the New Seniors Benefit and Reforming the Canada Pension Plan', in Gene Swimmer, ed., *How Ottawa Spends 1997–98: Seeing Red: A Liberal Report Card*. Ottawa: Carleton University Press.

————. 1998. 'New Money, New Mandate, New Politics: Federal Budgeting in the Post-Deficit Era', in Leslie A. Pal, ed., *How Ottawa Spends 1998–99: Balancing Act: The Post-Deficit Mandate*. Toronto: Oxford University Press.

'Report on Your Money Featuring Retirement Planning'. 1998. *Globe and Mail*, 9 May.

Robertson, Ann. 1997. 'Beyond Apocalyptic Demography: Towards a Moral Economy of Interdependence', *Ageing and Society* 17, 4: 425–46.

Ross, Ijeoma. 1997. 'Quarter of Boomers Want to Invest Bequests', *Globe and Mail*, 10 July, B4.

Statistics Canada. 1997. *Pension Plans in Canada, January 1, 1996*. Ottawa: Supply and Services Canada, Statistics Canada Catalogue No. 74–401–XPB.

————. 1998. 'RRSP Contributions and Withdrawals: An Update' and 'Tapping Unused RRSP Room', *The Daily,* 18 Feb.

Townson, Monica. 1996. 'Preparing for the Wave: The Baby Boom Generation Retires', presentation to the annual meeting of the Canadian Association of Pre-retirement Planners, Vancouver, Oct.

Turner, Garth. 1997. *2015: After the Boom. How to Prosper through the Coming Retirement Crisis*. Toronto: Key Porter Books.

Wood, Linda A., and Rolf O. Kroger. 1995. 'Discourse Analysis in Research on Aging', *Canadian Journal on Aging* 14 (Supp. 1): 82–99.

7 | # Alarmist Economics and Women's Pensions

A Case of 'Semanticide'

Lynn McDonald

Introduction

Although the Senior's Benefit—the benefit to replace Old Age Security, the Guaranteed Income Supplement, and tax benefits for seniors—was dropped by the Canadian government, the machinations surrounding its development and attempted implementation are instructive.[1] As a case study, the Senior's Benefit is illustrative of the worldwide retrenchment in state responsibility for social security and how this is implemented through indirect means designed to disguise the dismantling of the welfare state (Midgley, 1997; Ruggles and O'Higgens, 1987; Teeple, 1995; Workman, 1996). That the proposed Senior's Benefit was abandoned was not a victory for the proponents of the Canadian welfare state. Rather, it was abandoned because the financial community effectively argued that its 20 per cent clawback would militate against saving for old age, which in turn would have deleterious consequences for the economy (Slater, 1998). As noted by the president of the Canadian Chamber of Commerce, 'The Senior's Benefit breaks values that this nation has always held dear. It spells out disincentives to work and save.' (Janigan, 1997: 44).

The convergence of a number of factors—weak economies, the aging populations of Western industrial societies, and the rise of the political right, supported by religious fundamentalists—has been identified by many authors as the impetus behind the assault on the welfare state (Midgley, 1997).[2] It is no surprise, then, that the Senior's Benefit represents one of many assaults on Canada's social security system, and that the use of the *power* of the debt was the catalyst for the attack (Medoff and Harless, 1996). The surprise is the silence that accompanied the proposal. A significant shift in government policy such as the proposed Senior's Benefit is usually met with opposition from those adversely affected—and—the more extensive the change, the stronger the resistance. In the case of the Senior's Benefit, there was little opposition by older Canadians or by Canadian gerontologists—a strange development in light of the immense resistance generated by the previous government's proposal to overhaul Old Age Security in 1985.

The purpose of this chapter is to argue that the proposed Senior's Benefit sacrificed Canadian women, the most economically vulnerable seniors in Canada, in the name of deficit reduction. The method used was 'semanticide', the practice of redefining terms to make politically questionable activities appear acceptable (Margolin, 1997). The discourse about the alleged fiscal crisis facing the Canadian government was used to camouflage a policy that ultimately coddled corporations but had negative consequences for Canadian women. The proposed policy was gender blind; it did nothing to reduce the poverty of Canada's older women; it did not reflect the topography of women's lives (or men's, for that matter); and it was sexist through its lack of recognition of the contributions that women have made to Canadian society. Nevertheless, Canadians were silenced about this public policy by acts of semanticide perpetrated by the government, the media, and the financial sector. It is important to understand this process since it is likely to continue as the markets become more and more skittish and renewed attempts are made to shift the costs of pensions from government to the individual.

Silencing Canadians

The most effective forms of semanticide used by government, corporations, and the media included reframing the debt and the deficit into a daunting crisis, attributing the blame for the crisis to social spending by government, and cultivating the vision of the overtaxed Canadian who was on the verge of a tax revolt.

Canada's debt and deficit were redefined as a monstrous fiscal crisis (Cohen, 1997; McQuaig, 1995; Workman, 1996). This new fiscal crisis was a matter of grave importance, due serious respect. As Workman (1996) notes, the only appropriate way to discuss the debt was to talk in hushed and somber tones. Indeed, the dangers posed by the deficit to Canada's very sovereignty were to be kept in mind when setting public policy (McQuaig, 1995; Workman, 1996). All Canadians were to pull their weight in attacking the national crises, including seniors. The Finance Minister stated that seniors had 'to put their shoulder to the wheel' like all other Canadians, and the Senior's Benefit was to be the instrument of sacrifice (*Prime Time News*, 1994, cited in Workman, 1996). But the deficit and debt did not constitute a crisis. In fact, the debt hysteria was so out of control that Moody's Investment Services felt it had to issue a special commentary in June 1993 that described Canada's debt as 'grossly exaggerated' (McQuaig, 1995: 44).

The causes of the debt and deficit—high interest rates and lost tax revenues—were mystically transformed into unrestrained social spending by the federal government. In fact, this sleight of hand has been dubbed a 'Coyneism', after Andrew Coyne: the 'gross distortion of statistics put forward to support a regressive view' (Campbell, 1995: 15).[3] The dangerous magnitude of the debt became a 'given' in social policy discussions, taking precedence over all other concerns. The evidence pointed to the debt as a direct result of a shortage of tax revenues and high interest rates. Social program spending had not increased relative to GDP over the last 16 years, as demonstrated by Mimoto and Cross (1991). Nevertheless, while promising not to abandon seniors, the Finance Minister said that 'Ottawa has to face the impact that an aging population is having on the future of the Canada Pension Plan and the financing of the old-age pension' (Freeman, 1995: A4). In short, the $21.7 billion government spent on old age benefits had to be contained.

That Canadians were overtaxed, with a tax revolt looming on the horizon, was the rhetoric used to quell any talk of raising taxes as an alternative to social spending, even though Canada's tax rate of 37 per cent is below the average of 39 per cent for 24 OECD countries. An insidious version of this argument was an attempt to whip Canadians into a frenzy over intergenerational transfers embedded in pay-as-you-go pension plans and the spectre of an ensuing generational conflict (Courchene, 1997; Gunderson, 1998; Gunderson et al., 1996; Pesando, 1997; Robson, 1996). *Maclean's* popularized this idea with the comments of a typical 33-year-old Canadian, Michael Crichton, who stated, 'My mother thinks that the country should take care of her. . . . I am torn: I know we have to take care of them. But I am paying so much tax that I resent my country. The government just uses our generation' (Janigan, 1997: 42).

All of these instances of semanticide have been revealed for what they are by a number of respectable research groups such as Statistics Canada, the Canadian Council on Social Development, the Canadian Centre for Policy Alternatives, feminist scholars such as Isabel Bakker and Marjorie Griffin Cohen, economists such as Lars Osberg, Pierre Fortin, Frank Denton, and Byron Spencer, policy analysts such as Thom Workman, and the lone journalistic voice of Linda McQuaig (Bakker, 1996; Canadian Centre for Policy Alternatives, 1998; Canadian Council on Social Development, 1994; Cohen, 1996; Denton and Spencer, 1997; McQuaig, 1995; Mimoto and Cross, 1991; Osberg and Fortin, 1996; Workman, 1996).

A number of these authors offered reasons for the fatalistic acceptance of these myths by the Canadian public. Workman (1996) argued that the widely believed debt story was rooted in the everyday life of most Canadians and therefore appeared to be reasonable to most Canadians. Any Canadian could relate to 'being broke'. Cohen (1996: 35) suggested that a campaign was launched by the Tory government and business to convince Canadians that the government was hopelessly in debt in order to deflect their attention from the economic downturn resulting from free trade. Once the political left capitulated to the political right (e.g., the Liberals adopted the Conservative platform of the 1980s), most Canadians began to believe the deficit and debt were *the* issues. McQuaig argued that the anti-deficit campaign was presented as a 'modern-day morality play, a crusade for the future of the country' (McQuaig, 1995: 11). The sheer numbers and prominence of the persons discussing the debt overwhelmed Canadians into acceptance. McDonald (1997a) argued that, in academia, researchers both left and right of centre were so overtaken by economists and the astounding number of economic analyses generated on the cost-savings of different pension schemes, they were rarely heard (cf., Battle, 1996; Brown, 1995; Courchene, 1994; Lam et al., 1996).

While these authors knew that the fiscal crisis was a cover for the agenda of capital markets, which fervently believed that in a global economy there was only one valid position— namely, a roll back of the Keynesian welfare state and the unfettered movement of capital—their views were generally ignored. If anyone had the temerity to state this agenda, they were dismissed as unqualified, cavalier, unrealistic, unreasonable, emotional, and, for good measure, a member of a special interest group (Workman, 1996: 67). One of the first signs that alternative views would not be tolerated was the public flogging of Statistics Canada statisticians Mimoto and Cross, who published a refereed article in the *Canadian Economic Observer* that demonstrated that government spending was not the cause of the public debt (Mimoto and Cross, 1991). The Finance Department took swift action, forcing the editor to issue a disclaimer that the analysis was flawed. The editor duly noted that Mimoto and Cross's conclusion—'it was not explosive growth in program spending that caused the increase in the deficits after 1975, but a drop in federal revenues relative to the growth of GDP and rising debt charges'—'was not argued in the body of the article and should have not appeared in the conclusion' (Cross, 1991:3.17).

The upshot of semanticide was that many of us came to believe the arguments of 'false necessity'—arguments that market realities constrained our range of political and social choices (Block, 1990)—and the disbelievers, not surprisingly, were hesitant to speak out. Failing to question national monetary and social policy for fear that 'the money markets will be made nervous', is what we had come to accept—a type of apocalyptic economics that takes its place beside apocalyptic demography (McDonald, 1997b: 393). I am not suggesting an attack on fiscal prudence but rather that we, as Canadian citizens, in the face of apocalyptic economics sustained by semanticide, seemed to be at risk of losing our will 'to criticize, to reject conformity, passivity, and inevitability', which should be the normal expectations of any citizen living in a democracy (Saul, 1995: 36).

The Senior's Benefit: A Case of Semanticide

The Senior's Benefit was designed to replace Old Age Security, the Guaranteed Income Supplement, and age and pension credits. The benefit was to come into effect in 2001, with a maximum benefit of $11,420 for singles and $18,440 for couples. It would pay $120 more than the existing system to the poorest of the poor, but it would be clawed back at a rate of 20 per cent on each dollar of *household* income over $25,921 per year so that the payment would be completely clawed back at an annual income of $52,000 for an individual and $78,000 for a family. It is important to note that, because the new system would be assessed on the basis of household income and because it imposed a larger clawback, the Benefit would save the government millions of dollars.

Table 7.1: Distribution of Old Age Security, Canada/Quebec Pension
Plan Benefits, and Total Transfers and Income,
Senior Households, Canada, 1995

Pre-transfer Income Groups (Quintiles)	Income Range	Old Age Security (%)	Canada/Quebec Pension Plan (%)	Total Transfers (%)	Total Income (%)
lowest	less than $65	24.9	14.1	20.4	9.1
second	65 to 5,179	22.0	17.7	20.5	10.6
middle	5,180 to 13,432	18.1	21.7	19.6	14.2
fourth	13,433 to 28,835	17.8	22.9	19.8	21.3
highest	28,836 or more	17.2	23.6	19.7	44.8
total		100.0	100.0	100.0	100.0

Source: Calculations by the Centre for International Statistics at the CCSD based on micro-data from Statistics Canada's 1996 Survey of Consumer Finances (1995 income).

The form of semanticide that captured the Canadian imagination was the proclamation that old-age benefits must be slashed in order to save them, and hence talk of *sustaining* the future became part of this discourse. As the Prime Minister stated in response to the Speech from the Throne in 1996, 'The next step is to ensure that the support provided to seniors through the Old Age Security and Guaranteed Income Supplement program is sustainable and will be there for the future as well' (Government of Canada, 1996: 3). In his presentation of the 1998 budget, the Minister of Finance picked up the theme, noting that 'The Senior's Benefit will fully protect the pensions of all current seniors and near seniors. It will ensure that all those in need receive as much, if not more, than they would under the current system.' Later, when he announced the demise of the Benefit, he was still talking about the pension and its 'sustainability for future generations' (Finance Canada, 1998: 1).

Sustaining Poverty

The most significant aspect of the Senior's Benefit is that it would sustain poverty among Canadians. It is important to note that, while the overall economic situation of seniors has improved over the long run, this masks the current predicament of unattached older women. In 1994, poor unattached women aged 65 and older outnumbered poor unattached men of the same age by a margin of five to one (National Council of Welfare, 1996). Using census data, Moore and Rosenberg (1997) show that elderly women living alone are one of the most vulnerable groups economically. They find that being female and living alone increases the odds of being below Statistics Canada's low-income cut-offs almost seven times relative to being male and married. McDonald (1997c), in a study of retired widows who had previously worked, reports that approximately 49 per cent live below Statistics Canada's low-income cut-offs.

Table 7.2: Income for Retired Women, by Marital Status, 1994

	Widowed	Married	Separated/ Divorced	Ever Single
Retired Women				
Household income	$19,507.06	37,696.66	18,123.52	27,191.63
Personal income	$18,341.91	14,946.82	17,796.94	25,134.05
Below low-income cut-offs	Before/After + $120	Before/After + $120	Before/After + $120	Before/After + $120
Women	46.4%	22.6%	61.6%	34.9%
Men	31.7%	19.5%	41.4%	43.3%

Low-income cut-offs 1994 (1992 base)
1 Person: $16,482
2 Persons: $20,603

Source: General Social Survey, Cycle 9.

Table 7.1, which contains the distribution of transfer payments under the old system, shows the heavy reliance of Canadians on the public pension system. Most of Canada's seniors have no, or little pre-transfer income. For example, one-fifth of senior households receive less than $65 per year in pre-transfer payments, while 40 per cent collect less than $5,179. Only 20 per cent of senior households have pre-transfer incomes of more than $29,000. What is not shown here is that the poorest quintile of senior citizens rely on transfer payments for 90 per cent of their income, while the middle quintile rely on income security for 56 per cent of their income (Lochhead, 1998).

Women would be most hurt by the Senior's Benefit. Table 7.2 shows the exact effect it would have had on Canadian women. If $10 a month, or $120 a year, is added to the income figures, the proportion below the low-income cut-off *does not change*. It is also instructive to note the secondary poverty of married women—they are one husband away from poverty when we compare their personal income with their household income. A high proportion of the widowed and separated[4] live below the low-income cut-offs. And when we consider married women's *personal* income, we have a rough estimate of the income they would receive if they were not married. Looked at another way, married women's income comprises approximately 36 per cent of household income (McDonald, 1997c).

Whenever this poverty argument surfaces, the response from financial analysts is that the next generation of women will not have this problem because more work and will have their own pensions. For example, in the year 2015, 70 per cent of women are expected to receive benefits from the Canada/Quebec Pension Plan so they are unlikely to rely on the Senior's Benefit. Seventy per cent of women may, in fact, receive C/QPP but their level of income will not be much different in the future because their socio-economic circumstances have changed very little. A quick review of current trends will confirm this observation.

It is true that women's employment rates have increased, but this is not the whole picture. The employment rate for women aged 25–54 increased only 0.9 per cent between 1989 and 1997 (ibid.). Furthermore, women have experienced high rates of unemployment over the last decade, higher than the rates for men (ibid.). If we consider the distribution of employment by occupation, it is clear that the majority of women continue to work in occupations in which women have traditionally worked. 71 per cent of all working women are employed in teaching, nursing and health-related occupations, clerical work, or sales and services (compared to 78 per cent in 1982) (Hughes, 1995; Statistics Canada, 1994).

The growth of women in non-traditional occupations over the last two decades has been fairly slow. The greatest influx of women into non-traditional occupations from 1986 to 1991 was in management and administration, professional categories, and sales (Hughes, 1995). Their median incomes for full-time full-year work are consistently below their male counterparts. For example, the median income ratio (women's income as a proportion of men's) was 44 per cent for optometrists, osteopaths, and chiropractors and 88 per cent for inspectors and regulatory officers (Hughes, 1995). Essentially, women have made some progress, but the majority are doing the same work in the same occupations. Even when they break into non-traditional occupations, they still do not earn the same income as men.

The proportion of women in part-time work has not changed much either. In 1976, 70 per cent of part-time workers were women; in 1997, over 70 per cent of part-time workers were women (Statistics Canada, 1998). The instability of part-time jobs and the low salaries from part-time work have not changed. Twenty-eight per cent of part-time jobs are not permanent. In 1995, 43 per cent of all part-time workers earned less than $7.50 per hour. Less than 20 per cent of part-time jobs were covered by pensions and approximately 15 per cent fell short of the Year's Basic Exemption for the Canada Pension Plan (Schellenberg, 1997).[5]

Some would say women are within striking distance of pay equality with men. The female-to-male earnings ratio for full-time full-year workers inched up from .64 to .73 between 1981 and 1995. This modest increase means that women earn 73 cents for every dollar earned by men (Scott and Lochhead, 1997). Part of the reason for the gain, however, is because *men's incomes have been stagnant over the last decade* (Best, 1995). Furthermore, it is mainly the baby-boom women who saw small improvements in their incomes, while young women continued to fare very poorly.[6]

The majority of women continue to work in non-standard and contingent jobs that are likely to be part-time and in female occupations with little or no pension coverage, usually for low wages. The pensions of earlier generations of women were affected by the very same factors that operate today, albeit with less force (McDonald et al., 1997). Thus, tomorrow's seniors will be in marginally improved circumstances even if they have their own pensions because private pensions and the C/QPP depends on their earnings history. Also, one can see that the Senior's Benefit would not have lifted these women over the poverty line, as noted above.

The Mismatch between Women's Lives and Pension Policy

Adding to the burden of institutionalized lower earnings for women is a serious mismatch between the topography of women's lives and the proposed Senior's Benefit. Some scholars have argued that the tripartite nature of the life course is 'coming undone' (Guillemard, 1997). In the 'normal course of events' (which really means men's lives), school is followed by work, which is then followed by retirement, but this is no longer considered to be the norm. In short, retirement does not always represent an abrupt transition from work to non-work; it can be gradual, it can be part-time or full-time, and it can involve multiple exits (McDonald, 1996). It can also be argued that this version of the life course was *never* the norm for women.

For example, almost two-thirds of all women who have ever worked experience an interruption in paid work of six months or more. Regardless of the historical era, most such interruptions occur in the earlier years of a woman's life (Fast and Da Pont, 1997). Most women who have ever worked return to paid work after an interruption—about 71 per cent according to an analysis using 1995 General Social Survey data (ibid.). However, they are not as likely to return to the same job or to a full-time job if they had a full-time job prior to their interruption. In the 1950s, family-related reasons for work interruptions accounted for 88 per cent of women's work-leaving, while economic reasons accounted for about 1 per cent. In the 1990s, 47 per cent of interruptions are accounted for by family-related matters and 22 per cent by economic reasons (reflecting current shifts in the labour market and in the care of children) (ibid.). Employment discontinuities, of course, have serious ramifications for the future employability of women, their advancement, and their earnings.

While work interruptions tend to occur in the early twenties for women, there are also work interruptions for women in their fifties. The General Social Survey shows that women can be forced into retirement prematurely by poor health (21 per cent), unemployment (8 per cent), and caregiving (13 per cent) (McDonald et al., 1998a). Forced retirement frequently results in forgone wages and pension credits and ultimately reduced pensions. Using the Survey of Ageing and Independence, McDonald et al. (1998b) find that the individual annual retirement income of women who retire to caregive is, on average, almost $5,000 less than for those who retire for other reasons. Perhaps more important, the Senior's Benefit does not recognize early retirements, a serious matter when we consider that 13 per cent of women retire early to care for others. Such women would have to fill the 'retirement gap' with their own resources until they received the Spouse's Allowance or Senior's Benefit.

The Senior's Benefit is based on the conception of a nineteenth-century male industrial worker who supports a family—it does not take account of the realities of the lives of women with their multiple transitions in and out of the labour force and the caring and sharing that goes on between generations (McDaniel, 1997). These affect wages and ultimately the size of the benefit women would receive in retirement. The C/QPP and private pension plans are based on length of time in the labour force and on the amount of earnings. Even though the CPP has dropout clauses, private pensions do not, and because of their lower earnings women will not be able to create savings or make investments to the same degree as men. When the financial community (again committing semanticide) says the next generation of women will have their own pensions, it is clear that these pensions will not amount to much and that a sizable proportion of women will have to rely on the public pension system in their old age.

Familism

The amount of the Senior's Benefit was to be determined on the basis of the combined incomes of spouses. In the majority of cases, this would be determined more by the husband's income since men earn more money than women and the husband's larger income would push the amount of the Benefit downward. So we have the situation where women earn less over a lifetime because of wage discrimination and family responsibilities, yet their pensions will generally be lower than what they could expect if their contributions to Canadian society were fairly recognized. Monica Townson stated that for married women, the Senior's Benefit would 'take away the only pension they have ever received in their own name as a right and without reference to their husbands' (Townson, 1997: 193).

The Benefit, as family income-tested, represents what Margrit Eichler calls *familism*—a part of the sexist syndrome. The Senior's Benefit treats the family 'as the smallest unit of analysis in cases where it is, in fact, individuals within families . . . that engage in certain actions, have certain experiences, suffer or profit from particular costs or benefits' (Eichler, 1997: 90). She goes on to say: 'Assigning each adult the responsibility for economic well-being and care for inevitable dependents without giving any concomitant systematic public support for this central function mocks the notion of gender equality' (Eichler, 1997: 109).

Terminating the Senior's Benefit

Fortunately for Canadian women, the Senior's Benefit was abandoned in July 1998 with an announcement from the Finance Minister. In so doing, he contradicted the Prime Minister's promises to ensure that the support provided through the OAS and the GIS would be sustainable and would be there in the future. Paul Martin stated, 'Quite bluntly, in 1995 the option to fully preserve the OAS/GIS by simply choosing to fund it for the future did not practically exist' and that the decision was a result of the 'long range benefit arising out of the balanced budget and a declining debt-to-GDP ratio' (Finance Canada, 1998: 3).

His statements could be seen as another display of semanticide. The financial sector did not like the Benefit, not because it would perpetuate poverty but rather because it would discourage saving. What this really meant was that

Canadians would pay down their mortgages or buy things they would need in retirement rather than invest in RRSPs, which would reduce the profits of brokers and pension managers. The way they saw it, the taxes were far greater than the tax break Canadians would have received for contributions to their RRSPs before retirement. A hypothetical retired couple receiving $28,000 a year plus their Senior's Benefit would pay 25 per cent in federal and provincial taxes and 20 per cent for the clawback for a marginal tax rate of 45 per cent on each dollar of income (Janigan, 1997). Diane Ablonczy of the Reform Party said about the Benefit: 'We will fight this tooth and nail. It has negative effects on economic growth, on investment and capital formation' (ibid.). Lest the government forgot its promise to introduce the Senior's Benefit once the budget is balanced and lest they forgot the problems with taxes, the *Globe and Mail* (1998: A14) produced an editorial entitled 'Back to the Drawing Board on Senior's Benefit'. This editorial quoted David Slater of the C.D. Howe Institute and his 'startling tax rates' calculated on hypothetical Canadians. The editorial concluded that the Senior's Benefit 'needs a lot more work to avoid absurd marginal tax rates on senior's modest means'.

Conclusion

The dismantling of the social safety net at the expense of older Canadians for the purposes of enhancing the profits of investors needs to be exposed and discussed openly by experts and, more importantly, by the public. As Cohen (1996: 43) argues, we do not have to accept that 'economic policy will be removed from the democratic process.' We also do not have to accept the unbalanced and false pictures painted about the debt and the deficit, the excess in social spending by government, or the burden of unfair taxation—yet we embraced the message. The most disturbing feature of the process surrounding the Senior's Benefit was how easily Canadians were led to the brink of permanently disassembling their public pension system and how ineffective opposing groups were in terminating the Benefit. In the final analysis, the demise of the Benefit was a lucky coincidence that had little to do with concerns of seniors or gerontologists and everything to do with the agenda of capital markets.

Certainly, if Canadians knowingly decided that economic deficits were more important than social deficits, social policy should follow suit. However, the agenda of many, including myself, is to improve pensions, not reduce them. The reformulation of pension policies to take account of the caring responsibilities of women and the gender-segregated labour market in which they work is a starting point. For example, leaving the existing programs in place—the OAS, the C/QPP and the GIS—and making them gender-sensitive would help to alleviate many of the difficulties presented by the Senior's Benefit. The OAS pension could be increased to move women automatically above an agreed-upon poverty line, while longer periods of caregiving could be factored into the calculation of C/QPP benefits.

The case of the Senior's Benefit is important to consider because the war against the welfare state is not about to end. Even though the United Nations recently condemned the extent of poverty in Canada, the financial sector will not be stopped (Lawton, 1998). The Employment Insurance (EI) surpluses are the latest target of the business sector. When the federal government announced plans to reduce EI rates by up to $59 per worker, it was argued by business that the government could have gone much further in lowering the rates. The vice-president of the Federation of Independent Business, commenting on the battle over EI surpluses, stated that 'Our motto is, we don't quit and we don't go away. The government has nowhere to hide' (Lawton and Lu, 1998: A1). Closer to home, with regard to the increase in C/QPP contributions starting in January 1999, he claimed that 'The "outrage" won't really be hitting home until the new year' (Lawton and Lu, 1998: A1). Use of the word 'outrage' indicates that we are in for another round of semanticide. We might ask ourselves what is so outrageous about directing Employment Insurance surpluses to where they belong— namely, the workers. We might also want to prepare ourselves for another assault on the pension system. When the full effects of 'payroll taxes', a term inappropriately applied to the C/QPP,[7] are felt, our experience with the Senior's Benefit should fortify us for what is sure to ensue.

Notes

1. In July 1998 the Minister of Finance announced that the Senior's Benefit would be scrapped (Finance Canada, 1998).
2. A less noted explanation for the dismantling of social welfare is the inherent contradiction between the competing demands of capitalist interests and human welfare (Habermas, 1976; O'Connor, 1973; Offe, 1984).
3. Andrew Coyne was an editorial writer and columnist for the *Globe and Mail* and is now a columnist with the *National Post*.
4. About 47 per cent of married women 65 and older in 1991 were widows (McDonald et al., 1997).
5. To be eligible to contribute to the C/QPP, a worker's annual income must exceed the 'Year's Basic Exemption', which currently has been frozen at $3,500.
6. Between 1984 and 1994, more than one-tenth of women aged 40–54 who worked full-time and full-year moved out of the lowest annual earnings category of $24,000 or less (Scott and Lochhead, 1997).
7. C/QPP is a form of social insurance, not a payroll tax. Payroll taxes are based on the employer's total payroll while the C/QPP is based on employee earnings and entitles the worker to a benefit based on earnings (Townson, 1995: 17)

References

'Back to the Drawing Board on Senior's Benefit'. 1998. *Globe and Mail*, 27 Feb., A14.

Bakker, I., ed. 1996. *Rethinking Restructuring: Gender and Change in Canada*. Toronto: University of Toronto Press.

Battle, K. 1996. 'A New Old Age Pension', paper presented at the Conference on Reform of the Retirement Income System, Queen's University, Kingston, Ont.

Best, P. 1995. 'Women, Men and Work', *Canadian Social Trends* (Spring): 30–3.

Block, F. 1990. *Postindustrial Possibilities: A Critique of Economic Discourse*. Berkeley: University of California Press.

Brown, R.L. 1995. 'Achieving Stability and Equality and Paygo Financing', *Policy Options* 16, 6: 17–21.

Campbell, B. 1995. 'The Other Side of Coyne: Statscan Study on our Debt/Deficit "Crisis"', *CCPA Monitor* 1, 10: 14–16.

Canadian Centre for Policy Alternatives. 1998. *The Time Is Now: Alternative Federal Budget 1998*. Toronto: Canadian Centre for Policy Alternatives.

Canadian Council on Social Development. 1994. Submission to the Parliamentary Standing Committee on Finance. 15 Nov. Available at: http://www.ccsd.ca/finbrief.html

Cohen, M.G. 1996. 'New International Trade Agreements: Their Reactionary Role in Creating Markets and Retarding Social Welfare', in Bakker (1996: 187–202).

———. 1997. 'From the Welfare State to Vampire Capitalism', in P.M. Evans and G.R. Wekerle, eds, *Women and the Canadian Welfare State*. Toronto: University of Toronto Press, 28–67.

Courchene, T. 1994. *Social Canada in the Millennium: Reform Imperatives and Restructuring Principles*. Toronto: C.D. Howe Institute.

———. 1997. 'Generation X vs. Generation XS: Reflections on the Way Ahead', in K.G. Banting and R. Boadway, eds, *Reform of Retirement Income Policy: International and Canadian Perspectives*. Kingston: Queen's University, School of Policy Studies, 330–4.

Crompton, S., and L. Geran. 1995. 'Women as Main Wage-earners', *Perspectives* 7, 4: 26–9.

Cross, P. 1991. 'Note Regarding the Article "The Growth of the Federal Debt"', *Canadian Economic Observer* 4, 8: 3.17–3.18.

Denton, F.T., and B.G. Spencer. 1997. 'Population Aging and the Maintenance of Social Support Systems', *Canadian Journal on Aging* 16, 3: 485–98.

Eichler, M. 1997. *Family Shifts: Families, Policies, and Gender Equality*. Toronto: Oxford University Press.

Fast, J., and M. Da Pont. 1997. 'Changes in Women's Work Continuity', *Canadian Social Trends* (Autumn): 2–7.

Finance Canada. 1998. *Finance Minister's Statement on the Senior's Benefit*. Ottawa, 28 July. http://www.fin.gc.ca/newse98/98percent2D071e.html

Freeman, A. 1995. 'Ottawa Aims to Shrink Deficit', *Globe and Mail*, 28 Feb., A1, A4.

Galbraith, K.G. 1996. 'Foreword', in J. Medoff and A. Harless, eds, *The Indebted Society: Anatomy of an Ongoing Disaster*. Toronto: Little, Brown & Company (Canada).

Government of Canada. 1996. *The Senior's Benefit: Securing the Future*. Ottawa: Department of Supply and Services Canada.

Guillemard, A.M. 1997. 'Re-Writing Social Policy and Changes within the Life Course Organization: A European Perspective', *Canadian Journal on Aging* 16, 3: 441–64.

Gunderson, M. 1998. *Flexible Retirement as an Alternative to 65 and Out*. Toronto: C.D. Howe Institute.

————, D. Hyatt, and J.E. Psando. 1996. 'Public Pension Plans in Canada and the United States', paper presented at the Upjohn Institute Conference on Employee Benefits, Labor Costs, and Labor Markets in Canada and the United States, Kalamazoo, Mich.

Habermas, J. 1976. *Legitimation Crisis*. London: Heinemann.

Hughes, K.D. 1995. 'Women in Non-traditional Occupations', *Perspectives* 7, 3: 14–19.

Janigan, M. 1997. 'Making the Middle Class Pay: Ottawa's Plan to Revamp Old Age Benefits Raises Serious Issues of Fairness', *Maclean's* 29 Sept., 42–5.

Lam, N., J. Cutt, and M. Prince. 1996. 'The Canadian Pension Plan: Retrospect and Prospect', paper presented at the Conference on Reform of the Retirement Income System, Queen's University, Kingston, Ont.

Lawton, V. 1998. 'U.N. Condemns Canadian Poverty', *Toronto Star*, 5 Dec.

———— and V. Lu. 1998. 'EI Surplus Angers Business, Labour', *Toronto Star*, 4 Dec.

Lochhead, C. 1998. 'Who Benefits from Canada's Income Security Programs?', *Insight* 7: 1–6.

McDaniel, S.A. 1997. 'Serial Employment and Skinny Government: Reforming Caring and Sharing Among Generations', *Canadian Journal on Aging* 16, 3: 465–84.

McDonald, L. 1996. *Transitions into Retirement: A Time for Retirement*. Toronto: Centre for Applied Social Research, Faculty of Social Work, University of Toronto.

————. 1997a. 'The Link between Social Research and Social Policy Options: Reverse Retirement as a Case in Point, *Canadian Journal on Aging/Canadian Public Policy* (Supp.): 90–113.

————. 1997b. 'Editorial: Pension Questions that are Politically Out-of-the-Question', *Canadian Journal on Aging* 16, 3: 393–9.

————. 1997c. 'The Invisible Poor: Canada's Retired Widows', *Canadian Journal on Aging* 16, 3: 553–83.

————, P. Donahue, and B. Moore. 1997. *Widowhood and Retirement: Women on the Margin*. IESOP Research Paper No. 17. Hamilton: McMaster University.

————, ————, and ————. 1998a. *The Economic Casualties of Retiring Because of Poor Health*. IESOP Research Paper No. 29. Hamilton: McMaster University.

————, ————, and ————. 1998b. *The Economic Casualties of Retiring to Caregive*. IESOP Research Paper No. 28. Hamilton: McMaster University.

McQuaig, L. 1995. *Shooting the Hippo: Death by Deficit and Other Myths*. Toronto: Viking Penguin Books Canada.

———. 1998. *The Cult of Impotence: Selling the Myth of Powerlessness in the Global Economy*. Toronto: Penguin Books Canada.

Margolin, L. 1997. *Under the Cover of Kindness: The Invention of Social Work*. Charlottesville: University Press of Virginia.

Medoff, J., and A. Harless. 1996. *The Indebted Society: Anatomy of an Ongoing Disaster*. New York: Little, Brown.

Midgley, James. 1997. *Social Welfare in Global Context*. Thousand Oaks, Calif.: Sage.

Mimoto, H., and P. Cross. 1991. 'The Growth of the Federal Debt', *Canadian Economic Observer* 4, 6: 3.1–3.18.

Moore, E., and M.W. Rosenberg. 1997. *Growing Old in Canada: Demographic and Geographic Perspectives*. Toronto: International Thomson Publishing Co. with Statistics Canada.

National Council of Welfare. 1996. *A Guide to the Proposed Senior's Benefit*. Ottawa: Minister of Supply and Services.

O'Connor, J. 1973. *The Fiscal Crisis of the State*. New York: St Martin's Press

Offe, C. 1984. *Contradictions of the Welfare State*. Cambridge, Mass.: MIT Press.

Osberg, L., and P. Fortin. 1996. *Unnecessary Debts*. Toronto: James Lorimer.

Pesando, J.E. 1997. 'From Tax Grab to Retirement Saving: The Case for Privatizing the CPP', *C.D. Howe Institute Commentary 93*. Toronto: C.D. Howe Institute.

Robson, W.B.P. 1996. 'Ponzi's Pawns: Young Canadians and the Canada Pension Plan', in J. Burbidge et al., eds, *When We're 65: Reforming Canada's Retirement Income System*. Toronto: C.D. Howe Institute.

Ruggles, P., and M. O'Higgens. 1987. 'Retrenchment and the New Right', in M. Rein, G. Esping-Andersen, and L. Rainwater, eds. *Stagnation and Renewal in Social Policy*. Armonk, NY: M.E. Sharpe.

Saul, J.R. 1995. *The Unconscious Civilization*. Concord, Ont.: House of Anansi Press.

Schellenberg, G. 1997. *The Changing Nature of Part-time Work*. Ottawa: Canadian Council on Social Development.

Scott, K., and C. Lochhead. 1997. *Are Women Catching Up in the Earnings Race?* Ottawa: Canadian Council on Social Development.

Slater, D.W. 1998. *Fixing the Senior's Benefit*. Toronto: C.D. Howe Institute.

Statistics Canada. 1994. *Women in the Labour Force—1994 Edition*. Ottawa: Minister of Industry, Science and Technology, Statistics Canada Catalogue No. 75–507E.

———. 1998. *Labour Force Update—An Overview of the 1997 Labour Market*. Ottawa: Minister of Industry, Statistics Canada Catalogue No. 71–005–XPB.

Teeple, G. 1995. *Globalization and the Decline of Social Reform*. Toronto: Garamond Press.

Townson, M. 1995. *Our Aging Society: Preserving Retirement Incomes into the 21st*

Century. Toronto: Canadian Centre for Policy Alternatives.

———. 1997. *Independent Means: A Canadian Women's Guide to Pensions and a Secure Financial Future.* Toronto: Macmillan.

Workman, T. 1996. *Banking on Deception: The Discourse of Fiscal Crisis.* Halifax: Fernwood.

8 | 'What Did You Ever Do For Me?'

Intergenerational Linkages in a
Reconstructing Canada

Susan A. McDaniel

There is no doubt that population aging and intergenerational issues are much in the public eye in Canada in the late 1990s. Reading the daily news is almost like reading a long doomsday report. Social safety nets, education, and most notably publicly funded health care are argued to be threatened as much by aging populations as by deficits, debt, or the slashing by governments across the land. There is more myth and mysticism than reality to these prophecies.

Not all the world sees population aging in apocalyptic terms. The best demographic analysts in Europe, where the oldest of populations in the world live, are not worried. Researchers at the Netherlands Interdisciplinary Demographic Institute (van Solinge et al., 1998: 29) have this to say in a recently published report:

> One can easily view the aging process as a challenge, because deep-down it is not the aging of populations which primarily pose a threat to social protection systems. Rather, the finance principles on which those systems are based are flawed or not entirely shockproof. Aging populations are therefore no insurmountable threat, they merely lay bare the weaknesses of social arrangements in correcting market failures.

I will return later to the important point that population aging lays bare the weaknesses in correcting market failures.

Let me now ask a crucial question—if the oldest region of the world does not see population aging as a threat, why the preoccupation in Canada, one of the younger industrialized countries? Being an academic analyst in this area for many years, I have considered complex possibilities (e.g., McDaniel, 1986, 1987), and some have found their way into the media. However, simple explanations may suffice. Is it because we have David Foot in Canada, whose book, *Boom, Bust, and Echo*, was on the best-seller list for more than two years? No, voodoo demographics in Canada pre-existed Foot's best seller. In fact, I was writing about the profound worry Canadians have with respect to demographic aging as long ago as the mid-1980s (McDaniel, 1986).

Well, what could it be? I have two theories, both unacademically simple. First, Canada is being revealed to Canadians and to the rest of the world as a very contradictory place indeed. We are not what we see ourselves as being. Evidence can be found everywhere, but let's look briefly at the example of the Hepatitis C situation. The self-identity of Canadians is very much caught up in being caring, concerned, nice people who have accessible universal health care and a more advanced social safety net than south-of-the-border (which has almost none, so that comparison may not be much to boast about!). If pushed, as I was a few years ago when asked by a public school teacher in Vermont to describe for her students what was different about Canada, we might add our much lower crime rate than in the States, our peacekeeping role, and our safer and saner public blood system relying on volunteer donors rather than paid (sometimes desperate) donors. Alas, I mentioned these items to the class in Vermont, which embarrassingly shows that we are not what we think we are at all! In fact, it is these very *myths* about Canada and who we are that led in part to the continuing problem with tainted blood (Picard, 1998). That myths come back to haunt us is distinctly relevant to the issue of voodoo demographics, as we shall see. The reasons given by those in charge of the blood system in Canada for the steadfast refusal to test blood for the Hepatitis C virus in spring 1986 when countries around the world, whether profit or non-profit blood systems, were doing so, were two: cost (deep concerns about costs were expressed in Canada even in the mid-1980s); and the belief by those in charge that Canada's system was safer than others *because* of our caring approach in relying on volunteer blood donors. Preoccupation with bottom lines and abiding acceptance of myth has resulted in 60,000 Canadians (some, quoted by Picard [1998], suggest that the number could be as high as 400,000) contracting Hepatitis C from tainted blood transfusions, of whom 6,000 to 12,000 will die or have died (estimates Picard). This does not include the more than 2,000 Canadians who will die, or have died, from transfusion-caused AIDS. Given that Hepatitis C can lurk undetected for years and is transferable from shared toothbrushes and razors, the secondary infection rate could be huge.

So, the myth of Canada as safe and caring, as having a social safety net better than that in the United States, has led us to look for a culprit when public funding is slashed more sharply here than in any other industrialized country. The myth seems more enduring than the evidence to the contrary. The presumed culprit is another myth: population aging as motivator of restructuring. Canada is not the innocent in making huge changes to governments in the 1990s, being driven to it by the money traders on Wall Street. Canada is not being swept into the raging river of globalization as a little canoe, as one analyst suggested a few years ago in the NAFTA debate. Rather, Canada is leading the way in sharp reductions in 'big' government and is contributing to the river's rage. Population aging becomes a convenient scapegoat and cover for 'the weaknesses of social arrangements in correcting market failures' to which the Netherlands' analysts refer above (van Solinge et al., 1998; see also Myles, 1996). Myths about Canada led to the tainted blood scandal and are leading to perpetuation of another myth, the myth of voodoo demographics—of pensioners and sick elders popping out of closets unexpectedly demanding pensions and health care, thereby taxing our delivery systems. Our future has been said to be under 'house arrest', with uncertainty as all that is certain. I do not mean to be gloomy about these changes, but rather to present them as the backdrop to intergenerational interlinkages.

Second, Canada is concerned about population aging not because it is demographically old, but because it is *not*. If this seems paradoxical, it is. Fear of aging is a powerful force. Witness the immense popularity of Viagra, the impotence drug that hit the market recently and already has become the fastest-selling drug of all time, outselling Prozac. Fear of population aging is not much different. We may see ourselves as a society losing potency and becoming more feminized, less aggressive and dynamic, perhaps poorer. Canadians may worry about living in a society that may be less vibrant, and they point at what they fear (collective aging) with alarm (McDaniel, 1986, 1987).

'What Did You Ever Do For Me?'

We all exist in webs of intergenerational relationships that include older and younger people, whether in families, at work, or in society at large. What particularly interests me is the priority that has been given to generation as an identity signifier and what this means. When and how did I become a baby boomer? And some of you Gen Xers, and others seniors? How does this change the ways in which we relate to each other? How did generation replace so much else that we are? And why is it thought to matter so much?

'What Did You Ever Do For Me?' is the converse of the oft-cited slogan 'We do it all for you.' Virtually everything that is done in the 1990s, in policy in particular, is done in the name of the future, explicitly future generations. Government cutbacks? We do it all for you and the sake of your children. Social policy rewrite is supposedly done for the good of future generations. It is also invoked in families. Hard work by parents is not meant to deprive children of their parents, but to provide a better and brighter future for the children. Higher education is sacrifice by parents (and students themselves) who increasingly work and go into considerable debt to make better lives for their children.

Future generations and the well-being of future generations becomes 'that great beckoning project', by which almost anything can be justified. The fact of invoking future generations is telling unto itself. Images of caring, connection, and continuity might be more convincing with the addition of a futuristic family element. Whether current actions, in policy or in family, indeed are done with the best interests of future generations in mind is, of course, a real question. An American study looks at what we would get if some policy-makers' wishes for demographic change were instantly granted and finds that even more problems would result ('What If . . .', 1997).

In asking 'What Did You Ever Do For Me?' a strong sense of entitlement based on justice is expressed. There is also a sense of accusation that *you* gave less than *you* took. An accounting involving some notion of distributive justice is built into the statement, an idea of equity among generations, of individual entitlement rather than collective or public good. These expectations develop in a social and political context and are part, but not the entire story, of intergenerational interlinkages.

I have suggested that intergenerational issues are more spoken about than they are well conceptualized or analysed (McDaniel, 1998). As my thinking about the issues has deepened, I have become more convinced not only that this is the case, but that much that is spoken is based on half, or less, of the story.

In this chapter, I take a political economy perspective, broadly defined, on intergenerational interlinkage that questions the factors behind social trends, patterns, and actions. The questions themselves provide useful frameworks by which to analyse the perplexing dilemmas population aging and seniors pose to neo-liberal agendas of reconstructing Canada in the late 1990s, and to Canadian social cohesion.

First, neo-liberal agendas and the lessening of the welfare state call into question the place and value of seniors in society. Walker and Minichiello (1996: 3), for example, argue that exciting new research opportunities in gerontology are being created:

> the issue of relations between generations is emerging as a significant one in the sociology of aging. . . . The main reasons for this interest, which echo some of the early sociological inquiries of Mannheim [1968 (1952)], are that socio-demographic changes are having a profound impact on the duration and intensity of intergenerational relations between kin and, at the macro level, fiscal austerity is raising questions about the social contract between the generations which underpins all welfare states.

McDaniel (1997c: 2) argues similarly with respect to emerging policy research questions as the welfare state dismantles:

> Intergenerational transfers are the essence of societal reproduction, continuity, interaction and exchange. . . . Intergenerational transfers are also at the heart of the welfare state precept of redistribution of resources, and thus close to the centre of current social policy and economic restructuring in Canada. Yet, tensions, contradictions and insufficient clarity in the conceptualization and analysis of intergenerational transfers reveal vital unanswered questions, questions with crucial policy relevance.

Key here is that age, generation, and historical period are insufficient to understand the changing status of the aged in contemporary society, the effects on the aged of recent policy 'reforms', and what lies ahead (Osberg, 1998; Pampel, 1998). The focus must be on the profound and shifting interconnections among generations, both within families and in the wider society, which are shaped by the structures of the welfare state as well as by its dismantling (McDaniel, 1997d). Clark (1993a: 487) argues that a different way of seeing and doing is needed:

> the concept of 'moral economy' has been introduced . . . to describe the underlying, collectively shared basic moral assumptions making up a system of reciprocal relationships that reflect a society's social norms and obligations. This concept has been applied specifically to the gerontological context . . . to augment the more 'traditional' political economy perspective on policy and aging.

Although structure is spotlighted in this approach, individual actions also matter as seniors and others shape and reshape how the Canadian welfare state and its dismantling impinges on them, and they determine, to some extent, *that* the shifts occur and how they occur. It is in this intersection that perceptions and realities come to the fore as both expectations and social meanings, such as senses of entitlement and equity (Giddens, 1991). At the point where values meet change, values become transformed, transformative, and revealing of underlying social structures and cultural beliefs. This has happened with health care, as the National Forum on Health (1997) discovered.

Second, intergenerational relations transcend the usual research preoccupation with transfers (direct or indirect) and extend into the realms of transmission of ideas, technologies, social values, heritage, infrastructure, innovation, continuity, and possibility. Mannheim (1968 [1952]: 293–4), in his classic essay on generations, wrote:

> our culture is developed by individuals who come into contact anew with the accumulated heritage . . . a fresh contact (meeting something new) always means . . . a novel approach to assimilating, using and developing the proffered material . . . in the case of generations, the 'fresh contact' with the social and cultural heritage is determined not by mere social change . . . it facilitates reevaluation of our inventory and teaches us both to forget that which is no longer useful and to covet that which has yet to be won.

Canada is very different from the United States both in its lesser preoccupation with intergenerational justice issues (the 'Greedy Granny/Geezer' imagery in the United States) and in the different social contexts of intergenerational interrelations. Clark (1993b: 38–9) offers a compelling comparison of the United States and Canada:

> the highly individualistic nature of the United States promotes an apocalyptic view of the nature of population aging: conflict between individuals and age groups against a backdrop of shrinking social resources is seen as nearly inevitable. . . . Empirical data are presented in such a way as to reinforce this construction, and assumptions about the proper primacy of the traditional familial

model and the secondary responsibility of the government in addressing social problems are unquestioned. . . .

In Canada, by contrast, aging tends to be a more social issue, with the government response embodying collectivist principles set forth in such policies as universal health insurance. Greater reliance on social solutions defuses the apocalyptic aura of aging.... The definition and solution to the 'aging problem' is perceived within this collectivistic framework, undercutting the social polarization and the 'zero sum' thinking common south of the border.

This paper is constructed as a kind of quilt, where one corner or the middle is worked on and then the parts are sewn together and reworked as a part of the larger pattern. The work of putting the quilt squares into something larger is left to a group, in this case a group of fellow scholars and activists, as well as policymakers and fellow citizens. It is research and scholarly framing as quilting bee.

Dimensions of Intergenerational Linkages

Five underexplored dimensions of intergenerational interlinkages are considered here, extending the typology I developed in an earlier paper (McDaniel, 1997c).

One crucial dimension of the conceptualization of intergenerational relations is *the aperture through which we view intergenerational issues*. The usual script of intergenerational issues is written about *transfers only*, not really relations or interrelations, and about *public* transfers. The justifications are good ones; I have relied on them myself. We have excellent data on public transfers but less complete data on private transfers and not much that is comprehensive or detailed on social relations and interrelations among generations. What we have on social relations and private transfers is mainly from smaller or regional surveys, or small-scale case studies, or simulations, that are less well disseminated than are data on public transfers. Importantly, of course, policy decisions most often, but not always, take place in the realm of public transfers, if not among generations then among groups in society. Accounts of intergenerational transfers must take in the full range of such transfers—that is, more than the traditional cost/benefit accounting of financial transfers.

Another dimension of intergenerational issues is *the direction of the transfers and the nature of those transfers*. In a previous paper (McDaniel, 1997c) I developed a three-generation typology of intergenerational transfers using the terms 'receiving generations' and 'giving generations' to define the axes, but placing the prototypical children, parents, and grandchildren in both receiving and giving generations. I also expanded the nature of transfers beyond the monetary or the public (either redistributive or direct transfer) to include social transfers as well as intangibles such as attention and joy.

A third dimension of relevance is *the cohort/period conundrum* with which demographers are well acquainted. Change is occurring across two dimensions (and likely more) simultaneously. The clock of biographical pacing is ticking, as is the clock of historical change, and these interact in profound ways, as the insights of C. Wright Mills have compellingly revealed. There is also the clock of social hetero- or homogeneity (increasing similarity or difference), which relates to both history and biography but in cross-hatching and at times contradictory ways. The three clocks tick along simultaneously yet with very different beats. Intergenerational interlinkages in a reconstructing Canada are the means by which I can begin to detect the beats separately and in unison.

A fourth dimension of interest is *the multiple and layered interlinkages* among the various dimensions of intergenerational relations and transfers. Public intergenerational transfers may be connected with private transfers in ways as yet unknown (McDaniel, 1997c; Stone et al., 1998). Brodie (1994) argues that the boundaries between private and public are being radically adjusted in Canada. Both the domestic sphere and the market are being reprivatized, the latter through deregulation. The implications of these changes for intergenerational linkages and equity may be massive and are as yet mostly unassessed. This is but one linkage of many. I have yet to work through all the possibilities, but will share some of my thoughts on a quilt of interlinkages focusing on *family, work, and society* across generations.

A fifth dimension is *tension between perceptions and realities of intergenerational issues*. This tension often veils aspects of interlinkages that are not as visible as they might be. One example is the unfunded liabilities of Workers' Compensation funds, which transfer costs to future workers from governments and employers (Gunderson and Hyatt, 1998). Another example is public health insurance in Canada, which makes transfers from those in the middle to the young and the old.

Data and Analytical Approach

The goals of this chapter are three: (1) putting together disparate data and analyses on intergenerational interlinkages to see what story emerges from the previously unlinked pieces—filling in what is known, not yet known, and misknown; (2) reanalysing existing data on intergenerational linkages in light of the five dimensions discussed above; and (3) developing and nuancing a conceptual framework for analysing intergenerational interlinkages.

Data from diverse sources are used, including Statistics Canada, several research surveys and studies I have done over recent years, and archival and historical records. Analyses involve equally diverse approaches: trend and comparative analyses, decomposition analyses of contributors to intergenerational transfers, and analyses of data in new categories and combinations.

Family Intergenerational Linkages

Family intergenerational relations are, surprisingly, almost left out of the story of intergenerational accounting. There are two exceptions: a focus on caregiving and care-receiving that has dominated the research literature in gerontology; and, to a lesser extent, an interest in bequests, largely among economists, but recently among social historians.

Given the prevalence of belief in a supportive, multi-generational 'traditional family' in times past, not nearly as much is known about intergenerational relations in families past or present as might be expected. And much of what is known is incomplete, inaccurate, or mythologized (Hareven, 1991, 1994; McDaniel, 1997c, 1998; Montigny, 1997). Findings from one study (McDaniel and Lewis, 1998) analysing the censuses of pre-Confederation Newfoundland are telling, since Newfoundland is widely perceived as *the* most traditional and family-oriented of societies in North America, with presumed extended family support for the dependent, especially the aged. As a society thought to be isolated from collective institutions of elder support, such as pensions and long-term care, pre-Confederation Newfoundland offers a perfect circumstance to test family intergenerational interlinkages in the idealized past. The findings are surprising:

- There was little evidence of extended multi-generational families.
- Most aged lived alone or with spouses.
- When multi-generational households existed, they were either living together out of dire need, or supports were being provided *by* the elders.

Intergenerational relations in families involve, as Hareven (1991: 95) argues, 'the reconstruction of a multi-tiered reality' that moves away from grand theories of nature and of universalisms about family to the social construction of families in interaction with changing societies. There is little 'settled certainty' (Parr, 1996: 8) about intergenerational relations in families. In practice and perspective, temporariness (and temporality), dynamism, and social contexts, families and individuals as actors/agents in creating their own stories are characteristic of intergenerational relations (Levine, 1989). Precarious moments in the transfer and transformation of power from one generation to the next emerge, and at these moments it is possible to see clearly that generation is not age. People are products of their times and contribute (or not) to children and elders only insofar as they are able, whatever the culture or the times dictate.

These findings enable us to stitch in parts of the quilt squares on family for some of the five dimensions. In widening the aperture to look at families in the past, we find that our abiding understandings about past families are not true. We find that the direction of transfers is from old to young, contrary to what we might have anticipated. And we discover that there is nothing new in the tension between perceptions and realities of intergenerational supports and interlinkages.

Relations of young and old examined in family contexts enable exploration of the *contradictions* in the status of the old in relation to the young. For example, very rapid social change, as we are experiencing at present, could cause supports to the old to *increase* as they become more valued links to a receding and longed for past. So societies that revere the old may not be as traditional we have thought. This, of course, contrasts sharply with the grand theory that with modernization, the old lose status as their knowledge becomes less relevant.

How much do we know about generations in families? Again, not as much as we might think (Silverstein and Bengtson, 1997). We talk about the growth in three-generation families, but a recent study in France has shown that among women born in 1930, 26 per cent were in *four- generation* families at the age of 60 (Pennec, 1997), a proportion that is expected to increase. More than 90 per cent of the women who are in four-generation families at age 50 are in such families when they die. Images come to mind of family photos with four and five generations smiling together, but the real question is how those who provide care and support, usually middle-aged women, cope with so many generations at one time? Intergenerational interlinkages examined by numbers of generations in our families might yield a very different picture from what we have now of family interlinkages, which tend to presume that most families are smaller than they used to be and have limited intergenerational contacts.

Older couples' unions apparently develop in response to perceptions of intergenerational relations (Caradec, 1997: 66–7). Couples in France (the French seem to be ahead of us in the innovative examination of intergenerational interlinkages) who form when they are both over age 50 seem to prefer what they call 'semi-cohabitation', in which both partners keep their own homes but spend 3–4 nights a week together. This enables couples to maintain their familiar homes and not disrupt relationships with adult children and grandchildren, but at the same time to establish new ways to live in unions. Here, the quilt square pattern becomes more intricate as we learn about the multiple interlinkages in families between old and young. Concern about generational interrelationships leads older generations to invent new family forms.

The biggest overall research finding with respect to family incomes is that togetherness matters, as is apparent in Table 8.1. Being in a family, regardless of age, helps to insulate against poverty (Picot and Myles, 1995; Picot et al., 1998). It is important to keep this firmly in mind when one hears the litany from policymakers about rich seniors happily living in RVs, spending their children's inheritance on snowbird winters in Arizona, Florida, or Mexico. Although couples aged 65 and over tend to have the lowest incidence of low income among families, this changes markedly when one looks at non-family elderly, particularly women. While it is true that there has been a much touted decline in low income among seniors in Canada since 1980, this has been most marked among married seniors. Among single seniors, the news is much less good and much less touted. Almost as large a proportion of unattached women over 65 (53.4 per cent) as female lone parents were categorized as 'low income' in 1996 (Statistics Canada, 1997: 34–5).

That immediate family matters so much to poverty prevention leads to another possibility. We know that higher (or growing) inequalities in socio-economic

Table 8.1: Percentage Incidence of Low Income, Selected Family Types, Canada, 1980–1996

Family Types	1980	1985	1990	1996
Married Couple Only				
1 earner	11.9	13.8	11.6	12.8
2 earners	1.6	3.2	3.4	4.0
Parents with Children				
1 earner	16.6	21.1	23.2	25.0
2 earners	5.8	7.8	6.5	6.6
3+ earners	3.6	5.0	2.6	3.4
Lone Parent				
Male	25.4	26.9	25.5	31.3
Female	57.3	61.1	59.5	60.8
Elderly Unattached				
Male	60.7	50.2	41.0	33.3
Female	71.6	64.1	53.8	53.4

Note: Low-income cut-offs used here are based on an analysis of 1992 family expenditure data collected by Statistics Canada. Families who usually spend 54.7 per cent or more of their income on food, shelter, and clothing are considered below the low-income cut-offs, which are differentiated by size of area and family size.

Source: Statistics Canada (1997): Text Table IV, 34–5.

status in societies lead to overall lower life expectancies. Relative deprivation matters to well-being. Is it similarly worse or better to be poor in a poorer multi-generational family than to be poor in a better-off multi-generational family? What happens when inequalities are increasing, as they are now in Canada? We know very little about this. What we know is that transfers among generations in families are little understood (Stone et al., 1998). We also know that inequalities before government transfers (pensions, social assistance, etc) are much higher than after transfers, and that the gap has widened of late. This is good news about the effectiveness of Canada's social welfare system—until one remembers that it is being rapidly dismantled.

A Statistics Canada study (Zyblock, 1996) finds that the largest factor in family market income inequalities is increases that are occurring *within* age groups, not increasing inequalities *between* different age groups. The growing polarization of income in each age group matters more than population aging or shifting age structure. This is borne out by the 1996 census, which reveals that the growing numbers of baby boomers in the highest earnings group (those aged 45–54) *offset an even greater drop in earnings over the 1990–5 period* (the drop would have been 6 per cent overall instead of the actual 2.6 per cent decline) (Statistics Canada, 1998). Population aging therefore helped to prevent a further earnings drop in the early 1990s. This is not demographic aging as apocalypse, but its opposite. Zyblock and Tyrell (1997) assess the relative contributions of family type by age to income inequalities by means of decomposition analysis. The net largest contributor to growing inequality was lone-parent families with a head under age 45. Family type and gender of family head matter more than age or demographic change.

Inequalities in market income may be important (Picot, 1997), but in the 1990s a declining portion of our income comes from the market, both for the well-off and the less well-off. The 1996 census shows that employment income declined as a proportion of total income ($0.75 in 1996 compared to $0.86 in 1970) (Statistics Canada, 1998). If more people, particularly older people, depend more on transfers and/or investments, either directly through savings or indirectly through investments of their pension or other funds, a paradox emerges. Seniors, in many ways, are leaders in concern about the longer term and public good. Their belief in hard work for the sake of future generations, in self-sacrifice, in building infrastructure such as public education and public health, is well known. Robert Collins, in *You Had to Be There: An Intimate Portrayal of the Generation That Survived the Depression, Won the War, and Re-Invented Canada* (1997), wrote this about his own older generation (which he calls Generation M):

> We are bewildered, saddened, angered by the state of our country, the threat of a breakup, the lawlessness on its streets, the flagrant lack of discipline in its schools, the rash of personal bankruptcies, the staggering level of household debt (reportedly) nearly 88 per cent of personal income. What happened to the postwar Canada we lavished with so many hopes and dreams 50 years ago?

The paradox is that even with a strong long term and a more collective citizen-like outlook, increasing numbers of seniors and soon-to-be seniors are being forced by the need for cash flow into becoming 'stakeholders' (a word I do not like, in part because of its diminishing of the public interest) in pressuring for short-term gains. As money flows out of banks, trust companies, and credit unions and into mutual funds and stock and bond markets, more of us become stockholders who are interested in good short-term returns. Pension funds are the largest existing pool of capital. Unions, teachers, nurses, and professors, who may be very concerned about job security, about future savings, about boomerang children who have trouble locating secure jobs in the reconstructing and globalizing work world, are staking a hold in that world themselves in important ways, but without any real control. The upheaval in markets and pension funds, as well as the sharp decline in the Canadian dollar over the summer of 1998, revealed to many how vulnerable seniors are to the market and how their fates closely depend on what happens globally.

The question becomes, who is looking after the longer-term *public* interest? Government is not, business is not, and increasingly we ourselves are not. A paradox indeed, but there may be an unexpected bright spot here. The uncertainty of capital markets, or of public pensions or health care, may make one turn to the multi-generational family as insurance or a co-pooling of risks. Thus, a commonality of interests among multiple generations in families may be found among the uncertainty of globalized capital markets. However, this will not work for many, of course, whose extended families are not able to help. So, we have another complex stitch on the quilt square of multiple and layered intergenerational interlinkages.

Stone et al. make an important contribution to the consideration of intergenerational interlinkages by adding private intergenerational exchanges to public intergenerational transfers. These researchers suggest enticingly that intergenerational inequities created by the 'build-up of obligations for reciprocal giving based on dependency is a foundation of social cohesion' (Stone et al., 1998: 18). This certainly is in happy contrast with the prevalent, and I think wrong, notion that 'What did you ever do for me?' thinking of generational accounting will undermine social cohesion.

Work Linkages

We know little about work and intergenerational interlinkages. According to one analyst, we can be certain of four things (Price, 1997: 142):

1. There will be fewer workers supporting each retiree.
2. Costs for each retiree will be greater.
3. Average life lived after retirement will be greater, both because life expectancy is increasing but mainly because early retirement will continue.
4. We are not doing well in getting from here into the future.

This last bit of wisdom is important. It may not be the trend, but what we are not doing about it, that is the challenge.

John Ralston Saul (1995: 121) argues, that '[t]he economists and managers are the servants of god. Like the medieval scholastics, their only job is to uncover the divine plan' of the market and market forces. And indeed, worship of the market as a supreme force has been rapidly gaining ascendency over any other way to see things, and sometimes over any other supreme force. Otherwise reasonable people spout forth on the wisdom of the market, as if markets were a phenomenon imbued with both brains and souls.

Work insecurity is characteristic of our times. That job insecurity exists is not new; it is the breadth and depth of the insecurity people are facing in Canada in the 1990s that is new. Previously, layoffs were almost unknown among those aged 50 and over, but in the 1990s the rate of layoff in this age group has increased sharply, reaching deeply into the ranks of older white-collar managers and professionals, including public-sector workers. And many of these layoffs were permanent or of much longer duration than among younger workers. Sassoon (1997: 179–80) points out:

Changes in the labor market include the increasing insecurity of large sections of the population in Western Europe and North America, the shortening of working lives . . . and the phenomena of polarization between work-rich but time-poor households and work-poor households but (usually for women) also time-poor households in countries like Britain and the United States.

The ways in which work changes have resulted in interlinkages among generations are interesting and unexpected. Real earnings among younger workers have declined, particularly among men. Of course, this is among those younger workers who have work, a smaller proportion because of persistently high youth unemployment. Among older workers who keep jobs, there have been increasing earnings. Patterns of inequality within age groups have also shifted, with the widest increase in inequality among younger workers, but sharply growing inequalities have occurred among older workers as well, particularly among men (Finnie, 1997; Picot, 1997).

Shifts away from unionization and seniority policies in workplaces have meant shifts in intergenerational transfers. Seniority policies tend to make an implicit transfer from middle to older workers, presuming lesser productivity with aging (which may or may not be true). This transfer is lessened with decreased emphasis on seniority as a principle, and thus older workers benefit far less.

The pattern of shifting risks to individual workers and away from employers and governments is a transfer from older to middle or younger, as well as from better off to less well off. This counters the previous shift in some ways, as risks and responsibilities become greater among the middle-aged employed group, while older workers face fewer years of increased individual responsibility and benefit from the shared risks of earlier periods. This is an example of how the inadequacies of existing arrangements to cover market failures are brought out by, but not caused by, population aging.

Beliefs about older workers and what they can and cannot do can be an impediment to hiring, promotion, and retention. I asked about this in one part of a larger study I did of older workers in Alberta. The findings were surprising. It was only in regard to learning new technical skills and flexibility and willingness to change that people thought younger workers were superior. On all other fronts, older workers were thought to be equal to, or better than, younger workers. On dependability, dedication, and willingness to work hard, older workers were thought to be much superior. Interestingly, more women than men do not see age as a factor at all in their perceptions of who has superior skills. In addition, the common perception that technology transfer occurs from younger to older is not borne out in one study (Beaudry and Green, 1996), although many of us likely have had other experience in this regard.

Tensions between perceptions and realities come out in the quest for education by both older and younger people. The young are disadvantaged by their lack of experience, and older workers by that very experience and its presumed cost to the employer. Intergenerational mobility as an abiding motivation for hard work, too, is slipping away as youth find it harder to meet their parents' achievements, let alone exceed them.

So, in the quilt squares, we once again find surprises: unexpected transfers from old to young at work, privatization of risks that diminishes these transfers from old to young, but lessening seniority that increases risks for older workers and reduces them for younger. The stitches of this quilt square are as intricate and cross-hatching as they are for family intergenerational interlinkages.

Societal Intergenerational Linkages

Here is where the gaps between perceptions and realities become most pronounced. As Canadians, we think with our hearts about public transfers—remember social policy as a 'sacred trust'? Standing (1997: 1346) makes the point, in discussing social policy shrinkage in Eastern Europe, that 'The threshold of tolerance of impoverishment may have been higher than some expected, but the longer term consequences for social cohesion and distributive justice could be ugly.' His point may well apply to Canada.

Let's take a closer look at recent social policy shifts in Canada. Welfare state capitalism is purported to be premised on promoting equality of opportunities through access to education (mobility), health care (ability to contribute without the personal risks of ill health or injury), and income assistance (welfare and entitlement benefits such as pensions, unemployment [now employment] insurance, and workers' compensation, etc.). Social policy was never intended to be a major means of redistribution of income, wealth, or power. The premises of welfare state capitalism can only be secured on the basis of something close to full employment and where a strongly progressive income tax is feasible and widely accepted. When neither of these conditions is met, fiscal pressures make the welfare state difficult to sustain, so we start believing that targeting may be the answer and offer greater efficiency (Brodie, 1994; Handy, 1997). It is as if we are applying the early capitalist methods of producing more goods for less cost to the entirety of society, which is urged to move into the marketplace regardless of family circumstances or health problems and no matter the diminishing capacity of the market to provide a living wage. This is vividly apparent in the 1996 census, which indicated that employment income has dropped like a stone in Canada in the 1990s and that the market is capable of handling fewer and fewer full-time, full-year workers (Statistics Canada, 1998). This is another example of population aging laying bare the weaknesses of existing social arrangements in covering market failures.

To consider what the retreat from universality in social programs means for intergenerational interlinkages, consider first what targeting or selectivity does and its implications for intergenerational solidarity (Baker, 1996). Four points can be made. First, the quest for so-called efficiency often means that benefits are made more difficult to obtain, resulting in increased economic vulnerability for those who no longer receive benefits and in increased social inequalities.

Second, targeting benefits may *increase* social inequalities because it excludes those who are least able to make moral claims on political grounds for continuing benefits, i.e., families in poverty, the disabled, the working poor, those who are no longer searching for work, and the poor elderly. Pensions, on the other hand, are more likely to be seen politically as entitlements and can only be reduced with less enthusiasm. Third, the argument that targeting helps those who need help the most opens the door to paternalistic and often costly judgements of who *deserves* help (and it quickly becomes 'help', not entitlement). Do the elderly, for example, have their pensions reduced less because of need or because of fear of their voting power? By contrast, single mothers on social assistance have great need, but very limited political clout. Politicians and policy-makers may also identify readily with pensioners since their parents and often they themselves are pensioners or likely pensioners. Most politicians hope they will avoid single motherhood and certainly social assistance. Given the gender structure of legislatures in Ottawa and the provinces, single motherhood is not a risk for the overwhelming majority, and among those few who are single parents, social assistance is not much of a risk either.

Fourth, in moving towards targeting, entitlements often depend on means tests of some kind, increasingly often involving spreading to multiple generations. Eligibility for family benefits might be conditional on children staying in school, for instance, necessitating an intergenerational contract. Eligibility for senior benefits for home care may be contingent on the willingness of adult children to take on some caregiving, regardless of the preferences of either the senior or the adult children. Among the childless elderly, or those with geographically distant adult children or children who simply cannot help out, much as they might wish to, disadvantage may result, a kind of penalty for not having access to intergenerational resources.

In terms of intergenerational interlinkages, it is clear that social policy tendencies in a reconstructing Canada are shifting the grounds of relations and responsibilities among generations in families and in society in profound ways (Glossop, 1996). Recent social policy changes also create intergenerational dependencies that may not have existed previously. For example, coerced early retirement just prior to pension entitlement, with or without severance packages, places some men and women in their fifties into a category of unpensioned retirement. They are excluded by fiat both from the public transfer system and from the possibility of meaningful labour market activity because they are not expected to be looking for work. This is a generational phenomenon where highly capable people in mid-life are without work and without pensions, and thus unable to contribute societally or in terms of family resources to the benefit of older or younger generations. As Schulz (1988: 164), the originator of the term 'voodoo demographics', states, 'Everyone is in favour of keeping older people in the workforce except the unions, government, business and older people.'

Health-care infrastructure and the legacy of good health and longevity are vital but overlooked intergenerational societal transfers. Helliwell (1998: 142) argues that health care in Canada is a 'public good' often omitted from generational accounts and heritage, as are education and the inheritance of natural resources and a good environment. He suggests that 'investments in knowledge may well have much higher rates of return, seen from the perspective of the next generation, than any of the more obvious monuments to the energy and self-importance of the current generation'. De Broucker and Lavallee (1998) make a similar point with respect to education and literacy. With respect to health care, Helliwell (1998: 144) compellingly argues:

> the important point to make, however, is not the dollar value to attach to either the distributional equity or the administrative efficiency of the Canadian health care system, at least compared to the U.S. system, but that it matters to Canadians in the current generation, and is likely to matter to their successors. It is also likely, that if the Canadian system had not been established when it was, and if the spread of private insurers had followed the style and pattern seen in the United States, that there would by now be no realistic chance of starting again and getting to where we are now. This type of branching, where an opportunity not taken may be lost forever, poses great problems for the generational accounts.

Publicly funded health care in Canada disproportionately benefits the very old and very young, entailing indirect transfers from the middle generation to older and to younger generations. I have noted elsewhere (McDaniel, 1997c) that social benefits are demographically 'lumpy'.

An essential contradiction/tension in the intergenerational health legacy is that the very success of healthy aging and longevity, inherited from our parents and grandparents, which enables us both to live longer and to live longer in good health, is argued to *challenge* the public health-care system and is used by health-care reformers as a justification to reduce sharply public funds for health care (McDaniel and Chappell, 1999). Dilemmas and contradictions abound here. Without good health care and a sound and equitable society, people are less likely to live to old age and more likely to be in poorer health when old. Yet, the longevity of greater numbers of Canadians is defined by health-care reformers as problematic and challenging to the continuation of the health-care system in Canada as we know it. Success, in other words, is thought to be the undoing of what gave rise to it! The rhetoric of population aging as culprit is tuned up loudly with respect to health care.

A second key tension/contradiction is seniors pushing for private, quick access to health care, even if privatized. Yet they are the very architects of the current public system and most vividly store the motivations for developing the existing health-care system in Canada. This contradiction has been explored for Alberta, which has experienced health-care restructuring more profoundly than elsewhere in Canada (McDaniel, 1997b). Younger generations are the inheritors/ beneficiaries of the creations, ideas, wisdom, and political struggles of older generations, in ways similar to Mannheim's conceptualization of accumulated social and economic heritage. As well, younger generations tend to lose most in the future if seniors today are in the forefront, even inadvertently, as agents of health-care erosion, a process well under way in many parts of Canada today. In exploring this tension in Alberta, McDaniel (1997b) detects two central dimensions. First, there is the sense among some seniors, who tend to be affected, on average, more than younger people by cuts to public health care, that they have less time to wait in longer and longer queues in the public health-care system since they have less time left. McDaniel (ibid., 223) quotes a man of 81 who sums up this issue well: 'Six months wait for me is a larger portion of the time I have left than for someone younger.' Second, there is the structural 'reform' that, whether intentional or not, takes advantage of the greater apprehensions among seniors about longer queues in the public system (queues created largely by health-care 'reforms'). The most significant private-sector health-care growth area in Alberta has been in the development and expansion of eye clinics specializing in cataract surgery. Not surprisingly, these clinics disproportionately cater to the older population.

Seniors in Canada, even in 1989 before serious health-care restructuring and reforms had begun, were less enthusiastic than younger Canadians that health care have more funding (McDaniel and Chappell, 1999). Although the greatest proportion of seniors and of Canadians of all ages thought that government spending on health care was too little, seniors were considerably less likely to think that health care was underfunded than Canadians overall. This may reflect a greater conservatism among seniors, on average, who seem to be more supportive in the 1990s of 'reforming' health care under the impetus of fiscal necessity than are younger Canadians.

Although the National Forum on Health did not focus its values research explicitly on aging or seniors, several of its findings are relevant to intergenerational legacies and linkages. For example, one claim this body made was that:

> At a time when other traditional expressions of Canadian values have been placed under demonstrable stress, health and health care have increased in importance and prominence as a shared common value. In fact the health system has always engendered strong support among Canadians. (*National Forum on Health*, 1997: 5)

The Canadian health-care system, as both legacy and national symbol, emerges in the exploration of values by the National Forum on Health (1997: 7): 'People are proud of the existing system and see it as a source of collective values and identity.'

Tensions and contradictions emerge in the National Forum's research on values. While immense pride and confidence are expressed in the current system, yet health-care reform is viewed with apprehension by most Canadians:

> Cynicism about change is high and the public rejects many of the premises for 'reform'. They believe cost problems are rooted in mismanagement and abuse, and would prefer to see these issues dealt with first. This being said, people still

prefer using new public resources to preserve the integrity and core values of the system. (Ibid.)

The image of deception by those who seek reform as to the need and basis for the reforms is apparent, as is the sense of giving up on an inherited benefit for which previous generations fought and from which future generations would benefit (ibid., 9):

> Many people told us of their concern that health care would not remain the same in the future. A significant number believed that it was not as good as it had been because of government cuts in health care spending, longer waiting lists for doctors or procedures and the number of doctors leaving for the United States. . . . When participants in our research spoke about the future of the system, almost all did so in bleak terms.

The disjuncture between what is occurring with health-care reform in Canada and the values that underlie the legacy of the public system, created by older generations, is clear. Examined more closely with data from Alberta, it is seen that seniors much more strongly disagree with health-care reductions than do younger people (McDaniel, 1997b; McDaniel and Chappell, 1999). Seniors tend to agree a little less than do those under age 64 with the withholding of federal transfer payments to Alberta for Alberta's contravening of the Canada Health Act. In other data from the same 1996 Alberta survey, however, Smith (1996: 2) reports that the lowest levels of agreement with the statement, 'Budget cuts are reducing the quality of health care in Alberta', are found among respondents aged 60 and over. Yet 74 per cent overall think that the government should make a significant reinvestment in Alberta's health-care system (ibid., 2, 6). Seniors are deeply concerned about health-care reductions, yet they are not as likely as younger people to agree that penalties should be levied for contravention of the basic principles of Canadian health care. Seniors are least likely to see budget cuts as reducing the quality of health care, and they believe that government should reinvest in health care. It is easy to see the perplexing dilemmas seniors pose to the neo-liberal agenda of health-care reform.

Current trends towards deeper class polarization in Canada than has been known since World War II (Banting et al., 1995; Beach and Slotsve, 1996; Maxwell, 1996) have created an undermining of the general, broad-based, middle-class consensus that once characterized Canada (Lochhead and Shalla, 1996). '[P]olarization and the related developments in the labour market represent powerful changes, with important implications for poverty, inequality and the wider sense of social solidarity in Canadian life' (Banting et al., 1995: 16). The spectre of generation is raised more often in Canada as the possible basis of a new polarization. Class combined with age polarization is another dimension through which to analyse the tensions and contradictions posed by seniors and aging to the neo-liberal agendas (see, for example, Hicks, 1998).

A significant policy change in Canada has immense, thus far unknown, consequences for class/age polarization and generational interlinkages—the Canada Health and Social Transfer (CHST). Block funding to the provinces from the federal government was reduced by one-third over 1996 and 1997, with the federal transfer combined into a block consisting of health, post-secondary education, and welfare. The provinces then work out, each independently, how they allocate the substantially reduced funds among the three sectors (see McDaniel, 1997d). Seniors' claims to health care are placed in competition with the claims of aspiring university students and with those of poor lone parents and the disabled. The dilemmas raised here resonate with those mentioned earlier about the emergence of productivity and efficiency as the new ideals (Brodie, 1997). If there is little payoff for the provinces in terms of enhanced employment or GDP, it may be tempting to take monies away from the compelling needs of seniors to fund education. Public health care in Canada as the symbolic unifying 'railway' of the late twentieth and twenty-first centuries may be coming to an end.

The widespread policy and public perception that older people today are better off and no longer in need of public transfers raises another perplexing dilemma. In an analysis based on the experiences of the major cohorts of this century, McDaniel (1997d) finds that age is less important than cohort experience in shaping relative circumstances in later life. Thus, the current generation of elders is, on average (with wide variability, particularly by gender and region), better off than previous generations because of the benefits to which they had access while younger, including the benefits of a public health-care system in Canada. Future generations of elders will not have the same cohort experiences and could have greater needs for public transfers, which they will not have because of policies based on the situations of today's elders.

Wolfson et al. (1998: 18) find in a study based on the Statistics Canada LifePaths models, applied to all generations over the twentieth century and into the nineteenth, that 'heterogeneity swamps generation'. In other words, *generation per se matters less than socio-economic differences. Intra*generational polarizations are more important than *inter*generational polarizations. With respect to health-care reform in Canada and intergenerational interlinkages, this means that vertical equity, or redistribution from better off to less well off, matters more in public health care than the currently emphasized horizontal equity, that people in similar circumstances be treated equally. With health-care reform, the sweeping of seniors into a single 'similar circumstance' category may be distinctly inappropriate. This further disadvantages seniors who are already disadvantaged, widening the polarization within this generation.

The Future

So, in response to the title question, 'What Did You Ever Do For Me?', the multiple squares of the quilt reveal very different answers. It is not quite a crazy quilt that emerges, although the pattern is very complex. Intergenerational interlinkages are contradictory, hidden, and extend far beyond simple generational labels and public generational accounting. Interactions are apparent with gender and class as well as with other social factors, notably family situation.

Generation, however, emerges as an identity signifier in the 1990s that matters to the construction of generation as a socially and demographically meaningful concept. This is paradoxical. It is a self-fulfilling prophecy whereby the search for demographic category, as the astrological sign of the 1990s, becomes important, not because demographic categories such as generation are determining, but because they *become* real as the raw material of identity-building. Generation becomes the anchor for our self-identities when other signifiers, such as gender, ethnicity, and regional identification, have proven contentious or let us down.

The contradictory and unexpected directions of intergenerational transfers must be balanced against the concepts of equity and fairness of resource distribution. I conclude with an image from the late Bishop Adolphe Proulx, who used to say that a car accident looks very different depending on where you are at the time it occurs. If you are in a high-rise building looking down, you will experience it one way. If you are on the street, you will see it another way. And, of course, if you are sitting in the car that is hit, you will experience it in an entirely different way. Perhaps we have for too long been listening to those in the high-rise penthouses who tell us that no serious accident has occurred in Canada as it restructures. The key to seeing trends (and accidents) through the broad aperture of intergenerational interlinkages is that we start seeing ourselves all in the same car. As a consequence, we might drive much more cautiously.

Acknowledgements

Thanks to the Freisen Conference organizing committee for the opportunity to develop my thinking about generational interlinkages by their invitation to me to do the 1998 Freisen Lecture. Thanks to the late Sheryl McInnes and to Kerri Calvert for their assistance with references, to Teresa Abada for helpful suggestions, and to Lillian Zimmerman for originally suggesting the title question. I remain responsible for views expressed here and any errors that might occur.

References

Baker, Maureen. 1996. *Reinforcing Obligations and Responsibilities Between Generations: Policy Options from Cross-National Comparisons*. Ottawa: The Vanier Institute of the Family.

Banting, Keith G., Charles M. Beach, and Gordon Betcherman. 1995. 'Polarization and Social Policy Reform: Evidence and Issues', in Banting and Beach, eds, *Labour Market Polarization and Social Policy Reform*. Kingston, Ont.: School of Policy Studies, Queen's University, 1–20.

Beach, Charles M., and G.A. Slotsve. 1996. *Are We Becoming Two Societies?* Toronto: C.D. Howe Institute.

Beaudry, P., and D. Green. 1996. 'Cohort Patterns in Canadian Earnings and the Skill Biased Technical Change Hypothesis'. Vancouver: University of British Columbia, Department of Economics, Discussion Paper no. 97–03.

Brodie, Janine. 1994. *Politics on the Boundaries: Restructuring and the Canadian Women's Movement*. North York, Ont.: Robarts Centre for Canadian Studies, University of Toronto.

———. 1997. 'Meso-Discourses, State Forms and the Gendering of Liberal-Democratic Citizenship', *Citizenship Studies* 1, 2: 223–42.

Caradec, Vincent. 1997. 'Forms of Conjugal Life Among the "Young Elderly"', *Population* 9: 47–94.

Clark, Philip G. 1993a. 'Moral Discourse and Public Policy in Aging: Framing Problems, Seeking Solutions and "Public Ethics"', *Canadian Journal on Aging* 12, 4: 485–508.

———. 1993b. 'Public Policy in the United States and Canada: Individualism, Family Obligation, and Collective Responsibility in the Care of the Elderly', in Jon Hendricks and Carolyn Rosenthal, eds, *The Remainder of Their Days: Domestic Policy and Older Families in the United States and Canada*. New York: Garland, 145–67.

Collins, Robert. 1997. *You Had to Be There: An Intimate Portrait of the Generation That Survived the Depression, Won the War, and Re-Invented Canada*. Toronto: McClelland & Stewart.

Corak, Miles, ed. 1998a. *Government Finances and Generational Equity*. Ottawa: Statistics Canada, Catalogue No. 68–513–XPB.

———, ed. 1998b. *Labour Markets, Social Institutions, and the Future of Canada's Children*. Ottawa: Statistics Canada, Catalogue No. 89–553–XPB.

De Broucker, P., and L. Lavallee. 1998. 'Intergenerational Aspects of Education and Literacy Skills Acquisition', in Corak (1998b).

Finnie, Ross. 1997. 'Stasis and Change: Trends in Individuals' Earnings and Inequality in Canada, 1982–1992', *Canadian Business Economics* 6, 1: 84–107.

Giddens, Anthony. 1991. *Modernity and Self-Identity: Self and Society in the Late Modern Age*. Stanford, Calif.: Stanford University Press.

Glossop, Robert. 1996. 'Bailing Out on Future Generations', *Transition* (Mar.): 12–13.

Gunderson, Morley, and Douglas Hyatt. 1998. 'Intergenerational Considerations of Workers' Compensation Unfunded Liabilities', in Corak (1998a: 21–37).

Handy, Charles. 1997. *The Hungry Spirit: Beyond Capitalism, A Quest for Purpose in the Modern World*. New York: Random House.

Harevan, Tamara K. 1991. 'The History of the Family and the Complexity of Social Change', *American Historical Review* 96, 1: 95–124.

———. 1994. 'Aging, Generational Relations: A Historical and Life Course Perspective', *American Review of Sociology* 20: 437–61.

Helliwell, John F. 1998. 'What Will We Be Leaving You?', in Corak (1998a: 141–7).

Hicks, Chantal. 1998. 'The Age Distribution of the Tax/Transfer System in Canada', in Corak (1998a: 39–56).

Levine, David. 1989. 'Recombinant Family Formation Strategies', *Journal of Historical Sociology* 2, 2: 89–115.

Lochhead, Clarence, and Vivian Shalla. 1996. 'Delivering the Goods: Income Distribution and the Precarious Middle Class', *Canadian Council on Social Development* 20, 1: 15–19.

McDaniel, Susan A. 1986. *Canada's Aging Population.* Toronto: Butterworths.

———. 1987. 'Demographic Aging as Paradigm in Canada's Welfare State', *Canadian Public Policy* 13, 3: 330–6.

———. 1995. 'The Family Lives of the Middle-Aged and Elderly', in Maureen Baker, ed., *Families: Changing Trends in Canada,* 3rd edn. Toronto: McGraw-Hill Ryerson, 194–210.

———. 1996. 'Family/Work Challenges Among Older Working Canadians', in Marion Lynn, ed., *Voices: Essays on Canadian Families.* Toronto: Nelson, 195–214.

———. 1997a. 'Caring and Sharing: Demographic Change and Shifting State Policies', in Monica Verea, ed., *Women in North America at the End of the Millennium.* Mexico City: Universidad Nacional Automona de Mexico.

———. 1997b. 'Health Care Policy in an Aging Canada: The Alberta "Experiment"', *Journal of Aging Studies* 11, 3: 211–28.

———. 1997c. 'Intergenerational Transfers, Social Solidarity, and Social Policy: Unanswered Questions and Policy Challenges', *Canadian Public Policy/Canadian Journal on Aging* (joint issue): 1–21.

———. 1997d. 'Serial Employment and Skinny Government: Reforming Caring and Sharing among Generations', *Canadian Journal on Aging* 16, 3: 465–84.

———. 1998. 'Intergenerational Transfers and Social Institutions: Social Policy Directions', in Corak (1998b).

——— and Neena Chappell. 1999. 'Health Care in Regression: Implications for Canadian Seniors', *Canadian Public Policy* 25, 2: 100–10..

——— and Ellen M. Gee. 1993. 'Social Policies Regarding Caregiving to Elders: Canadian Contradictions', *Journal of Aging and Social Policy* 5, 1–2: 57–72.

——— and Robert Lewis. 1998. 'Did They or Didn't They?: Inter-generational Supports in Canada's Past and A Case Study of Brigus, Newfoundland, 1920–1949', in Lori Chambers and Edgar-André Montigny, eds, *Family Matters: Papers in Post-Confederation Canadian Family History.* Toronto: Canadian Scholars Press, 475–97.

Mannheim, Karl. 1968 [1952]. 'The Problem of Generations', in Paul Kecskemeti, ed., *Essays in the Sociology of Knowledge.* London: Routledge & Kegan Paul.

Maxwell, Judith. 1996. 'Social Dimensions of Economic Growth', *The Eric John Hanson Memorial Lecture Series,* vol. 8. Edmonton: University of Alberta, 25 Jan.

Montigny, Edgar-André. 1997. *Foisted Upon the Government? State Responsibilities, Family Obligations and the Care of the Dependent Aged in Late Nineteenth Century Ontario*. Montreal and Kingston: McGill-Queen's University Press.

Myles, John. 1996. 'Public Policy in a World of Market Failure', *Policy Options* 17, 6: 14–19.

National Forum on Health. 1997. Ottawa: National Forum on Health.

Osberg, Lars. 1998. 'Meaning and Measurement in Intergenerational Equity', in Corak (1998a: 131–9).

Pampel, Fred C. 1998. *Aging, Social Inequality and Public Policy*. Thousand Oaks, Calif.: Pine Forge Press.

Parr, Joy. 1996. 'Gender History and Historical Practice', in Parr and Mark Rosenberg, eds, *Gender and History in Canada*. Toronto: Copp Clark, 8–27.

Pennec, Sophie. 1997. 'Four-Generation Families in France', *Population* 9: 75–101.

Picard, André. 1998. *This Gift of Death: Confronting Canada's Tainted Blood Tragedy*. Toronto: HarperCollins.

Picot, Garnett. 1997. 'What is Happening to Earnings Inequality in Canada in the 1990s?', *Canadian Business Economics* 6, 1: 65–83.

——— and John Myles. 1995. 'Social Transfers, Changing Family Structures, and Low Income Among Children', No. 82, Research Paper Series. Ottawa: Analytical Studies Branch, Statistics Canada.

———, ———, and Wendy Pyper. 1998. 'Changing Labour Market Conditions, Government Transfers, and Poverty Among the Young and Old', in Corak (1998b).

Price, Matthew C. 1997. *Justice Between Generations: The Growing Power of the Elderly in America*. Westport, Conn.: Praeger.

Sassoon, Anne Showstack. 1997. 'Comment on Jane Lewis: Gender and Welfare Regimes, Further Thoughts', *Social Politics* (Summer): 178–81.

Saul, John Ralston. 1995. *The Unconscious Civilization*. Concord, Ont.: House of Anansi.

Schulz, James. 1988. *The Economics of Aging*. Belmont, Calif.: Wadsworth.

Silverstein, Merril, and Vern L. Bengtson. 1997. 'Intergenerational Solidarity and the Structure of Adult Child-Parent Relationships in American Families', *American Journal of Sociology* 103, 2: 429–60.

Smith, Pamela. 1996. *The 1996 Alberta Survey: Public Attitudes about Changes in the Health Care System*. Edmonton: Population Research Laboratory, University of Alberta.

Standing, Guy. 1997. 'The Folly of Social Safety Nets: Why Basic Income Is Needed in Eastern Europe', *Social Research: An International Quarterly of the Social Sciences* 64, 4: 1339–79.

Statistics Canada. 1997. *Income Distributions by Size in Canada, 1996*. Ottawa: Statistics Canada, Catalogue No. 13–207–XPB.

———. 1998. '1996 Census: Sources of Income, Earnings and Total Income, and Family Income', *The Daily*, 12 May.

Stone, Leroy O., Carolyn J. Rosenthal, and Ingrid Arnet Connidis. 1998. *Parent-Child Exchanges of Supports and Intergenerational Equity*. Ottawa: Statistics Canada, Catalogue No. 89–557–XPE.

van Solinge, Hanna, Harry van Dalen, Pearl Dykstra, Evert van Imhoff, Hein Moors, and Leo van Wissen. 1998. *Population, Labour and Social Protection in the European Union: Dilemmas and Prospects*. The Hague: Netherlands Interdisciplinary Demographic Institute.

Walker, Alan. 1996. *The New Generational Contract*. London: UCL Press.

————— and Victor Minichiello. 1996. 'Emerging Issues in Sociological Thinking: Research and Teaching', in Minichiello, Neena Chappell, Hal Kendig, and Walker, eds, *Sociology of Aging: International Perspectives*. Melbourne: International Sociology Association Research Committee on Aging, 1–7.

'What If . . . ?'. 1997. *American Demographics* (Dec.): 39–41.

Wolfson, Michael C., Geoff Rowe, X. Lin, and Stephen F. Gribble. 1998. 'Generational Accounting and Government Policy with Heterogeneous Populations', in Corak (1998a: 107–26).

Zyblock, Myles. 1996. 'Why Is Family Market Income Inequality Increasing in Canada? Examining the Effects of Aging, Family Formation, Globalization and Technology'. Working Paper No. W–96–11E. Ottawa: Applied Research Branch, Human Resources Development Canada.

————— and Iain Tyrell. 1997. 'Decomposing Family Income Inequality in Canada, 1981–93', *Canadian Business Economics* 6, 1: 108–19.

Index

aging population: excuse for welfare state retrenchment, 5, 60, 130–1; three images, 100
'apocalyptic demography', 2, 5–25, 100–2, 129; deconstruction of, 7–14: examples, 6–7; population and politics, 14–16; and social policy, 16–20, 21

Bank of Canada, 17
birth control movement, 16
'boomerang kid'. *See* home-returning

Canada Pension Plan (CPP): operation of, 18; suggested strategies, 111; uneasiness over, 107, 108
caregiving: by men, 76–7; by women, 11–12, 20, 41, 56, 57–9, 64–5; extent of help to parents, 56–7; and family life, 45, 46–7, 64–8, 73, 76; inter-generational. *See* intergenerational caregiving; a public issue, 61; questions about use of the term, 65–8; sandwich generation, 57–9

debt, national, 16–17; causes, 115–16, 117; excuse for welfare state retrenchment, 115–17, 130–1
dependency ratio (DR), 8–13; elderly, 8–9; shortcomings, 11–13; total DR, 9, 10–11; youth, 9–10, 11
disability rates among the elderly, 39

'eldercare', term questioned, 66–7
Employment Insurance (EI), 124
eugenics movement in Canada, 14–15

family relations: intergenerational links, 134, 135–40; a part of 'caregiving', 45, 46–7, 64–8, 73, 76; young adults living with parents. *See* home-returning. *See also* reciprocity
family structure, changing, 45–63; ages

with living parents, 46–7; decreasing size of family, 49–51; female paid workers, 54–5, 59, 108, 119–20; generational structure, 51–3; marital status trends among women, 47–9; scattering of the family, 53–4
financial assistance to parents, 56–7
Foot, David, 2, 3n2, 57, 103, 129

generational accounting, 13–14
generational overlap, 47

health-care system: Canada Health and Social Transfer, 147; costs, and apocalyptic demography, 19–20; health promotion and disease prevention, 40; home-care services, increasing needs, 41, 42; impact of population aging, 26–7, 39–41, 42; restructuring, 42, 143–7; tainted blood scandal, 130. *See also* hospitals and population aging
home-returning: popular images, 80–1, 88, 93; positive views of parents and children, 90–4; prevalence, 83–4; reasons for, 84–8; social policy issues, 94–5; support by parents or children, 88–90
hospitals and population aging: closure of hospitals, 41–2; hospitalization days, 32–7; hospital morbidity, 27, 37–9; population projections, 29–30; projections for acute-care days, 26–9; separation rates (patient releases), 30–1; trends in length of stay, 31–2

'ideas of the day', 15
income inequalities, 137–9; intra-generation differences, 138–9, 147. *See also* poverty
interdependence. *See* reciprocity
intergenerational caregiving, 64–79; child